First World War
and Army of Occupation
War Diary
France, Belgium and Germany

4 DIVISION
Divisional Troops
406 Field Company Royal Engineers
(formerly 1/1 Renfrew)
24 June 1914 - 21 June 1919

WO95/1470/1

The Naval & Military Press Ltd
www.nmarchive.com
Published in association with The National Archives

Published by

The Naval & Military Press Ltd

Unit 10 Ridgewood Industrial Park,

Uckfield, East Sussex,

TN22 5QE England

Tel: +44 (0) 1825 749494

www.naval-military-press.com

www.nmarchive.com

This diary has been reprinted in facsimile from the original. Any imperfections are inevitably reproduced and the quality may fall short of modern type and cartographic standards.

© Crown Copyright
Images reproduced by permission of The National Archives, London, England, 2015.

Contents

Document type	Place/Title	Date From	Date To
Heading	4 Division. Troops. 406 Field Coy R.E. (Formerely 1/1 Renfrew) 1916 Apr To 1919 June. 526 Field Coy R.E. (Formerely 1/1 Durham) 1915 Sept To 1919 Feb.		
Heading	WO95/1470/1 406 Field Co. RE. 1916 April-1919 June.		
Heading	406 Fld Coy R.E. 4th Division War Diaries 1/1 Reference Field Coy R.E.S. 23-4 To 31-12-16, Joined 1-5-16		
Heading	4th Division. I/1st Renfrew Field Company. Royal Engineers. 23/4/16 To 31/5/16		
War Diary		23/04/1916	23/04/1916
War Diary	Marseilles	24/04/1916	24/04/1916
War Diary	In Train	26/04/1916	27/04/1916
War Diary	Saulty	28/04/1916	02/05/1916
War Diary	Lucheux	03/05/1916	07/05/1916
War Diary	Beaumetz	08/05/1916	15/05/1916
War Diary	Beauquesne	16/05/1916	16/05/1916
War Diary	Bertrancourt	17/05/1916	31/05/1916
Heading	4th Division. I/1st Renfrew Field Company. Royal Engineers. June 1916		
War Diary	Bertrancourt	01/06/1916	22/06/1916
War Diary	Camp At P.6.a Ref. Map. Beaumont No. 2 By B. 1/20000	24/06/1914	24/06/1914
War Diary	Camp	25/06/1916	26/06/1916
War Diary	Camp P.6.a	27/06/1916	27/06/1916
War Diary	Camp	27/06/1916	29/06/1916
War Diary	Camp P.6.a	30/06/1916	30/06/1916
Heading	4th Division. I/1st Renfrew Field Company. Royal Engineers. July 1916		
War Diary	Camp P.6.a. Reference Map 54 D 1/40000	01/07/1916	04/07/1916
War Diary	Camp P.6.A.	05/07/1916	05/07/1916
War Diary	Camp P.6.a. Ref. Map Sheet No. 54 D 1/40000	06/07/1916	06/07/1916
War Diary	Camp	07/07/1916	08/07/1916
Miscellaneous	Camp P.6.a. Ref. Map Sheet No. 54 D.	09/07/1916	09/07/1916
War Diary	Camp	10/07/1916	10/07/1916
War Diary	Camp P.6.A. Ref. Map Sheet No. 57 D 1/40000	11/07/1916	11/07/1916
War Diary	Camp	12/07/1916	12/07/1916
War Diary	Camp P.6.A. Ref. Map Sheet No. 57. D 1/40000	13/07/1916	13/07/1916
War Diary	Camp	14/07/1916	15/07/1916
War Diary	Camp P.6.A. Ref. Map Sheet No. 57. D. 1/40000	16/07/1916	16/07/1916
War Diary	Camp	17/07/1916	18/07/1916
War Diary	Camp P.6.A. Ref. Map Sheet No. 57. D 1/40000	19/07/1916	19/07/1916
War Diary	Camp	20/07/1916	20/07/1916
War Diary	Camp P.6.A. Ref. Map Sheet No. 57. D 1/40000	21/07/1916	21/07/1916
War Diary	Bus	22/07/1916	22/07/1916
War Diary	Amplier	23/07/1916	23/07/1916
War Diary	Camp D.7.c.5.2. Ref. Sheet No. 27 1/40000	24/07/1916	26/07/1916
War Diary	Camp A.15.b.9.5. Ref. Map Sheet No. 28 M W	27/07/1916	27/07/1916
War Diary	Camp A.15.b.9.5. Ref. Map Belgium Sheet No. 28 N W	28/07/1916	28/07/1916

War Diary	Camp	29/07/1916	29/07/1916
War Diary	Camp A.15.b.9.5. Ref. Map Belgium Sheet No. 27 N.W.	30/07/1916	30/07/1916
War Diary	Camp	31/07/1916	31/07/1916
Map	Sketch Shewing New Road		
Map	Plan Of Decauville Railway Laid In Sector		
Diagram etc	Corps O.P. 5th Avenue.		
War Diary	Hdqrs At Camp H. A 15.b.9.5. Ref. Map Belgium Sheet No. 28 N.W.	01/08/1916	01/08/1916
War Diary	Camp H.	02/08/1916	03/08/1916
War Diary	Hdqrs At Camp H. A 15.b.9.5. Ref. Map Belgium Sheet No. 28 N.W.	04/08/1916	04/08/1916
War Diary	Camp. H.	05/08/1916	06/08/1916
War Diary	Hdqrs at Camp. H. A.15.b.9.5. Ref. Map Belgium Sheet No. 28 N.W.	07/08/1916	07/08/1916
War Diary	Camp H.	08/08/1916	08/08/1916
War Diary	Hdqrs At Camp H. A15.b.9.5. Map Ref. Belgium Sheet No. 28 N.W.	09/08/1916	09/08/1916
War Diary	Camp. H.	10/08/1916	11/08/1916
War Diary	Hdqrs At Camp H A15.b.9.5. Ref. Map. Belgium Sheet No. 27 N.W.	12/08/1916	12/08/1916
War Diary	Camp. H.	13/08/1916	13/08/1916
War Diary	Hdqrs At Camp H A15.b.9.5. Ref. Map. Belgium Sheet No. 28 N.W.	14/08/1916	14/08/1916
War Diary	Camp H.	15/08/1916	16/08/1916
War Diary	Hdqrs At Camp H A15.b.9.5. Ref. Map. Belgium Sheet No. 28 N.W.	17/08/1916	17/08/1916
War Diary	Camp H.	17/08/1916	18/08/1916
War Diary	Hdqrs At Camp H. A15.b.9.5. Ref. Map No. Sheet 28 N.W. Belgium	20/08/1916	20/08/1916
War Diary	Camp H.	21/08/1916	22/08/1916
War Diary	Camp J.	23/08/1916	24/08/1916
War Diary	Hdqrs At Rly Dug Outs I 20.c.4.1 Ref. Map Sheet No. 28 N.W Belgium	25/08/1916	25/08/1916
War Diary	Hdqrs At I 20.c.4.1 1 Ref. Map No. Sheet 28 N.W.	26/08/1916	26/08/1916
War Diary	Hdqrs At I 20.c.4.1	27/08/1916	27/08/1916
War Diary	I 20.c.4.1	29/08/1916	30/08/1916
War Diary	Hdqrs At I 20.c.4.1	31/08/1916	31/08/1916
Diagram etc	Willows Dugout		
Diagram etc			
War Diary	Hdqrs At I 20.c.4.1 Ref. Map Belgium Sheet No. 28 N.W.	01/09/1916	01/09/1916
War Diary	Hdqrs At Camp G H.13 Ref. Map Belgium Sheet No. 28 NW	02/09/1916	03/09/1916
War Diary	Hdqrs At Camp G	04/09/1916	04/09/1916
War Diary	Hdqrs At H.8.a.4.8. Ref Map Belgium Sheet No. 28 N.W. 1/20000	05/09/1916	05/09/1916
War Diary	Hdqrs At H.8.A.4.8	06/09/1916	06/09/1916
War Diary	Hdqrs At H.8.a.4.8. Ref. Map Belgium Sheet No. 28. N.W.	07/09/1916	07/09/1916
War Diary	Hdqrs At H.8.A.4.8	08/09/1916	08/09/1916
War Diary	Hdqrs At H.8.A.4.8. Ref. Map Belgium Sheet No. 27 N.W.	09/09/1916	09/09/1916
War Diary	Hdqrs At H.8.A.4.8	10/09/1916	12/09/1916
War Diary	Hdqrs At H.8.a.4.8. Ref. Map Belgium Sheet No. 27 N.W.	13/09/1916	13/09/1916

War Diary	Hdqrs At H.8.A.4.8	14/09/1916	15/09/1916
War Diary	Hdqrs At H.8.a.4.8. Ref. Map Belgium Sheet No. 27 N.W.	16/09/1916	16/09/1916
War Diary	Hdqrs At H.8.A.4.8	17/09/1916	18/09/1916
War Diary	Longpre	19/09/1916	24/09/1916
War Diary	Allonville	25/09/1916	26/09/1916
War Diary	Corbie	27/09/1916	29/09/1916
War Diary	Vaux	30/09/1916	30/09/1916
Diagram etc			
Heading	4th Division. I/1st Renfrew Field Company. Royal Engineers. October 1916		
War Diary	Vaux Sur Somme	01/10/1916	08/10/1916
War Diary	Ref. Map France Sheet No. 57 C S.W.	09/10/1916	09/10/1916
War Diary	Hdqrs At S.29.c.5.2. Ref. Map Sheet No. 57 C S.W.	10/10/1916	10/10/1916
War Diary	Hdqrs At S.29.c.5.2	11/10/1916	11/10/1916
War Diary	Hdqrs At S.29.c.5.2 Ref Map Sheet No. 57 C S.W.	12/10/1916	14/10/1916
War Diary	Hdqrs At S.29.c.5.2. Ref. Map Sheet No. 57 C. S.W	15/10/1916	24/10/1916
War Diary	Hdqrs At F.19.c.9.3. Ref. Map Albert 1/40000	25/10/1916	30/10/1916
War Diary	Hdqrs At Doudelainville	31/10/1916	31/10/1916
Heading	4th Division. I/1st Renfrew Field Company. Royal Engineers. November 1916		
War Diary	Hdqrs At Doudelainville Ref Map N.W. Europe Sheet No. 3	01/11/1916	01/11/1916
War Diary	Hdqrs At Doudelainville	02/11/1916	02/11/1916
War Diary	Hdqrs At Villeroy Ref Map Dieppe Sheet No. 16	03/11/1916	30/11/1916
Heading	4th Division I/1st Renfrew Field Company. Royal Engineers. December 1916		
War Diary	Villeroy Ref. Map Nieppe Sheet No. 16	01/12/1916	03/12/1916
War Diary	Camp 112 L, 2A Ref. Map Albert	04/12/1916	04/12/1916
War Diary	Camp At A25, C	05/12/1916	06/12/1916
War Diary	Hdqrs At A.12. Central Ref Map Albert	07/12/1916	07/12/1916
War Diary	Camp At A 12, Central Ref Map Albert Sheet	08/12/1916	08/12/1916
War Diary	Hdqrs At T.24.c.b.8 Ref. Map 57 C S.W. 4. Combles	09/12/1916	10/12/1916
War Diary	Hdqrs At T.24.c.b.8 Ref. Map Combles Sheet No. 57 S.W. 4	11/12/1916	30/12/1916
War Diary	Hdqrs At B.14 Ref. Map Albert	31/12/1916	31/12/1916
Heading	4th Division War Diaries 40th Field Coy RE. Late 1/1 Renfrew. January To December 1917		
War Diary	Hdqrs At Maurepas B.14.a.54 Ref Map No. 62 C N.W.	01/01/1917	08/01/1917
War Diary	Hdqrs At B, 14, A, 5, 4 Ref Map 62 C N.W.	09/01/1917	31/07/1917
War Diary	Hdqrs At B. 30.b.7.6. Ref Map No. 62 C NW 1/20000	01/02/1917	08/02/1917
War Diary	Hdqrs At B 20.b.7.6. Ref Map Sheet No. 62 C N.W. 1/20000	09/02/1917	11/02/1917
War Diary	Hdqrs At B. 30.b.7.6 Ref Map Sheet No. 62C N.W. 1/20000	12/02/1917	21/02/1917
War Diary	Hdqrs At Limber Camp	22/02/1917	22/02/1917
War Diary	Hdqrs At Camp 12	23/02/1917	28/02/1917
War Diary	Hdqrs At Camp 12 Chipilly H. 2. Ref Map. Amiens 1/10000	01/03/1917	07/03/1917
War Diary	Hdqrs at Savy Ref Map Lens 11	08/03/1917	05/04/1917
War Diary	Hdqrs at C.21.d.9.2 Ref. Map Arras Sheet No. 51B N.W. 1/10000	06/04/1917	20/04/1917
War Diary	Hdqrs at Montenes Court Ref Map Len 11	21/04/1917	21/04/1917
War Diary	Hdqrs at Lattre St. Quentin Ref Map Lens. 11	22/04/1917	23/04/1917
War Diary	Hdqrs at Berlen Court Ref Map Lens 11	24/04/1917	28/04/1917
War Diary	Hdqrs at Haute Avesnes Ref Map Lens.11	29/04/1917	29/04/1917

War Diary	Hdqrs G.17.a.1.4 Ref. Map France Sheet 51 B N.W. 1/20000	30/04/1917	30/04/1917
War Diary	Hdqrs At H.13.d.9.9. Sheet France 51B NW 1/20000	01/05/1917	12/05/1917
War Diary	Hdqrs At G17.d. Sheet 51b NW 1/20000 and Frances Lens 11. 1/100000	13/05/1917	13/05/1917
War Diary	Tilloy-Les-Hermaville Sheet Frances Lens 11 1/10000	15/05/1917	31/05/1917
War Diary	Coy Hdqrts at Moncheaux Map Ref Sheet Lens 11. 1/100000	01/06/1917	10/06/1917
War Diary	Coy Hdqrts at Arras G 22 b.2/1/2.9 Reference Arras Sheet 51B N.W. 1/10000	11/06/1917	11/06/1917
War Diary	Coy Hdqrts at Blangy G24 a.8.6. (Ref. Arras Sheet 51 B.N.W. 1/10000	12/06/1917	12/06/1917
War Diary	Coy Hdqrts at Railway Embankment H.13.b.9.0. (Arras Sheet 51 B.N.W.) 1/10000	13/06/1917	13/06/1917
War Diary	Coy Hdqrts at Railway Embankment H.13.b.9.0. Sheet France 51 B.N.W. 1/20000	14/06/1917	30/06/1917
War Diary	Map References Sheet 51B NW. Hdqrs At H.13.b.8.1	01/07/1917	03/07/1917
War Diary	Hdqrs At H.13.b.8.1 Sheet No 51.B N.W.1/20000	04/07/1917	31/07/1917
Miscellaneous Diagram etc	Demolition of Tank No. 780		
War Diary	Hdqrs At H.13.b.9.0. Ref. Map 51B NW 1/20000	01/08/1917	08/09/1917
War Diary	Hdqrs At Ransart Ref Map No. 51C 1/40000	09/09/1917	18/09/1917
War Diary	Hdqrs At Pas Ref. Map Lens. 11. F.5	19/09/1917	20/09/1917
War Diary	Hdqrs At Salem Camp X.29.C.2.4. Ref. Map Sheet 19. S.E. 1/20000	21/09/1917	26/09/1917
War Diary	Hdqrs At Salem Camp X29,C,24	27/09/1917	28/09/1917
War Diary	Hdqrs At Canal Bank B.24.b.9.5	29/09/1917	30/09/1917
War Diary	Hdqrs At B.24.b.9.5. Ref Map Sheet 28. NW.	01/10/1917	06/10/1917
War Diary	Hdqrs At Candle TR	07/10/1917	09/10/1917
War Diary	Hdqrs At Candle Tr C.9.a.1.7. Ref Map Sheet No. 28. NW.	10/10/1917	14/10/1917
War Diary	Hdqrs At Proven Portsdown Camp Hazebrook Sheet No. 5	15/10/1917	15/10/1917
War Diary	Hdqrs At Proven Portsdown Camp Hazebrook Sheet No. 5	16/10/1917	16/10/1917
War Diary	Hdqrs At Road Camp Hazebrook Sheet No. 5	17/10/1917	19/10/1917
War Diary	Hdqrs At Gouves Ref Map Lens. 11	20/10/1917	24/10/1917
War Diary	Hdqrs At M.2.c.4.6. Ref Map 51B. 1/40000	25/10/1917	31/10/1917
Miscellaneous	C.R.E. 4th Division		
Heading	War Diary		
War Diary	Hdqrs At M.2.c.8.3. Ref Map 51 B. 1/40000	01/11/1917	23/11/1917
War Diary	Hdqrs At Fosse Cave Ref Map N.11.b.4.3. Sheet 51.B 1/40000	24/11/1917	30/11/1917
War Diary	Hdqrs At Fosse Cave Map Ref N.12.a.3.3. Sheet 51.B 1/40000	01/12/1917	31/12/1917
Heading	4th Division 406th Field Company R.E. 1918 Jan-1919 June		
Heading	War Diary January 1918		
War Diary	Headquarters At Les Fosses Cave N12.a.3.3. Sheet 51B N.W. 1/40000	01/01/1918	31/01/1918
Heading	War Diary Feby 1918		
War Diary	H Qrs at Les Fosses Coal N.12.a.3.3. Sheet 51 B NW 1/40000	01/02/1918	06/02/1918
War Diary	Coy H. Qrs. Schramm Barracks Arras" Lens. 11. Sheet	07/02/1918	16/02/1918
War Diary	Coy H. Qrs at No. 1 Rue De Beaufort Arras	17/02/1918	28/02/1918

Heading	4th Div. 406th (Renfrew) Field Company. R.E. March 1918		
Heading	406th (Renfrew) Field Coy RE		
War Diary	Cav Situated H Qrs At No. 1 Rue De Beaufort Arras. Reference Map Lens 11. 1/100000 And Sheet France 59B NW 59B SW 1/20000	01/03/1918	22/03/1918
War Diary	Coy H. Qrs at Railway Embankment (A 13 b 90 10 Sheet 59 B.N.W. 1/20000	23/03/1918	23/03/1918
War Diary	Coy H. Qrs at Etrun Reference Sheet 51 C 1/40,000	24/03/1918	31/03/1918
Heading	4th Divisional Engineers 406th (Renfrew) Field Company R.E. April 1918		
Heading	War Diary 406th (Renfrew) Field Coy RE April 1918		
War Diary	Coy H. Qrs Situated at Stirling Camp (Near Fampoux) H.13.b.90.10 Sheet 51 B N.W. France	01/04/1918	08/04/1918
War Diary	Coy H Qrs Simencourt Lens II 1/100000	09/04/1918	12/04/1918
War Diary	Coy H Qrs Busnes Sheet France 36 A 1/40000 Cantraines Sheet France 36A 1/40000 Gonnehem V 23-b.7.8. Sheet France 36A. 1/40000	13/04/1918	18/04/1918
War Diary	Coy H Qrs at Gonnehem V23.b.7.8. Sheet France 36A 1/40000	18/04/1918	18/04/1918
War Diary	Coy H Qrs at Gonnehem V 23 B.7.8 Sheet France 36 A 1/40000 and Cense La Vallee V 11.c.o.8. Sheet France 36 A. 1/40,000	18/04/1918	30/04/1918
Miscellaneous	C.R.E. 4th Division.	18/04/1918	18/04/1918
War Diary	Hdqrs At Cense La Vallee Ref Map Sheet No. 36 A 1/40000 V 11 C.1.7	01/05/1918	31/05/1918
War Diary	Hdqrs At Cense La Vallee V.11.c.1.7. Map 36 A 1/40000	01/06/1918	31/07/1918
Heading	War Diary August 1918 406th (Renfrew) Field Coy RE.		
War Diary	Coy Hdqrs at Cense-La-Vallee V.11.c.1.7. Sheet France 36A 1/40000	01/08/1918	23/08/1918
War Diary	Rely Sheet Hazebrouck 1/10000	24/08/1918	24/08/1918
War Diary	Hericourt Sheet Lens 11. 1/100000	25/08/1918	26/08/1918
War Diary	ACQ Lens 11 1/100000	27/08/1918	28/08/1918
War Diary	H Qrs. Spade Trench O 7.b.4.1 Sheet 51B 1/40000	29/08/1918	01/09/1918
War Diary	Coy Hdqrs at O.9.b.5.4	02/09/1918	03/09/1918
War Diary	Hdqrs At M.4.D.3.4. Ref Map Sheet 51 B 1/40000	04/09/1918	05/09/1918
War Diary	Hdqrs At Houvelin	06/09/1918	20/09/1918
War Diary	Hdqrs At Monchy Le Preux	21/09/1918	21/09/1918
War Diary	Hdqrs At P.13.c.4.2. Ref. Sheet 51B 1/40000	22/09/1918	06/10/1918
War Diary	Hqrs at Monchy Le Preux	07/10/1918	07/10/1918
War Diary	Hqrs at Moyellette Ref Map Lens 11	08/10/1918	11/10/1918
War Diary	Hdqrs. At E.9.b.9.1. Sheet 57C 1/40000	12/10/1918	13/10/1918
War Diary	Hdqrs at Maves T.23.c.4.9. Ref Map Sheet 51A 1/40000	14/10/1918	19/10/1918
War Diary	Hdqrs at Villers en Cauchie U.5.a.5.7. Ref Map Sheet 51A 1/40000	20/10/1918	20/10/1918
War Diary	Hdqrs. at Villers en Cauchie	21/10/1918	21/10/1918
War Diary	Hdqrs at Saulzoir P.2.b.a.7.3 Ref Map 51A 1/40000	24/10/1918	26/10/1918
War Diary	Hdqrs at Verchain P.11.d.6.6. Ref. Map. 51 A 1/40000	27/10/1918	02/11/1918
War Diary	Hdqrs at Saulzoir P.2.6.d.7.3 Ref Map 51 A 1/40000	03/11/1918	08/11/1918
War Diary	Hdqrs at Saulzoir	09/11/1918	09/11/1918
War Diary	Hdqrs At Preseau	10/11/1918	10/11/1918
War Diary	Hdrs at Roisin Belgium A 29 D 7 7 Ref Sheet 51 1/40000	11/11/1918	19/11/1918

War Diary	Hdqrs at St Saulve Vallencienes	20/11/1918	30/11/1918
War Diary	Coy H Qrs Situated at St Saulve Valenciennes Ref Map Valenciennes 1/100000	01/12/1918	31/12/1918
War Diary	Hdqrs At St. Saulve Valenciennes	01/01/1919	04/01/1919
War Diary	H Qrs at Morlanweltz Belguim Sheet 46 1/40000	05/01/1919	05/01/1919
War Diary	Coy H Qrs Morlanwelz Belgium Map 46 1/40000	01/02/1919	28/02/1919
War Diary	Hdqrs at Binche Belgium Map 46 1/40000	01/06/1919	21/06/1919

4 DIVISION. TROOPS.
406 FIELD COY R.E.
(FORMERELY 1/1 RENFREW)
1916 APR TO 1919 JUNE.

526 FIELD COY R.E.
(FORMERELY 1/1 DURHAM)
1915 SEPT TO 1919 FEB.

WO 95 1470/1

406 FIELD CO. RE

1916 APRIL - 1919 JUNE

(406 FLD COY RE)

4th Division

War Diaries

1/1 Renfrew Field Coy R.E.s
(Changed to 406 Feb 17)
23-4 To 31-12-16. Joined 1-5-16.

1916

FROM - EGYPT. 9 CORPS TROOPS.
No. 1. CANAL SEC.

4th DIVISION.

1/1ST RENFREW FIELD COMPANY.

ROYAL ENGINEERS.

23/4/16 to 31/5/16.

WAR DIARY or INTELLIGENCE SUMMARY

(Erase heading not required.)

1/1 Renfrew Fd Coy R.E.

Army Form C. 2118

Instructions regarding War Diaries and Intelligence Summaries are contained in F.S. Regs., Part II. and the Staff Manual respectively. Title Pages will be prepared in manuscript.

Place	Date	Hour	Summary of Events and Information	Remarks and references to Appendices
At Sea	23/4/16	4-0 PM	Arrived Marseilles on board H.M.T.S. Transylvania.	
		8-0 "	Ship brought up in roads owing to weather being too stormy to enter docks.	
Marseilles	24/4/16	5-4.30 AM	Ship docked in docks of Marseilles.	
		9-0 AM	Entraining orders received. Stores & Waggons disembarked.	
		6-0 PM	Coy disembarked & marched to Gare St. Charles.	
		7-0 "	Entrained & left Marseilles.	
In train	25/4/16	1-0 AM	Passed through Orange. Halt 45 min.	
		12-0 noon	Arrived Macon. Halt 1 hour.	
		9-0 PM	Arrived at Les Laumes ". 50 min.	
In train	26/4/16	5-45	Arrived Juvisy Station. Paris. Rations served, left at 7-0 AM.	
		11-0 AM	Arrived Epluches.	
		4-10 PM	Arrived Amiens.	
		6-10 PM	Arrived Abbeyville, remained overnight in train. Orders received to proceed to Doullens on the 27 Inst.	
In train	27/4/16	8-17 AM	Left Abbeyville by train. Arrived Doullens 9-15 AM. Disentrained on arrival as Doullens to proceed to Talby arrived shortly at 11-0 AM. Detrained at Lastrat Station & marched to Sarilly.	Major Hodgson Cmdg 5th ...

Army Form.C. 2118.

WAR DIARY
or
INTELLIGENCE SUMMARY

(Erase heading not required.)

Instructions regarding War Diaries and Intelligence Summaries are contained in F.S. Regs., Part II and the Staff Manual respectively. Title Pages will be prepared in manuscript.

Place	Date	Hour	Summary of Events and Information	Remarks and references to Appendices
Sailly	28/4/16		Arrangements made for unit to be attached to 55th Division & Letters of instructions in this area. & Major to take over the Workshops & Park. Coy found Working parties for Bailly & Gorey.	
Sailly	29/4/16		Parties of Units visited Front line trenches in area. Working parties of Bailly, Gorey, & Divisional Park, Laribert.	
Sailly	30/4/16		Working parties at Bailly, Gorey, & Divisional Park, Laribert. All Company transport arrived by road from Abbeyville.	
Sailly	1/5/16	10.0am	Orders received that all arrangements received for 55th Div were cancelled.	
		2-0pm	Orders received Unit would proceed to Lucknow under the C.R.E. 4th Division. Working parties employed at Gorey, Bailly, & Deer Park	
Sailly	2/5/16	9-0pm	All working parties brought back to Unit. Unit marked out from Sailly. Were inspected en route by the C.R.E. 4th Division.	
		5-0pm	Unit arrived at Lucknow.	

J.N. Hodgard Captain
for Lieut. Colonel, R.E.
1/1st Renfrewshire
O. C. 1/1st Renfrewshire
Field Coy. R.E.

Army Form C. 2118

WAR DIARY
or
INTELLIGENCE SUMMARY
(Erase heading not required.)

Instructions regarding War Diaries and Intelligence Summaries are contained in F. S. Regs., Part II. and the Staff Manual respectively. Title Pages will be prepared in manuscript.

Place	Date	Hour	Summary of Events and Information	Remarks and references to Appendices
Lucheux	3/5/16		Company employed on Instructional work, Gas attacks & uses of Anti-Gas appliances.	
Lucheux	4/5/16	9-0 am	Company inspected by G.O.C. 4th Division. Company employed on Instructional work. Repairing equipment & overhauling tools.	
Lucheux	5/5/16		Company employed on Instructional work. Lectures on Gas attacks. Orders received for Hqrs & 2 Sections to proceed to Beauval by road & 2 Sections to move to BERTRANCOURT to be attached to the 4th Durham R.E.	
Saturday	6/5/16	9-30 am	Hqrs & 3rd Section moved out from Lucheux via Doullens – Hem – Beauvillers & Bernaville. Coy halts about 3h. outside BERNAVILLE to allow 11th B.G. troops from JAMES to pass on by road. Lucheux for BERTRANCOURT.	
		9-15 am	No. 1 & 2 Sections marched out from Lucheux for BERTRANCOURT.	
Sunday	7/5/16		Remainder of unit at BEHUMETZ.	

JM Hodgson Capt R.E.
for Lieut-Colonel, R.E.(I.)
O.C. 7/1st Renfrewshire
Field Coy. R.E.

Army Form C. 2118

WAR DIARY
or
INTELLIGENCE SUMMARY

(Erase heading not required.)

Instructions regarding War Diaries and Intelligence Summaries are contained in F.S. Regs., Part II. and the Staff Manual respectively. Title Pages will be prepared in manuscript.

Place	Date	Hour	Summary of Events and Information	Remarks and references to Appendices
Beaumetz	8/5/16		Company employed on Instructional Work. Special attention paid to Gas helmet drill, & Instruction. Working parties employed on repairing wells in district. No 1 & 2 Sects. employed with 3rd Durham R.E., 2 Sect. Durham R.E. attached to 1st Reserve R.E. at Beaumetz.	
Beaumetz	9/5/16		Unit employed on Instructional Work & Repairing Pontoon & Bridging Equipment. Working parties on repairs to wells. Making wash troughs &c.	
Beaumetz	10/5/16		Company Route March with Vehicles. 1 Sect. Durham R.E. left for VAUCHELLES at 5-0 AM.	
Beaumetz	11/5/16	9 am	Medical Inspection of Unit. Working parties making water troughs for attachments. Remainder of Coy employed repacking Coy stores & waggon drill. attached to Reed & Jouille.	
Beaumetz	12/5/16		Company Route March. Working parties on Water troughs, tables &c. Capt. H.W. Hodgart rejoined Unit from hospital.	
Beaumetz	13/5/16		Company employed on Instructional Work. Lectures on Field Engineering. Working parties erecting water troughs, repairing Pontoon & Rigging Equipment of Unit. Quantity of Ordnance Stores received.	

H.W. Hodgart Capt R.E.
for Lieut-Colonel, R.E.(I.)
O.O. 71st Renfrewshire
Field Coy., R.E.

Army Form C. 2118

WAR DIARY
or
INTELLIGENCE SUMMARY
(Erase heading not required.)

Instructions regarding War Diaries and Intelligence Summaries are contained in F. S. Regs., Part II. and the Staff Manual respectively. Title Pages will be prepared in manuscript.

Place	Date	Hour	Summary of Events and Information	Remarks and references to Appendices
BEAUMETZ.	14/5/16	11-0AM	Company employed on repairing & overhauling tools. Received orders for HW & 2nd Sect Renfrew R.E. & 1st Durham R.E. to proceed to BERTRANCOURT on the 15th inst.	
BEAUMETZ	15/5/16	9-0AM	HW & 2 Sect. Renfrew R.E. & 1st 1st Durham R.E. moved out from BEAUMETZ. Route via BERNAVILLE – FIENVILLERS – CANDAS – BEAUVAL. Units arrived at BEAUQUESNE. Halt made for the night & Troops billeted in Town.	
BEAUQUESNE.	16/5/16	9-0AM	March to BERTRANCOURT resumed via MARIEUX – VAUCHELLES – ACHEUX. Arrived BERTRANCOURT at 3-30 PM.	
BERTRANCOURT	17/5/16	9-0AM	Preparations made for starting work on Artillery positions under the VIII Corps Artillery. No 2 Sect. Renfrew R.E. rejoined unit from 4 Durham. Sapping No 1 Sect attached to 4 Durham R.E. for work.	
BERTRANCOURT	18/5/16		Working parties sent out to work on O.P.s at HECHONVILLERS and COLINCAMPS. 16 sappers at work on each position in three shifts day and night, for No 14 Siege Battery and	

J M Hodgart Capt R.E.
for Lieut.-Colonel, R.E.(I.)
O. C. 71st Renfrewshire
Field Coy., R.E.

Army Form C. 2118

WAR DIARY
or
INTELLIGENCE SUMMARY
(Erase heading not required.)

Instructions regarding War Diaries and Intelligence Summaries are contained in F. S. Regs., Part II. and the Staff Manual respectively. Title Pages will be prepared in manuscript.

Place	Date	Hour	Summary of Events and Information	Remarks and references to Appendices
BERTRANCOURT	19/5/16		Working parties at Work on O.P.s at COLINCAMPS & AUCHONVILLERS. Section of 11th Army front Working party sent out to O.P.s at SAILLY-au-BOIS. Enemy seem lately not much concernedly retorted owing to partly contined M.G. fire.	
BERTRANCOURT	20/5/16		Parties working at COLINCAMPS, AUCHONVILLERS, SAILLY-au-BOIS, on O.P.s	
		3-5pm	Party of 2 N.C.O.s 14 Sappers sent out to ENGLEBELMER to erect O.P.s for Heavy Siege Battery R.M.A.	
BERTRANCOURT	21/5/16		Working parties on O.P.s at COLINCAMPS - AUCHONVILLERS - SAILLY-au-BOIS. Materials for construction very slow in coming up to Line.	
BERTRANCOURT	22/5/16		Working parties on O.P.s at COLINCAMPS - AUCHONVILLERS - SAILLY-au-BOIS. ENGLEBELMER. Head cover started on O.P. at ELLIS SQUARE in COLINCAMPS. Sect.	
BERTRANCOURT	23/5/16		Working parties on O.P.s & Dug-Outs at COLINCAMPS, AUCHONVILLERS, SAILLY-au-BOIS, ENGLEBELMER & MENSIL.	
BERTRANCOURT	24/5/16		Working parties on O.P.s & Dug-Outs at COLINCAMPS, AUCHONVILLERS, SAILLY-au-BOIS, ENGLEBELMER & MENSIL. Party of 1 N.C.O. & 5 Sappers detailed for work on Gun Emplacements for 1st Divisional Artillery at COLINCAMPS.	

H. M. Hogg(?) Lieut.
for Lieut.-Colonel, R.E.(J.M.)
O.C. 1/1st Renfrewshire
Field Coy. R.E.

1875 Wt. W593/826 1,000,000 4/15 J.B.C. & A. A.D.S.S./Forms/C. 2118.

Army Form C. 2118

WAR DIARY
or
INTELLIGENCE SUMMARY
(Erase heading not required.)

Instructions regarding War Diaries and Intelligence Summaries are contained in F. S. Regs., Part II. and the Staff Manual respectively. Title Pages will be prepared in manuscript.

Place	Date	Hour	Summary of Events and Information	Remarks and references to Appendices
BERTHANCOURT	25/7/16 to 31/7/16	3 pm	Company working on O.P.'s Dug Outs at COLINCAMPS, SAILLY au BOIS, AUCHONVILLERS, ENGLEBEAMER & MENSIL for VIII Corps Artillery. HQ working parties withdrawn & returned to Company HQ, BERTRANCOURT. O.P. & Dug Outs handed over at Epsom, Delancey, Attack in AUCHONVILLERS Sector, ELLIS SQUARE, TAUPIN, HASRU in COLINCAMP Sector. RITZ & SANDOWN in ENGLEBEAMER. POPLAR & PALESTINE in SAILLY au BOIS.	

M.M. Hodgson O.N.C.E.
(acting) for Lieut. Col.
O.C. 175th Tunnelling Coy R.E.

4th DIVISION.

1/1ST RENFREW FIELD COMPANY.

ROYAL ENGINEERS.

JUNE 1916.

Army Form C. 2118

1/1 Renfrew ???
R.E.

WAR DIARY
or
INTELLIGENCE SUMMARY
(Erase heading not required.)

Instructions regarding War Diaries and Intelligence Summaries are contained in F.S. Regs., Part II. and the Staff Manual respectively. Title Pages will be prepared in manuscript.

Place	Date	Hour	Summary of Events and Information	Remarks and references to Appendices
BERTRAN COURT	1/6/16	4 pm	Rest day for Company. All Company equipment inspected & checked. No 3 Section left BERTRANCOURT to proceed to MAILLY-MAILLET	
BERTRAN COURT	2/6/16		Work started for 4th Division. New track started from BERTRANCOURT to POMMIERS on MAILLY RR. Decauville Rail from ORCHARD, MAILLY to SUCERERIE for Ration Dump. Ammunition Dump started in ACHEUX Rd at BERTRANCOURT for 4th Divi Artillery.	
BERTRAN COURT	3/6/16		Work continued on New track BERTRANCOURT to POMMIERS & Decauville Track ORCHARD – SUCERERIE. New trucks in course of erection. T.M. dug outs in QUARRY started. Ammunition Dump. Training carried for weather cover	
BERTRAN COURT	4/6/16		Work continued on New track. Decauville track, Ammunition Dumps & T.M. Dug-outs. 3 trucks completed & put on railway. T.M. Dugouts started in ROMAN RR. All work being carried on by continuous shifts.	

J.M. Hodges.
O.C. 1/1st Renfrew
Field Coy. R.E.

1875 Wt. W593/826 1,000,000 4/15 J.B.C. & A. A.D.S.S./Forms/C. 2118.

Army Form C. 2118

WAR DIARY
or
INTELLIGENCE SUMMARY
(Erase heading not required.)

Instructions regarding War Diaries and Intelligence Summaries are contained in F.S. Regs., Part II. and the Staff Manual respectively. Title Pages will be prepared in manuscript.

Place	Date	Hour	Summary of Events and Information	Remarks and references to Appendices
BERTRAN COURT	5/6/16		Work continued on tracks. Becourt track ORCHARD — SUCERERIE. Galleries in T.M. Dug-outs in QUARRY started. 2nd T.M. Dug-out in ROMAN Rd started. AMMUNITION Dump in ACHEUX Rd.	
BERTRAN COURT	6/6/16		Work on tracks continued. Becourt track ORCHARD — SUCERERIE. ROMAN Rd started. Cover on Ammunition Dumps completed. Work started roadways for Dumps. Work on T.M. Dugouts in ROMAN Rd & QUARRY continued. Corps O.P. Dug-out & Tunnel under 5th Avenue taken over from 1/Durham L.I.	
BERTRAN COURT	7/6/16		Work continued on CORPS O.P. DUG-OUT & TUNNEL under SUNKEN Rd. Track from BERTRANCOURT to POMMIERS completed. Becourt track ORCHARD — SUCERERIE. Rails laid on track up ROMAN Rd. New road cut of Ammunition Dumps ACHEUX Rd. Excavations for T.M. Dug-outs ROMAN Rd.	

Jno Hodgson Capt R.E.
No 1 Int. RENDE...
FIELD COY. R.E.

1875 Wt. W593/826 1,000,000 4/15 J.B.C. & A. A.D.S.S./Forms/C. 2118.

Army Form C. 2118

WAR DIARY
or
INTELLIGENCE SUMMARY
(Erase heading not required.)

Instructions regarding War Diaries and Intelligence Summaries are contained in F. S. Regs., Part II. and the Staff Manual respectively. Title Pages will be prepared in manuscript.

Place	Date	Hour	Summary of Events and Information	Remarks and references to Appendices
BERTRAN COURT	8/6/16		Work carried on CORPS O.P. Dugouts & TUNNEL under SUNKEN R?. New track started from POMMIERS - SUCRERIE. Deauville track ORCHARD - SUCRERIE & ROMAN R?. Ammunition dumps in AMIENS R?. T.M. Dug-outs in ROMAN R? & QUARRY.	
BERTRAN COURT	9/6/16		Work carried on CORPS O.P. Dug-out & TUNNEL 5th AVENUE. This work was greatly hindered at night owing to heavy shelling of dumps & stores could not be brought up. Deauville tracks ORCHARD - SUCRERIE & ROMAN R? tracks. New loop road started from BERTRANCOURT - BEAUSART - MAILLY.	
BERTRAN COURT	10/6/16		Work carried on CORPS.O.P. Dug-outs & TUNNEL 5th AVENUE. BEAUSART road cleared & ramps made for level crossings. Deauville tracks, ROMAN R?. - ORCHARD - SUCRERIE. T.M. Dugouts in ROMAN R? & QUARRY. Start made on R.E. Dug-out on MAILLY - BEAUSART loop road.	

J M Hodgson
Major 1/1st Renfrew??
FIELD COY. R.E.

1875 Wt. W593/826 1,000,000 4/15 J.B.C. & A. A.D.S.S./Forms/C. 2118.

Army Form C. 2118

WAR DIARY
or
INTELLIGENCE SUMMARY
(Erase heading not required.)

Instructions regarding War Diaries and Intelligence Summaries are contained in F.S. Regs., Part II. and the Staff Manual respectively. Title Pages will be prepared in manuscript.

Place	Date	Hour	Summary of Events and Information	Remarks and references to Appendices
BERTRAN COURT	11/6/16		Works carried on CORPS O.P. Dugout & TUNNEL in 5th AVENUE. BEAUSART Loop completed. Ramps made & level crossing completed over railway MAILLY - BEAUSART at East end of BEAUSART. Decauville track up ROMAN Rd & ORCHARD - SUCERERIE, work on that named tramway could only be carried on by night. Lifting platforms erected at Ammunition dumps ACHEUX Rd. Work started on T.M. dugouts in QUARRY & platform erected for storage of bombs (etc.) Excavation of R.E. dug-out on MAILLY - COLINCAMPS Rd.	
BERTRAN COURT	12/6/16		Work carried on at CORPS O.P. dugout & TUNNEL in 5th AVENUE. Decauville tracks ROMAN Rd, ORCHARD - SUCERERIE. T.M. dug outs on ROMAN Rd. R.E. Dugout work was severely impeded on both these works owing to serious flooding. BEAUSART - MAILLY - BERTRANCOURT track completed.	
BERTRAN COURT	13/6/16		Work carried out at CORPS O.P. Dug out & TUNNEL 5th AVENUE. Decauville tracks ROMAN Rd. ORCHARD - SUCERERIE. T.M. dugouts in ROMAN Rd, R.E. dug out on BEAUSART loop road for R.E. dump. Repairs to ACHEUX Rd at Ammunition Dump.	

H.M. Hoggan.
Capt. R.E. (T)
O.C. 1/1st [illegible]
FIELD Coy. R.E.

1875 Wt. W593/826 1,000,000 4/15 J.B.C. & A. A.D.S.S./Forms/C. 2118.

Army Form C. 2118

WAR DIARY
or
INTELLIGENCE SUMMARY
(Erase heading not required.)

Instructions regarding War Diaries and Intelligence Summaries are contained in F. S. Regs., Part II. and the Staff Manual respectively. Title Pages will be prepared in manuscript.

Place	Date	Hour	Summary of Events and Information	Remarks and references to Appendices
BERTRAN COURT	14/6		Works carried on at CORPS O.P. Dug-out & TUNNEL in 3rd AVENUE. Deauville track ROMAN Rd, ORCHARD - SUCRERIE, work stopped on last named track owing to continuous shelling. Track broken in two places, repairs effected before dawn. T.M. Dug-outs in ROMAN Rd. & repairs to ACHEUX Rd. 10 tons metal laid. O.C. 2nd Lot A.H. Anderson transferred to hospital.	
BERTRAN COURT	15/6	9 am	Major HORDERN R.E. took over command of unit. Works continued on CORPS O.P. Dug out & TUNNEL in 3rd AVENUE, Deep out roofed. Deauville tracks. ROMAN Rd., ORCHARD - SUCRERIE. T.M. Dugouts in ROMAN Rd. New track started from BERTRANCOURT to SUCRERIE. Repairs to road at Ammunition Dump ACHEUX Rd., 30 tons metal laid. O.C. visited all works & offrs. 12 to 1 PM.	
BERTRAN COURT	16/6		Works continued on CORPS O.P. Dug-out & TUNNEL. Concrete roof of O.P. started. Deauville track ORCHARD - SUCRERIE completed & linked up with old track from SUCRERIE - VAILROE. 5 new trucks put on roads. Deauville track in ROMAN Rd. ramp made from F end of ELLES Sq. for track to HYDE PARK CORNER. Start made with track from 3rd AVENUE to WHITE CITY. T.M. Dugouts in ROMAN Rd. half roofed & galleries framed. R.E. Dugout gallery framed. New track BERTRANCOURT - SUCRERIE about ⅔ complete. Working teams for roads mostly.	H.W. Hordern

1875 Wt. W593/826 1,000,000 4/15 J.B.C. & A. A.D.S.S./Forms/C. 2118.

WAR DIARY or INTELLIGENCE SUMMARY

(Erase heading not required.)

Army Form C. 2118

Instructions regarding War Diaries and Intelligence Summaries are contained in F.S. Regs., Part II. and the Staff Manual respectively. Title Pages will be prepared in manuscript.

Place	Date	Hour	Summary of Events and Information	Remarks and references to Appendices
BERTRAN COURT	17/6		Works carried on CORPS O.P. Dug out & TUNNEL in 3rd Avenue. Takes roof on rails to aid concealment. Roof of Tunnel propped. Deccauville track. ROMAN R4. to HYDE PARK CORNER. 3rd AVENUE & WHITE CITY. Bridge erected for last named. R.E. & T.M. Dug outs. New road to SUCRERIE completed. Hand bridges on MAILLY - AUCHONVILLERS track erected. Water troughs erected at B.O.S. water point.	
BERTRAN COURT	18/6		Works carried on. CORPS O.P. dug out & TUNNEL. Roof of O.P. completed (concrete). Deccauville tracks. ROMAN R4. 2 hand bridges built. WHITE CITY LINE 9 direct hits, line repaired. T.M. Dug out & R.S. Dug-out framework erected. MAILLY - AUCHONVILLERS road completed & extension beyond SUCRERIE started. Metal put on MENEUX R4. at Ammunition Dumps. 20 tons metal laid on MENEUX R4. at Ammunition Dumps.	
BERTRAN COURT	19/6		Works carried out on CORPS O.P. Dug-out & TUNNEL. Ventilator shaft from O.P. to Dug out started. Steps up to 3rd Avenue completed. Deccauville tracks. ROMAN R4. 2 bridges erected & loops laid from ramps to WHITE C. LINE T.M. Dug outs & R.E. Dug-out. NEW TRACK SUCRERIE to NEW TRENCH completed. Road at Ammunition Dumps repaired.	

A.M. Hodgard
CAPT. R.E.
O.C. 1/1st SHEFFIELD
FIELD COY. R.E.

Army Form C. 2118

WAR DIARY
or
INTELLIGENCE SUMMARY

(Erase heading not required.)

Instructions regarding War Diaries and Intelligence Summaries are contained in F. S. Regs, Part II. and the Staff Manual respectively. Title Pages will be prepared in manuscript.

Place	Date	Hour	Summary of Events and Information	Remarks and references to Appendices
BERTRAN COURT	20/6		Works carried on. CORPS O.P. Dug out & TUNNEL in 3rd AVENUE. Beaucourt tracks. 2 trenches bridged & 15" tracks completed & repaired on rails. T.M. & RE Dugouts. Framing made & galleries stepped. ROADS. Guide posts made & erected on BEAUSART-MAILY track. 10 tons metal laid on HAIFUX R^d.	
BERTRAN COURT	21/6		Work carried on. CORPS O.P. Dug-out & tunnel now nearing completion. T.M. Dugouts framing erected. R.E. Dug-out framing completed & 2nd gallery commenced. Beaucourt track. ROMAN R^d — HYDE PARK completed, forward dump for rails made. Name boards erected in Trenches.	
BERTRAN COURT	22/6		Works carried out. CORPS O.P. Dug-out & TUNNEL in 3rd AVENUE R.E. Dugout completed. T.M. Dug outs ROMAN R^d framing in 8 shelters completed. Name boards & marking posts for forward trenches & forward roads made. French bullion wall & wirelss in INFERNO TR^{ch}.	
		6 pm	Company concentrated in ORCHARD on BEAUCOURT-BEAURAMCOURT R^d. at P.C.R.	

A.M.Hodgard
CAPT.
FIELD CO^Y. R.E.

Army Form C. 2118

WAR DIARY
or
INTELLIGENCE SUMMARY
(Erase heading not required.)

Instructions regarding War Diaries and Intelligence Summaries are contained in F.S. Regs., Part II. and the Staff Manual respectively. Title Pages will be prepared in manuscript.

Place	Date	Hour	Summary of Events and Information	Remarks and references to Appendices
CAMP at P.B.2. Nr ranch BEAUMONT No 2 4 B. zone	24/6/14		Work completed on PUMPS, OP Dug-out & TUNNEL in 5th Avenue. Fresh O.P. constructed during night 33/24" in ELLES SQUARE. Decauville track ORCHARD - SUCERERIE - HYDE PARK completed. Tractor line over SEBRE R? from ROMAN R? to WHITE CITY & 5th AVENUE started. Two concrete dugouts at SUCERERIE developed for R? Artillery.	
CAMP	25/6	11-0 am	Company employed overhauling vehicles, stores, tools(etc). Inspection by O.C. Company. Trenches in rear of CAMP dug with the view of providing shelter of camp by the enemy.	
		12.0 noon	Railway patrol reports all lines up to 12 midnight 24/25th. Patrol reports 1 break in ROMAN R? repairs effected. Bridge patrol reports all correct on SEBRE R? bridges.	
CAMP	26/6/10	4 pm	Company completes overhauling stores, vehicles. Gas helmet drill & lectures by O.C. Lecture. Rail patrol reports bridge over SERRE R? broken down by shell fire. Bridge rebuilt by night. Forward dumps for tools & stores completed & some stores taken up & dumped.	
		5.30 pm	MAILLY keenly shelled & R.E. store set on fire.	

A.M. Hodgart
O.C., 173rd RENGLER HIRE
CAPT. R.E. (?)
FIELD ?

Army Form C. 2118

WAR DIARY
or
INTELLIGENCE SUMMARY
(Erase heading not required.)

Instructions regarding War Diaries and Intelligence Summaries are contained in F. S. Regs., Part II. and the Staff Manual respectively. Title Pages will be prepared in manuscript.

Place	Date	Hour	Summary of Events and Information	Remarks and references to Appendices
CAMP P.6.a.	27/6/16	5.0am	Action rehearsed parade, with full company stores.	
		10.0am	Party sent out to repair dug out at ration dump on ORCHARD–SUCERERIE road. Repairs to AUCHONVILLE R.E. signal cable buried. Dug out at NORTHERN telephone exchange in BOW ST. Rail patrol reported break in WHITE CITY LINE. Repairs effected at night. EXIT ladders made & erected in BORDEN TRENCH.	
CAMP	28/6/16	7.0am	Action rehearsal parade, with Tools, Equipment slung ready for action. Gas helmet drill & inspection. Letters by O.P. section. Repairs to telephone exchange & dug out effected by night. Trench sign boards completed & erected & posts for forward roads made.	
		8-0pm	Patrol reported No.2 bridge over SERRE R⁴ damaged, repairs effected.	
CAMP	29/6/16	7.0am	Action rehearsal parade with rehicles & details of assembly given. Roads repaired MAILLY–AUCHONVILLERS. Patrols reported breaks in line on ORCHARD–SUCERERIE track, repairs effected by night. O.P. in ELLES S.B. damaged by shell fire, repaired, also gun emps to connect at EUSTON.	
		4.0pm		

J.M. Hodgson

Army Form C. 2118

WAR DIARY
or
INTELLIGENCE SUMMARY
(Erase heading not required.)

Instructions regarding War Diaries and Intelligence Summaries are contained in F. S. Regs., Part II. and the Staff Manual respectively. Title Pages will be prepared in manuscript.

Place	Date	Hour	Summary of Events and Information	Remarks and references to Appendices
CAMP P.6.A.	30/6	7/40am	Company inspected by G.O.C. who addressed the units on the coming attack.	
		9-30am	Action rehearsed forwards.	
			Ammunition & Ammonal charges made up.	
			Bengal torpedos filled & taken up to Dump.	
			All tools & stores taken up & forward dumps completed.	
		6pm	No. 1 Section. Lieut. A.D. Bell in command marched out of camp to take up position in Assembly Trench.	

H. Hodgart
Capt. R.E.
O.C. 171st Rt...
Field Coy. R.E.

4th DIVISION.

I/IST RENFREW FIELD COMPANY.

ROYAL ENGINEERS.

JULY 1916.

WAR DIARY or INTELLIGENCE SUMMARY

Army Form C. 2118

1/1 Renfrew & Coy R.E.

Place	Date	Hour	Summary of Events and Information	Remarks and references to Appendices
BLANP	1/7/16	7-15 am	Company parade (less 1 section) in fighting order. All of but transport & R.E. Limbered waggons stopped away to go forward with stores.	
P.G.H.		8-15 am	No.4 Lieut Jones marched out of camp, to repair & reconnoitre MAILLY - SUCRERIE Rd & SERRE Rd. One load road material sent up to SUCRERIE.	
Huns Map SyD 1/40000		11 am	No.2 Sect under Lieut McWilliam moved up to SUCRERIE to assist in repairing Roads.	
		12 noon	Beaucourt rail Patrols reported line all correct.	
		12 noon	SERRE Rd Bridges reported all correct.	
		4 pm	Patrols reported SERRE Rd Bridges Beaucourt track & MAILLY Rd all correct.	
		4.30 pm	No.2 Sect ordered to return to P.G.H.	
		6-15 pm	No.4 Sect ordered to return to P.G.H via MAILLY Rd reported road in good order.	
		8-0 pm	SERRE Rd Bridges & Beaucourt track reported all correct.	
		12-0 midnight	Beaucourt Track reported 2 breaks, these were immediately repaired	
		12-30 pm	SERRE Rd Bridges all correct.	
			Unit in Bivouac at P.G.H.	

1086   1155   1045   12/8
Capts M. Keller, N. Aitken, W/R M. B. & O'Connell Wounded.

H.M. Hodgard CAPT. R.E. (T).
O.C. 1/1 RENFREW
FIELD COY. R.E.

Army Form C. 2118

WAR DIARY
or
INTELLIGENCE SUMMARY
(Erase heading not required.)

Instructions regarding War Diaries and Intelligence Summaries are contained in F. S. Regs., Part II. and the Staff Manual respectively. Title Pages will be prepared in manuscript.

Place	Date	Hour	Summary of Events and Information	Remarks and references to Appendices
CAMP P.C.H. Ref. Map Sheet No 57d 1:40000	2/7/16	6-30 AM	All animals harnessed & needles yoked ready to move.	
		8-0 AM	SERRE Rd. & Decauville portals reported all correct.	
		8-30 AM	No 4 Sect left camp & proceeded to TAUPIN TRENCH to effect repairs	
		9-0 AM	O.C. visited 12 Bn HQrs & inspected all trenches in sector. Trenches were in a ruinous condition owing to shelling.	
		12-30 PM	No 1 Sect withdrawn from Line. They aid not leave the forward dug during the attack on previous day.	
		8-30 PM	No 2 Sect left camp for work on deepening pumps was taken in order to pump out trenches.	
		9-0 PM	No 3 Sect left camp with pumps for work on BORDEN AVE.	
		9-30 PM	All 1 Line transport left to fetch water stores from SERRE Rd. On arrival there heavily shelling, the enemy using 1MHR/1MTRY shells, resulting in seriously wounding of Driver Houston & 1 Riding Horse. 1 PD Horse slightly wounded. Driver Houston after being wounded showed great pluck by driving his vehicle out of danger until the dressing station HALLY was reached.	
		11-45 PM	9/D Corpl Peebles, D. wounded. (Shrapnel)	

A. M. Hodgart
Capt, R.E. (T.)
O.C. 1/1st RENFREWSHIRE
FIELD COY., R.E.

Army Form C. 2118

WAR DIARY
or
INTELLIGENCE SUMMARY
(Erase heading not required.)

Instructions regarding War Diaries and Intelligence Summaries are contained in F.S. Regs., Part II. and the Staff Manual respectively. Title Pages will be prepared in manuscript.

Place	Date	Hour	Summary of Events and Information	Remarks and references to Appendices
Camp	3/4/16	5-30 AM	3 Sections returned to camp from Loos-elles	
P.G.H. Reference Map Sheet 54 D 1/40,000		3-15 pm	4 Sections left camp for work repairing 2nd line trenches & entry covers in B.6. area.	
			1 line transport engaged conveying stores to point K 33. L. 5. 2. By Sheet 11. S.W. D 6740. Whilst unloading all 8 line tr. wagon at this point the wagon was struck on the Yser portion by an H.E. Shell, which detonated resulting in the death	
		11-45 pm	of N° 1083 Corp¹ Lyon P. 1115 Cap¹ Hamilton W. 1242 S¹ Shelton, S. who were killed outright, also 2 S.D. Mules were killed. 1/4 Home [illegible] tops blown away which was afterwards shot. Wagon & stores were completely destroyed	

H W Hodgart
CAPT., R.E. (T.),
O.C., 1/1st RENFREWSHIRE FIELD COY., R.E.

Army Form C. 2118

WAR DIARY
or
INTELLIGENCE SUMMARY
(Erase heading not required.)

Instructions regarding War Diaries and Intelligence Summaries are contained in F.S. Regs., Part II. and the Staff Manual respectively. Title Pages will be prepared in manuscript.

Place	Date	Hour	Summary of Events and Information	Remarks and references to Appendices
Camp P.G.H.	4/4/16	4-15PM	Sections returned to camp	
		9-0AM	Working parties sent out to pump water out of CHEEROH AVE. 6th AVE. & VALLADE as these trenches were flooded to a depth of 2'6".	
Reserve Hy Luisnoyd L/1800		8-0PM	Working parties sent out to repair breaks in parapet of TURPIN TRENCH, clearing foreground from ELLES SQUARE to NEWGATE & wiring reformed. Wiring around FORT HOYSTED, ELLES SQ. VIEW TRENCH renewed & repaired. 30 yards new fire step in 6th AVENUE added. Breaks in DECAUVILLE line on ORCHARD–SUCRERIE repaired. 140 yds of old wood track down SERRE Rd replaced by metal track.	
Camp P.G.H.	5/4/16	4-15AM	Working parties returned to camp.	
		9-0AM	Working parties sent out to pump out CHEEROH AVE. 6th AVE. & VALLADE water in these trenches was reduced to a depth of 6".	
		9-0PM	Night parties sent out for work on entanglements in front of VIEW TR. & VELLES SQ. Remainder of wooden track down SERRE Rd. replaced by metal track. 1 break in DECAUVILLE on SUCRERIE–HYDE PARK CORNER repaired.	

Lieut. J. M°WILLIAM wounded by shrapnel.

H M Hodgart
Capt...
O.C., 1/1st RENFREWSHIRE
FIELD COY. R.E.

Army Form C. 2118

WAR DIARY
or
INTELLIGENCE SUMMARY
(Erase heading not required.)

Instructions regarding War Diaries and Intelligence Summaries are contained in F.S. Regs., Part II. and the Staff Manual respectively. Title Pages will be prepared in manuscript.

Place	Date	Hour	Summary of Events and Information	Remarks and references to Appendices
Camp P.C.H. Rly Head Martinsey D 1/40,000	6/10		Parties at work pumping out CHEEROH AVE, 6th AVE & PALLIADE. Drainy trenches. Trench boards laid in CHEEROH TRK. Party repairing the steps in BORDEN TR. Start made with new Deauville line from SUNKEN RD. Hut erected in camp. R.E. Workshops at MAILLY repaired. O.C. Major C. HOADERN transferred to hospital sick.	
Camp	7/10		No return could be effected in trenches owing to heavy rains causing serious flooding. All available men & pumps were employed to keep water as low as possible. A few trench boards were laid in CHEEROH TRK & sumps pits dug. 150 yds new Deauville track laid at night.	
Camp	8/10		Pumping operations on CHEEROH AVE, PALLIADE, 6th AVE. Good progress made & nearly all water pumped out. Trench boards laid in CHEEROH AVE & sumps dug & trench drainage started. One hut erected in camp. R.E. WORKSHOP trench frames made ready for trench heads prepared. Pistons & over-heads erected in workshops by 9th Field Coy R.E.	

J.M. Hodgard
CAPT. R.E. (T.)
O.C. 1/1st RENFREWSHIRE
FIELD COY. R.E.

WAR DIARY
or
INTELLIGENCE SUMMARY

(Erase heading not required.)

Army Form C. 2118

Instructions regarding War Diaries and Intelligence Summaries are contained in F. S. Regs., Part II. and the Staff Manual respectively. Title Pages will be prepared in manuscript.

Place	Date	Hour	Summary of Events and Information	Remarks and references to Appendices
Camp P.C.H At Huf Hill N°5 y.d.	9/10		Pumping continued on LEGEND Tr. Trench boards laid on BUFFALO Tr. deepening of trench & drainage continued. Gas hut erected in Camp. 1-9p Night party started work on T's improving VALLADE Tr. Ramp completed for Decauville track across SUNKEN Rd & stores carried up.	
Camp	10/10		Day parties at work on CHEEROH AVE trench boards & clearing of trench. This trench had been badly hit by shell during night & 70 places were repaired by monthly work (?) w. sandbags. 14 T's more dug in I LEGEND Tr. Work started at night on trench BURROW Tr. This portion of trench was completely flooded. Work cont'd on Decauville track rails carried up from ROMAN Pl Lair to SERRE Rd. Loose trenches repaired in line between SUNKEN Rd & 6th AVE crossing. Gas hut erected in Camp. French frames made in Workshop. & Loopers of revent tank pasteur rivet on enemy trenches. Reciting party returned to camp as usual. A.M. Hodgart. CAPT., R.E. (T.) O.C., 1/1st RENFREWSHIRE FIELD COY., R.E.	

1875 Wt. W593/826 1,000,000 4/15 J.B.C. & A. A.D.S.S./Forms/C. 2118.

Army Form C. 2118

WAR DIARY
or
INTELLIGENCE SUMMARY
(Erase heading not required.)

Instructions regarding War Diaries and Intelligence Summaries are contained in F.S. Regs., Part II. and the Staff Manual respectively. Title Pages will be prepared in manuscript.

Place	Date	Hour	Summary of Events and Information	Remarks and references to Appendices
Camp P.L.H. Hq Staff Shaft No 5 9.D. 1/1,1000	9/11/16		Work of deepening, draining, & keeping French boards in CHEEROH AVE cont. Shaft "J's" completed in LEGEND T? with fire steps & communications deepened. Tunnel in BURRON T? cutting made through SERRE R? and tunnel filled in, trench made passable. 135' of the Deserire Trench had heavy rights 11/12". Work on bay-nest frames in workshop.	
Camp	10/11/16		Light "T's" completed in LEGEND T? Shoes taken up for dug-outs in LEGEND T? Work started on dug-outs by continuous shifts. Trench boards laid in CHEEROH AVE & trench closed on forms in LEGEND T? Work started on 6"A.T.F. deepening & cleaning trench. Large trees repaired in Beaverville Line ORCHARD-SUCRERIE, mine cut & road prepared for main track. Carpenters Trench frames & dug-out frames in Reg Workshop MAILLY.	

A.W. Hodgart
CAPT. R.E. (T).
O.C. 1/1st HIGHLAND
FIELD COY., R.E.

Army Form C. 2118

WAR DIARY
or
INTELLIGENCE SUMMARY
(Erase heading not required.)

Instructions regarding War Diaries and Intelligence Summaries are contained in F.S. Regs., Part II. and the Staff Manual respectively. Title Pages will be prepared in manuscript.

Place	Date	Hour	Summary of Events and Information	Remarks and references to Appendices
Camp P.U.H. Dot Madh Dud N° 54 D. Ypres	13/4/16		Work carried on Line "G" completed in LEGEND TR & now started gallery in Dug-Out. Frames overhauled & put crossents in each gallery. Trench boards laid & revetting in CHEFROH AVE. Refixing & laying 6th AVE. 215 yds new Decauville track laid over SUNKEN RR. Dug-out & trench frames made in Workshops.	
Camp	14/4/16		Work continued in CHEFROH AVE clearing & deepening & laying trench boards Work on new dug-outs in LEGEND T.R. excavating galleries. No work done on 7" in LEGEND or Decauville tracks owing to working parties being wanted back at 3.30 p.m. N° 1073 Sapper Duguid R. wounded by shrapnel in CHEFROH AVE. Lieut. ARK Shutter fought very few Cals.	
Camp	15/4/16		Cleaning of CHEFROH AVE & 6th AVE continued, refixing BAP.D.F.N AVE at AMIAN RR end. "G" completed in LEGEND TR making a total of 112 7ft. laid to date 3 rafter. Elephant shelter for 8th Wyo at MANLY started. Making Dug-out & trench frames in R.E. Workshops New Decauville track. Trenches drifted & stores carried up. The party were heavily shelled during night 14/15 little progress made. N° 1135 Sapper Jamieson wounded by shrapnel McFadzeal.	OC. 176 Res. BEY.... Capt. R.E. (T) FIELD COY. R.E.

1875 Wt. W593/826 1,000,000 4/15 J.B.C. & A. A.D.S.S./Forms/C. 2118.

Army Form C. 2118

WAR DIARY
or
INTELLIGENCE SUMMARY
(Erase heading not required.)

Instructions regarding War Diaries and Intelligence Summaries are contained in F. S. Regs., Part II. and the Staff Manual respectively. Title Pages will be prepared in manuscript.

Place	Date	Hour	Summary of Events and Information	Remarks and references to Appendices
Camp P.b.A. Rd works Pead N°5 y.a. ???	16/4/16		Work carried on Dug-outs in LEGEND T? galleries attained 5 feet. Work started on Dug-out in BURROW T? Deepening & laying French pocards in CHEEROH & 6" AVE. Deepening & laying French pocards in CHEEROH & 6" AVE? New T?? lack to hold 6 rifles started in CHEAPSIDE. 135 yards new Decauville track laid to MAHONVILLERS. Work on B?? Hqrs NAILLY continued. Dug-out & track elements made in R.g. Workshops. NAILLY. Capt M.E. Hodgart joined unit from Lit.	
Camp	17/4/16		Work on Dug-outs in LEGEND & BURROW T?? continued & frames in galleries erected. Dug-out in MOUNTJOY T? started. New T?'s in CHEAPSIDE completed. Repairing of CHEEROH AVE & 6 AVE continued. Work on all tunnel BURROW T?? old frames removed & temporary revetment to match. 165 yards new Decauville track laid.	
Camp	18/4/16		Work on Dug-outs in LEGEND, BURROW, MOUNTJOY T?? continued. Deepening tunnel in BURROW T?? shored frames put in. No work was done on Decauville track as stores taken up owing to a Bombardment ?????	

F.M. Hodgart
CAPT. R.E. (T).
O.C., 1/1st RENFREW???
FIELD COY

WAR DIARY or INTELLIGENCE SUMMARY

Army Form C. 2118

(Erase heading not required.)

Instructions regarding War Diaries and Intelligence Summaries are contained in F.S. Regs., Part II. and the Staff Manual respectively. Title Pages will be prepared in manuscript.

Place	Date	Hour	Summary of Events and Information	Remarks and references to Appendices
Camp P.6.A Ref group Sheet N.57.D	19/7/16		Work on Dug Outs in LEGEND, BURROW, & MOUNTJOY T⁴ continued. Dug out in CHATHAM T⁴ started. Men were sent from 6ᵗʰ H.L.I. out to MAILLY R⁹ started. Were evacuated to a depth of 3 ft. for about 215 yards. Work of deepening 6ᵗʰ avenue & tunnel towards continued. Land drainage for Dernancourt made over SUNKEN R⁴ & MAILLE MAILLY R⁴. Rails lifted from old MAILLY line & taken to HAMEL–HUM HAMMELVILLERS R⁴ station.	
Camp	20/7/16		Work on N⁰⁵ 1, 2, 3, 4 & 5 Dug outs continued Galleries well advanced & framed. Deepening of 6ᵗʰ ave completed. Heads trace laid in 6ᵗʰ ave & CHATHAM. Deepening of tunnel in BURROW T⁴. Elements frames erected & revetment prepared. Stores for Dernancourt track taken to BUCHONVILLE R.S. Station Orders received to find our work in sects. N 63 by R.8. All work was visited by the O.C. Coys & Liaison officers of relieving Coy.	
		7 pm	All tools withdrawn & working parties returned to HQ of each.	

H.M. Hodgart
CAPT., R.E. (T.)
O.C., 1/1st RENFREWSHIRE
FIELD COY., R.E.

Army Form C. 2118

WAR DIARY
or
INTELLIGENCE SUMMARY
(Erase heading not required.)

Instructions regarding War Diaries and Intelligence Summaries are contained in F. S. Regs., Part II. and the Staff Manual respectively. Title Pages will be prepared in manuscript.

Place	Date	Hour	Summary of Events and Information	Remarks and references to Appendices
Camp P.C.A 104 Ypres Dist N°51 D Ypres	21/7/16		All Company stores packed & Company marched out at 4-30 am. The relieving Coy marched in at 8-30 am all stores, camp, correspondence (etc.) handed over, relay completed at 9 am. Then N.C.O's left & other parties for relieving Coys working parties. Company arrived at camp in BUS 1.30.2.3.H at 9-15 am onwards.	
		2-0 pm	Inspection of arms & equipment by O.C. West.	
BUS	22/7/16	7-30 AM	Company marched out route via LOUVENCOURT, MARIEUX, BARTON for AMPLIER arriving at 11-25 am. Coys arrived in Billets 3 officers	
		9 pm	Billets at gas helmets & gas drill.	
AMPLIER	23/7/16	4.45 AM	Company 1st Line Transport left AMPLIER along with by cyclists & cyclists for entrainment at DOULLENS, arrived DOULLENS at 8.50 am started to entrain. Remainder of unit left AMPLIER at 9-30 am arrived DOULLENS 10.55 am all & wheels & animals entrained. Entrainment completed ready to move at 12 noon. Train left at 12.19 pm. Arrived ESQUELBECQ at 6-30 pm. Detrainment & proceeded to billets in WORMHOUDT at D. of D.C.S.2. Ref. Sheet 1939 Ypres, Belgium.	

H.W. Hedgard, CAPT, R.E. (T),
O.C., 1/1st RENFREWSHIRE
FIELD COY., R.E.

Army Form C. 2118

WAR DIARY
or
INTELLIGENCE SUMMARY
(Erase heading not required.)

Instructions regarding War Diaries and Intelligence Summaries are contained in F.S. Regs., Part II. and the Staff Manual respectively. Title Pages will be prepared in manuscript.

Place	Date	Hour	Summary of Events and Information	Remarks and references to Appendices
Camp D.4. C.5.2. Belgium M/Sheet 1/134	24/10	10.00	Company in camp, employed on fatigues. Gas helmet drill. Camp visited by C.R.E. & orders received for move on following day.	
"	25/10		Company marched out at 2-opm & proceeded to Camps K at L.3.A.5.3. Refreshments may stop arriving there at 6-30 pm. All animals & vehicles parked. Bivouacs erected. Advance party consisting of 2 Officers & 4 N.C.O.'s proceeded to meet Guide from Grenade Line at POPERINGHE Town Hall at 8 pm for the purpose of taking over work in the Line. Party returned to Camp K at 5-30 am morning 26th inst.	
"	26/10		Company Hdqrs & 2 sections left camp at 2 pm proceeding to Camp K1a POPERINGHE arriving there at 4-45 pm. Camp reached at 9.05. via Msp Belgium Sheet N° B & N.W. All stores & maps taken over from 96th Field Coy R.E. 2 Sections left Camp K at L.3.A.5.3. at 6 pm arriving at railway overhead crossing met & section moved to BRIELEN. Relief complete & new line at midnight 26/27.	

W.M. Hodgart CAPT, R.E. (T).
O.C. 1/1st RENFREWSHIRE
FIELD COY., R.E.

Army Form C. 2118.

WAR DIARY
or
INTELLIGENCE SUMMARY
(Erase heading not required.)

Instructions regarding War Diaries and Intelligence Summaries are contained in F.S. Regs., Part II. and the Staff Manual respectively. Title Pages will be prepared in manuscript.

Place	Date	Hour	Summary of Events and Information	Remarks and references to Appendices
Camp Hts. L.9.5 Ref Map Belgium Sheet 14 S.W.NW	24/4/16	7-0 am	Company less 2 sections in Hutments at Camp A.15.2, 9, 5. Relieved by normal rest. Huts taken over & vehicles parked. Sections employed cleaning camp & washing vehicles. Lectures on line employed on day-Rest in BOAR-LANE & CONEY T.R. & carrying up stores. No Coys Working parties available.	
Camp Hts. L.9.5. Ref Map Belgium Sheet 14 S.W.NW	28/4/16		Sections in camp employed on Rifle Exercises, gas helmet drill. Overhauling stores & repairs to vehicles. Sections in huts on work at night. Dug-outs EMMELINE, LA BELLE ALLIANCE, WILLOWS. & Revet drains at WILLOWS. Four day-outs started at the WILLOWS.	
Camp	29/4/16		Sections in Camp at work clearing repairing weapons. Gas drill & rifle exercises. Sections in huts employed at night on drainage work at LA BELLE ALLIANCE. & at WILLOWS.	

H.W. Hodgach
Capt., R.E.
O.C. 1/1st RENFREW...
FIELD COY., R.E.

Army Form C. 2118

WAR DIARY
or
INTELLIGENCE SUMMARY
(Erase heading not required.)

Instructions regarding War Diaries and Intelligence Summaries are contained in F.S. Regs., Part II. and the Staff Manual respectively. Title Pages will be prepared in manuscript.

Place	Date	Hour	Summary of Events and Information	Remarks and references to Appendices
Camp H.15.c.9.5 Ref Map Belgium Sheet N° 27 NW	30/7/16		Sections in Camp overhauling stores in forenoon, rest during afternoon. Listons in Lines employed on night 29/30 on Drainage of dug-outs at HABELLE-ALLIANCE. Excavation & drainage of dug-outs at WILLOWS. N° 1218 Sapper Brunell.S. Wounded 29/16 Reported died of wounds at 39th Canadian General Hospital.	
Camp	31/7/16		1 Section employed on Icemaker & trench for pipe line at Camp & overhauling vehicles & improving Camp well duck-walks & Section in Line employed on night of 30/31, in carrying tools & stores & timber from Railway Cottage to forward portion of STIRLING-LANE.	

WMHodgard — O.C. O.O., 1/1st Renf............ 4 FIELD COY., R.E.

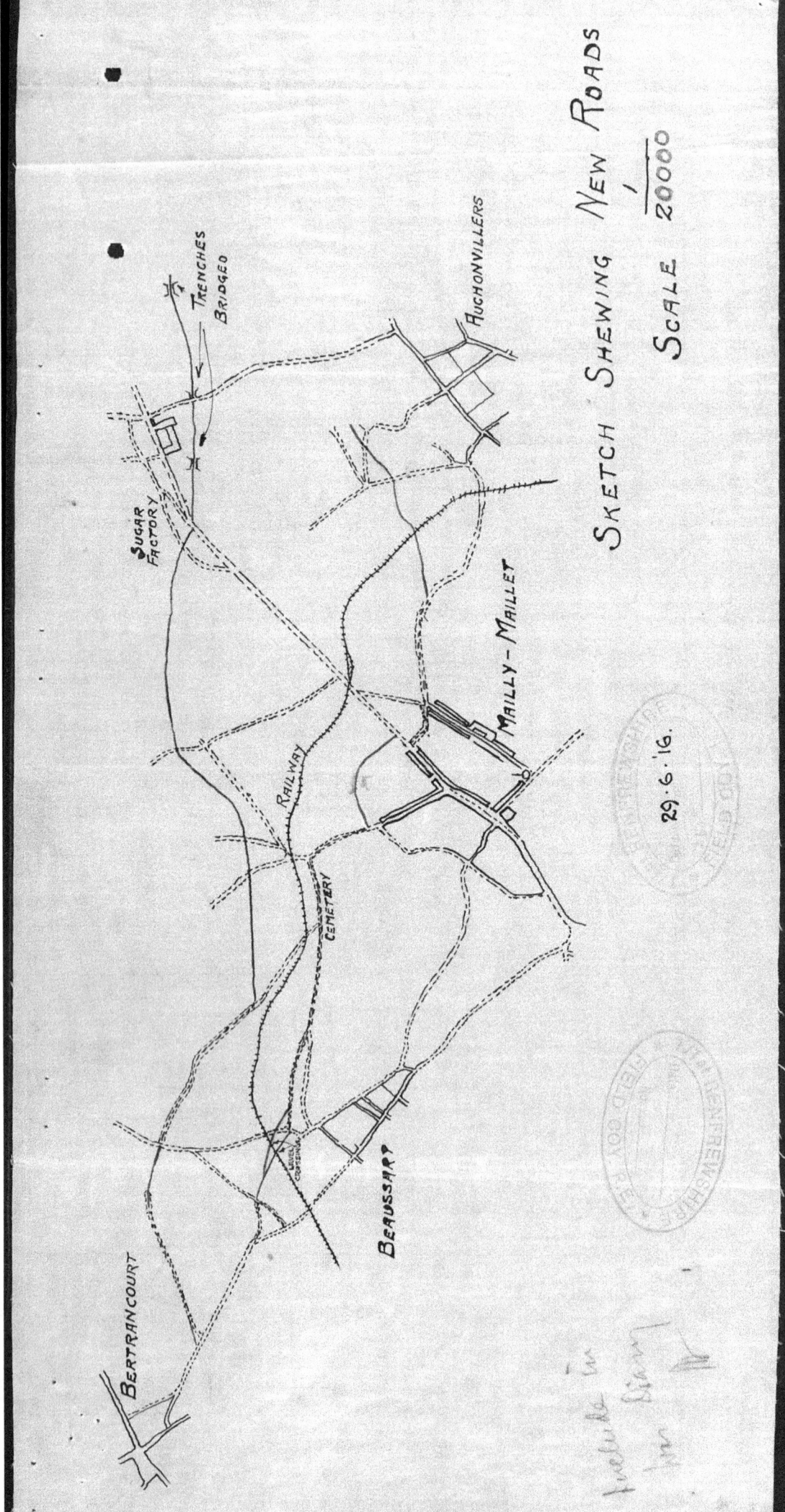

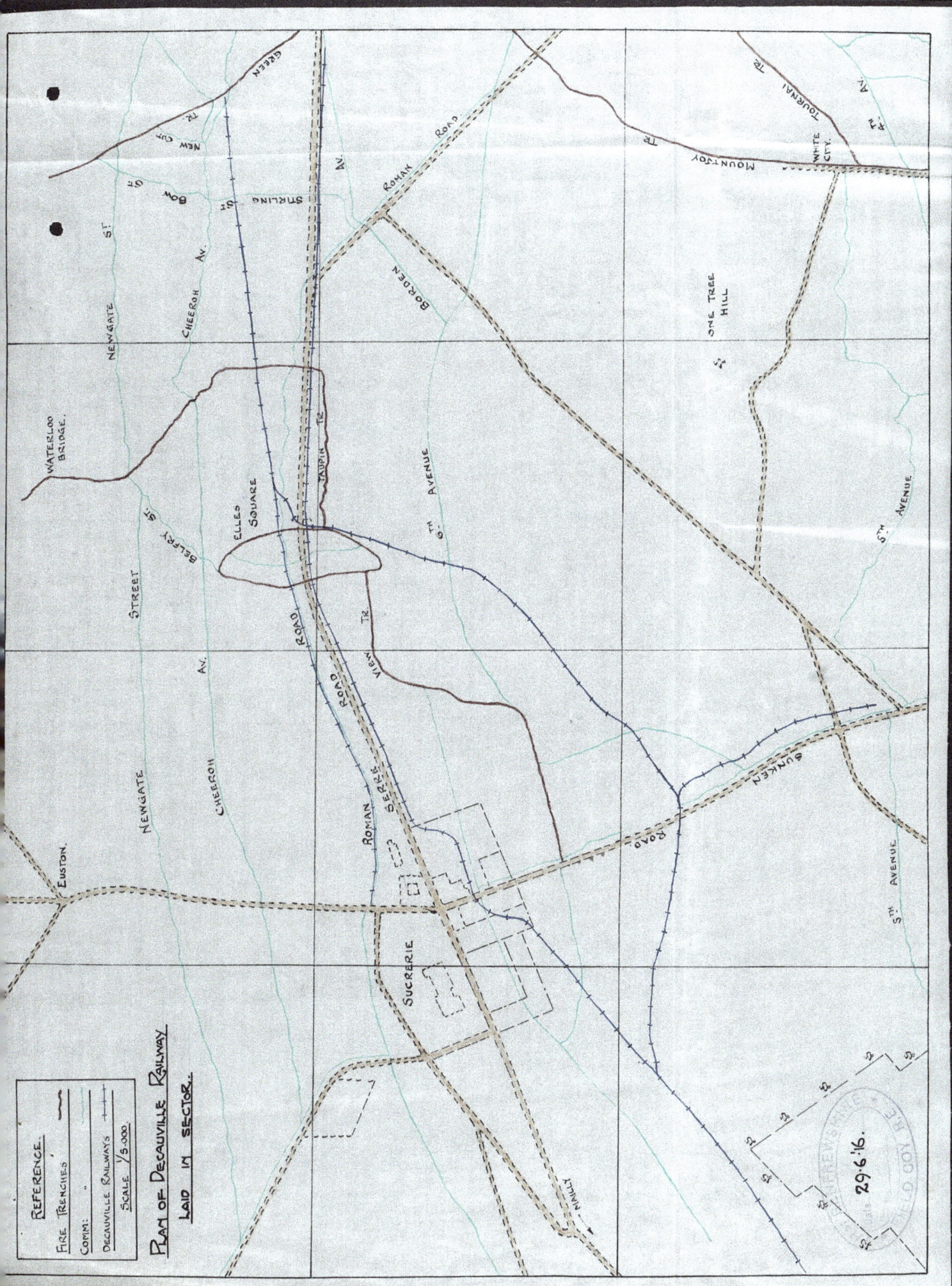

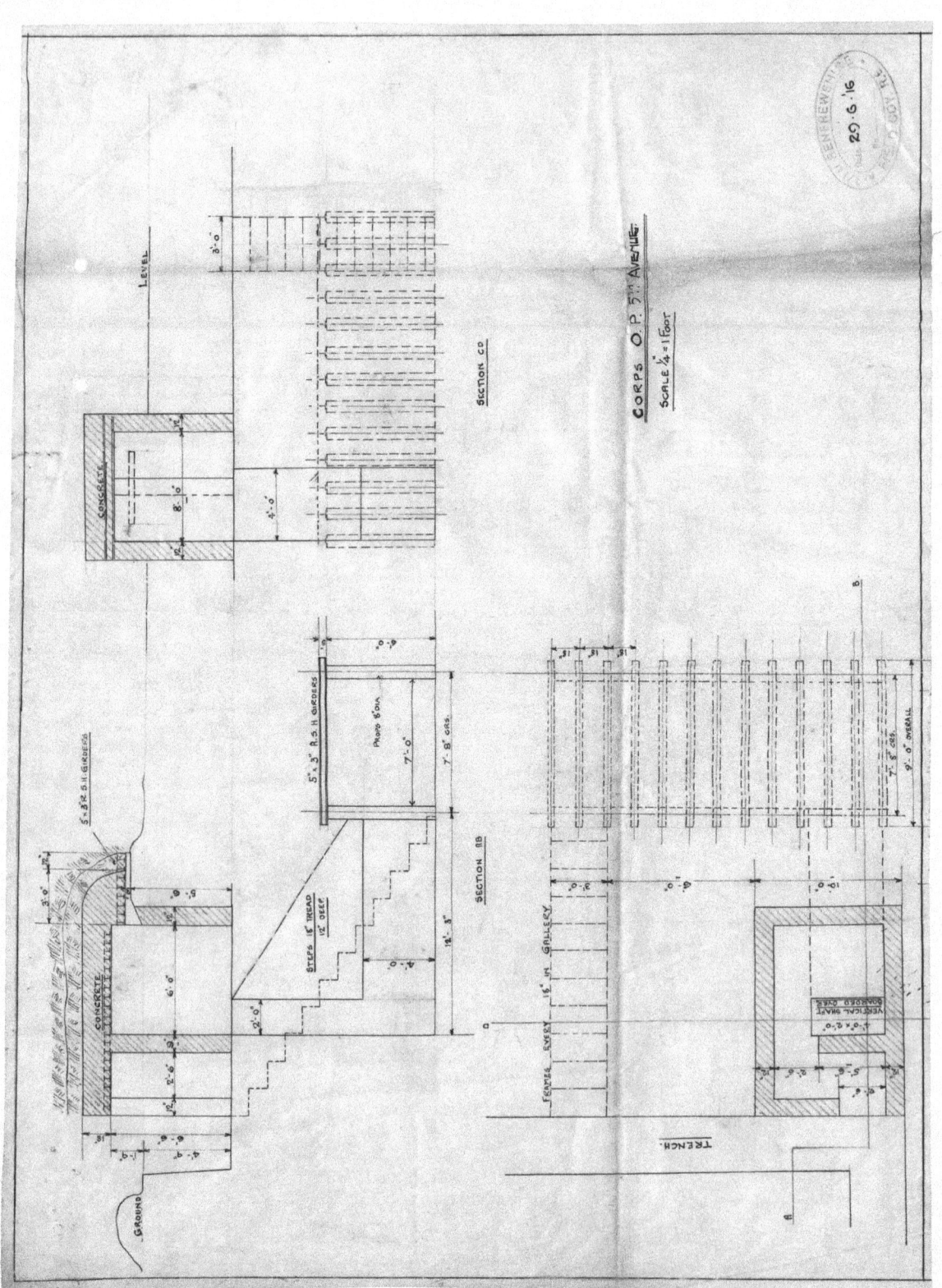

WAR DIARY or INTELLIGENCE SUMMARY

Army Form C. 2118

1/1 Renfrew 2nd Coy R.E. Vol 9

(Erase heading not required.)

Instructions regarding War Diaries and Intelligence Summaries are contained in F.S. Regs., Part II. and the Staff Manual respectively. Title Pages will be prepared in manuscript.

Place	Date	Hour	Summary of Events and Information	Remarks and references to Appendices
Hdqrs at CAMP.H. H15.2.9.5. Ref Maps Belgium Sheet N: 28NNW	1/7/16		SECTIONS at Hdqrs. Employed on improvements in CAMPS F.P.T.H. at B29.H42. Fitting A frames, revetting, laying trench boards & drainage of STIRLING LANE. Stores taken from Ply Cottage	
CAMP.H.	2/7/16		SECTIONS at Hdqrs. CAMP.P. Roadmaking & ablution bench. Repairs to fencing of horse standings at CAMP H. SECTIONS at B29.a.42. Erecting frames, revetting, heightening parapet & drainage of STIRLING LANE.	
CAMP.H.	3/7/16		SECTIONS at Hdqrs. CAMP.P. roadmaking, erecting water pipe & ablution bench. CAMP.H. Erecting incinerators & repairs to horse standings. SECTIONS at B29.a.42. Revetting, drainage & preparing trench for A frames on ground. STIRLING LANE. Bridge over PILKEM Rd removed & prepared to make bridge 2 ft. to suit heightening of parapet. WILLOWS. Communication trench widened & trench boards laid on dump prepared for stores.	

WmHodyal CAPT. R.E. (T.S.)
O.C. 1/1st RENFREWSHIRE FIELD COY, R.E.

1875 Wt. W593/826 1,000,000 4/15 J.B.C. & A. A.D.S.S./Forms/C. 2118.

WAR DIARY or INTELLIGENCE SUMMARY

Army Form C. 2118

(Erase heading not required.)

Instructions regarding War Diaries and Intelligence Summaries are contained in F.S. Regs., Part II. and the Staff Manual respectively. Title Pages will be prepared in manuscript.

Place	Date	Hour	Summary of Events and Information	Remarks and references to Appendices
Hdqrs at CAMP. H.	4/5/16		SECTIONS at Hdqrs. Roadmaking, carry water-pipes & ablution bench in CAMP. H. Repairing roads & drainage in CAMP. H.	CAMP. P.
Hrs 4,9,5 at Hdqrs between Huts 28MM			SECTIONS at B.29.a.4.2. Bridge over PIKKEM A4 relaid, heightening parapet & drainage of STIRLING LANE. Frames & stores taken up from Pdy Cottage Dug-outs at WILLOWS. Trench closed to dug-outs, parapet cleaned & new extension marked out.	
CAMP. H.	5/5/16		SECTIONS at Hdqrs. Roadmaking, new curb laid & 20 yds metalled. CAMP. P. Trench repaired for ablution bench; 1 hut taken down for transfer to CAMP H. SECTIONS at B.29.a.4.2. Bridge over PIKKEM A4 completed, heightening & revetting in STIRLING LANE. All dug-out parties employed conveying up stores.	CAMP. P.
CAMP. H.	6/5/16		SECTIONS at Hdqrs. Pathmaking, fitting pipes & pumps foundation bench CAMP. P. 2nd hut taken down & removed to CAMP. H. SECTIONS at B.29.a.4.2. Fitting A frames, revetting & drainage of STIRLING LANE. Dug-outs at WILLOWS. Excavation of dug-outs, stores taken up for concrete work.	

H M Hodgab.
CAPT., R.E. (T).
D.O., 1/1st RENFREWS
FIELD COY., R.E.

WAR DIARY
or
INTELLIGENCE SUMMARY

(Erase heading not required.)

Army Form C. 2118

Instructions regarding War Diaries and Intelligence Summaries are contained in F.S. Regs., Part II. and the Staff Manual respectively. Title Pages will be prepared in manuscript.

Place	Date	Hour	Summary of Events and Information	Remarks and references to Appendices
Hdqrs at CAMP. H. A.15.L.9.5. Mt Kemmel Belgium Sh.11 N° 28 N.W.	5/7/16		SECTIONS & Hdqrs. Roadmaking & erecting Cook-House in CAMP.P.P. Rests removed to CAMP H. Stores taken to ECHMP to start work. Telephone stores removed from CAMP.H. to N.B. Park RESERVOIR. SECTIONS at B.29.a.4.2. Hutting frames & revetting taken to STIRLING LINE. Dug-outs at WILLOWS. No cart for carrying stores taken up to CAMP KANE. Work was considerably delayed owing to large water party being required. Officer N°s 2 & 4 Sects visited line to take over work ready to relieve infantry. 89th	
CAMP.P.H.	6/7/16		SECTIONS & Hdqrs. Roadmaking & erecting Cook-House in CAMP.P.P. Huts carried to site & ground levelled off in CAMP.H. Working parties ceased work in CAMPS at 12 noon. Kit inspected. Gas helmet drill & inspection. SECTIONS at B.30.a.4.2. Erecting frames, revetting & carrying parapets in STIRLING LINE. Excavation of dug-outs at WILLOWS. Stores taken up from Rly Cottage.	
		6.30 pm	Letter R.E.O. AC/2 4/4. Lieut. Revill to take over work for the night 9/10 N°s 1 & 3 Sects marched out of camp for BRIELEN to relieve N°s 1 & 3 Sects.	
		8 pm		
		12.45 am	Relief completed at 10 pm N°s 1 & 3 Sects arrived in CAMP.P.H.	

N.M. Hodgart, Capt., R.E. (T).
O.C., 1/1st RENFREWSHIRE
FIELD COY., R.E.

Army Form C. 2118

WAR DIARY
or
INTELLIGENCE SUMMARY
(Erase heading not required.)

Instructions regarding War Diaries and Intelligence Summaries are contained in F. S. Regs., Part II. and the Staff Manual respectively. Title Pages will be prepared in manuscript.

Place	Date	Hour	Summary of Events and Information	Remarks and references to Appendices
Hqrs at CAMP.H. A15.d.9.5. Prov. Ret. Belgium Sheet 11° 28 NW.	9/6		Sections at Hqrs. Erecting huts in CAMP.F. Ventilating hut in CAMP.P. Excavation for concrete floor of cook house. No work done in line - on night 8/9th owing to section relief. 3 O.R. joined unit from N°2 Res. Park.	
CAMP.H.	10/6		Sections at Hqrs. Erecting huts & Officers cook house in CAMP.H. Roadmaking & making cures for fitter for Abbleton Beek in CAMP.P. Laying trench - boards in CAMP.F. Sections at B29.a.4.2. Erecting H frames, laying trench boards, revetting & widening STIRLING LANE. Excavation of dug-outs at WILLOWS. Floor moved up to site.	
CAMP.H.	11/6		Sections at Hqrs. Framework of Officers cook house & legs't hut erected in CAMP.H. Roadmaking. Laying cement floor in cook house & everything for roof of Ableton house in CAMP.P. Laying trench boards in CAMP.F. Horsefall protector assembled at ELVERDINGHE CHATEAU. Framing for shelter dug-outs at WILLOWS started. Sections at B29.a.42. Erecting H frames, laying trench boards & erecting center in STIRLING LANE. Dug-outs at WILLOWS 40 cu.ft. excavated & broken tools & rubble carried up to dug-out dump.	W.M. Hodge A.L. Capt. R.E. (T.) 1/171st ???

1875 Wt. W593/826 1,000,000 4/15 J.B.C. & A. A.D.S.S./Forms/C. 2118.

WAR DIARY or INTELLIGENCE SUMMARY

Army Form C. 2118

Place	Date	Hour	Summary of Events and Information	Remarks and references to Appendices
Hdqrs at CAMP H. Hos: b.g.5 Ref. Map Belgium Westroog NW.	12/5/16		Sections at Hdqrs. Laying concrete floor in cook-house, ventilating huts & roadmaking in CAMP.H. Water trough connected up & boiled, pipes covered, new pump fitted in D.H.C. lines. Officers storeroom completed & floor laid of kyft hut in CAMP.H. Trench boards laid in CAMP.F. Waterfall destructor meetn at ELVERDINGHE Chateau. Sections at B.30.a.4.2. Erecting frames, revetting & netting screens in STIRLING LANE. Dug-out at WILLOWS. 500 ft excavated & stores moved up to dump. Eighty meter posts in BRIELEN-BOESINGHE-BURG.Rd. Upper Kitchen (improved?)	
CAMP.H.	13/5/16		Sections at Hqrs. Water trough completed in D.H.C. lines. CAMP.H. One hut completed, frames erected for officers cook house & floor laid. CAMP.F. Erecting cook-house floor. Laying ablution trenches with zinc. Sections at B30.a.42. Erecting trench frames & laying trench boards. Gear dump at BRIELEN. Rebuilt & completed. Dug-outs at WILLOWS. 400 cub ft excavated & stores dumped on site.	

J.M. Hodger.
CAPT, R.E. (T.),
O.C., 1/1st RENFREWSHIRE
FIELD COY., R.E.

Army Form C. 2118

WAR DIARY
or
INTELLIGENCE SUMMARY
(Erase heading not required.)

Instructions regarding War Diaries and Intelligence Summaries are contained in F.S. Regs., Part II. and the Staff Manual respectively. Title Pages will be prepared in manuscript.

Place	Date	Hour	Summary of Events and Information	Remarks and references to Appendices
Hdqrs at CAMP.H. A/50 R.E. Hdqrs Poperinghe Hussingh N.H.	14/7/16		Sections at B.20.a.4.2. Erecting trench frames, laying duck boards, withdrawing trench & sand-bag covers invited in STIRLING LANE. No. 3 Gun Emplacement being rebuilt at BRIELEN. R.A.M.C. dug-outs at WILLOWS. Not out yet excavated & stores carried up to site.	
CAMP.H.	15/7/16		Sections at Hdqrs. CAMP.P. second hut built and 4 floor joists laid. CAMP.P. Cook-house 90 sq ft rough cement laid 100 sq ft flooring laid. Eight troughs for abbuter troughs completed, internals & roof erected. Sections at B.20.a.2. Erecting frames & laying trench boards in STIRLING LANE. No 3 Gun Emp at BRIELEN. Roof stiffened & brickwork completed. Dug-outs at WILLOWS. 300 cu ft excavated. Progress on this work very slow owing to flooring causing continuous flooding. Stores carried up to site.	
CAMP H	16/7/16		Sections at Hdqrs. Officers cook-house & store room completed CAMP.H. All floors standing in 10 ft huts Transport Lines arranged & ragged out. concrete floor completed in Cook-house & Smithy Latrines in CAMP.P. Sections at B.20.a.2. Erecting frames & laying trench boards in STIRLING LANE. Work on No 3 Gun Empt at BRIELEN completed. Section on YPRES Rd completed B.A.M.C. dug-outs 550 cu ft excavated & stores taken up to Birkhoshe from Ply Cottage.	

N.W. Hodgash, CAPT., R.E.
O.C. 1/1st

Army Form C. 2118

WAR DIARY
or
INTELLIGENCE SUMMARY
(Erase heading not required.)

Instructions regarding War Diaries and Intelligence Summaries are contained in F. S. Regs., Part II. and the Staff Manual respectively. Title Pages will be prepared in manuscript.

Place	Date	Hour	Summary of Events and Information	Remarks and references to Appendices
Hqrs at CAMP H. R.15, B9.5. Ref. Map Belgium No 28 N.W.	14/7/16		Sections at Hdqrs. Erecting huts in CAMP.H. Horse standings in D.A.C Lines ground levelled & curbs for trackwork laid. Bootmakings huts completed for cookhouse. Latrine floors prepared for concrete & sedimentation tanks made in CAMP.P. Sections at B20. & 9. Erecting frame laying trench boards & erecting screens in STIRLING LANE. R.A.M.C. Dug-outs 450 cu. ft. excavated & stores moved to site.	
CAMP.H.	18/7/16		Section at Hdqrs. Erecting huts in CAMP.P.H. Horse standings in R.A.M.P. started. Roadmaking 172 sq yds brushwood & 132 sq yds metal laid in CAMP.P. Horse standings levelled & laid out in D.A.C. CAMP. & road repaired. Sections at B20. & 2 STIRLING LANE. Four corners revetted, framed & completed. No 3 Gun Empt at BRIELEN. Ammunition dug out and prepared & structure R.A.M.C. Dug-outs All parties employed conveying stores from Billettage to BURR. LANE.	
CAMP.H.	19/7/16		Sections at Hdqrs. Huts completed in H. CAMP. 16th Bn Transport Lines. Wire netting sides & standings pegged out. CAMP.P.142 sq yds brushwood & metal laid on track. 360 sq ft concrete floor laid in Latrine. D.A.C Lines curbs completed. Sections at B20.&2 STIRLING LANE. Side corners revetted, framed & completed. Sand bag screen erected. R.A.M.C. Dug-outs. 300 cu. ft. excavated, stores taken to site. Framing & shoring for cement sides of Dug-outs completed, marked in sections & conveyed up to BRIELEN. Sketches attached.	

N.M.Hodgar. CAPT. R.E.(T.)
O.C. 1/1st Lowland

1875 Wt. W593/826 1,000,000 4/15 J.B.C. & A. A.D.S.S./Forms/C. 2118.

Army Form C. 2118

WAR DIARY
or
INTELLIGENCE SUMMARY
(Erase heading not required.)

Instructions regarding War Diaries and Intelligence Summaries are contained in F.S. Regs., Part II. and the Staff Manual respectively. Title Pages will be prepared in manuscript.

Place	Date	Hour	Summary of Events and Information	Remarks and references to Appendices
Hdqrs at CAMP.H. A.15. 8.9.5 Ref Map N° Sheet 28 N.W. Belgium	20/6/16		Sections at Hdqrs. P.CAMP. Making roadways, laying concrete floors in latrines & Officers Rest house. Laying out horse standings in N° 4th line, erecting curbs on R.R. & R.R.F. transport lines. Sections at B.20.a.4.2. STIRLING LANE. Revetting & laying in trench boards, erecting A.frames, dugouts, & WILLOWS. 200 W.F.R. excavated & store for concrete moved. Work in two sectors taken over by Field Recces 38 Division nights of 19/21st	
CAMP.H.	21/6/16		Sections at Hdqrs. P.CAMP. Officers cook-house completed & recommendation for additional benches. All repairs to Proton Wagons completed & new wheels fitted. All big tools withdrawn from stores and returned to Hdqrs.	
		11.30 pm	N°s 2 & 4 Sections rejoined Company at Hdqrs. from B.20.a.4.2.	
CAMP.H.	22/6/16		N° 1 & 3 Sects employed roadmaking & completing latrines in CAMP.H. Repairing Military Road through CAMP.H.	
		11.15 pm	Orders received for Unit to vacate CAMP.H. & proceed to CAMP.J. at P.&.C.2.5. All stores & vehicles packed.	
		2 pm	Company left CAMP.H. arrived at CAMP.J. at 9 p.m.	

A.M. Hodgson.
Capt, R.E.
O.C. 1/1st RENFREWSHIRE

Army Form C. 2118

WAR DIARY
or
INTELLIGENCE SUMMARY
(Erase heading not required.)

Instructions regarding War Diaries and Intelligence Summaries are contained in F.S. Regs., Part II. and the Staff Manual respectively. Title Pages will be prepared in manuscript.

Place	Date	Hour	Summary of Events and Information	Remarks and references to Appendices
CAMP J.	23/5/16		Company Drill, Gun behind Drill & inspections.	
		4 pm	2 Officers & 10 Other Ranks left CAMP.J. for MILLWAY Dug-outs at I.30.C.4.1. to take over workmen huts from 9th Canadian Field Coy R.E.	
CAMP. J.	24/5/16		Company & Physical Drill. Company Stores overhauled & checked.	
		6-30 pm	Company Hors, Stables & Mounted Shed. Marched out of CAMP.M.J. for MILLWAY Dug-outs route via WINNERTINGHE-YPRES arriving at 11-15 pm. Distribution of Unit as follows:- No9 pr No1 Section Railway Dug-outs at I.30.C.4.1. Nos 2 & 3 Sects at Bluffs Dug-outs at I.33.a.6.2 No4. Mounted Sect at CAMP.J. A.8.C.52 Advance parties within the line during the day & took over workmen huts.	
HDQRS at Railway Dug-outs 25/5/16		6-0 am	Left HQ, visited line & took over work. Stores carried up for myself/staff.	
I.30.C.4.1		7-30 pm	Working parties left stores carried at dumps from Divisional Park. O.C. visited all works in Lector & Bois Noyr.	
Pdt. HQ. 2nd Hs 25 NH Belgium				

A.W. Hodgard
CAPT. O.C.
173rd RENFREWS
FIELD COY. R.E.

WAR DIARY or INTELLIGENCE SUMMARY

Army Form C. 2118

(Erase heading not required.)

Instructions regarding War Diaries and Intelligence Summaries are contained in F.S. Regs., Part II. and the Staff Manual respectively. Title Pages will be prepared in manuscript.

Place	Date	Hour	Summary of Events and Information	Remarks and references to Appendices
HdQrs at I.20.c.4.1. Ref. Map N° Sheet 28 N.W.	26/7/16		Working parties employed carrying stores to dumps. night of 25/26 #	
			VERBRANDMOLEN TR. Revetting, reutting traces & improving parapet.	
			INTERNATIONAL TR. Revetting & draining trench & excavations for dug outs.	
			GRAND FLEET ST. Revetting & improving parapet.	
			RAT ALLEY. Revetting & laying heavy trench boarding.	
			R.LINE. Revetting & erecting new fire step with timber.	
			DINGOHAL & DRIVE. Erecting trench frames & improving parapets.	
			THAMES ST & WYND. Cleaning & clearing trenches. Excavations for Stokes Gun Emplacement	
	10-30 pm		N°4 Sec? & Mounted Sec? with transport marched out from CAMP J for CAMP G arrived CAMP G at 12-15 p.m.	
HdQrs at I.20.c.4.1.	27/7/16		R.LINE (RIFR) Digging Mess Landing, Officers dug out + shafts in DEAD GATE. M.R. Dig out in PRESENT TR. pumped out & work started. INTERNATIONAL TRENCH. reuetting & new shutter completed. Night parties work continued improving parapets.	
			DIAGONAL, KINGST & DRIVE. Erecting frames, laying trench boards, & draining trench.	
			STOKES GUN EMP?. Excavations & 1 frame fitted.	
			BRIDGE N° 42. Changes relaid.	
			Night parties for VERBRANDEN Sec? employed carrying stores to dumps & repairing wagon damaged on road the night 26/7/y 27	

N° 1133 Sapper Shaw J. Wounded in action by a Rifle bullet.

A.M. Hodgart. Capt.
O.C. 171st Renfrew
Field Coy. R.E.

Army Form C. 2118

WAR DIARY
or
INTELLIGENCE SUMMARY
(Erase heading not required.)

Instructions regarding War Diaries and Intelligence Summaries are contained in F. S. Regs., Part II. and the Staff Manual respectively. Title Pages will be prepared in manuscript.

Place	Date	Hour	Summary of Events and Information	Remarks and references to Appendices
Hdqrs at T.20.c.4.1. Ref Map Sheet 28 S.W. 1/20,000 Belgium	28/7/16		THAMES ST. INTERNATIONAL TR. DIAGONAL, 3g RESERVE. Revetting trenches, evetting frames. Getting drains, laying trench boards, & improving parapets. 2 dug-out shelters made. 3g SUPPORT Traverses rebuilt & timber revetted. Excavation of dug-out in DEANSGATE. GRAND FLEET ST. & RAT ALLEY Trench boarding & revetting. Deauville track repaired at the BLUFFS. BRIDGES Nos 23 & 25 Genecotton – Chaze horses repaired.	
T.20.c.4.1.	29/7/16		Work on THAMES ST. INTERNATIONAL TR. revetting, erecting frames, 1 Lewis trench boards. Steps taken up for 8 gun Empl. GRAND FLEET ST. Cross sections laid & frames erected & trench boarding laid. Excavation for dug out in DEANSGATE completed. R.LINE River. Revetting & draining trench. DRIVE. Traverses rebuilt. Considerable difficulty has been experienced in getting wagons with stores up to Dumps owing to heavy rains & wagons have been frequently overturned or stuck fast. Parties of 2nd Australian Field Coy visited all works in R.Line with a view of relieving unit.	
		10.15pm	Gas attack. All ranks turned out Anti-gas appliances complete. No casualties.	
T.20.c.4.1.	30/7/16		Works continued THAMES ST. INTERNATIONAL TR. DIAGONAL & 3.2 RESERVE. Revetting, erecting frames & laying trench boards. Steps for dug-out in DEANSGATE carried up. Plan works considerably flooded during day. GRAND FLEET ST. Revetting erecting frames & trench boards. Night parties at work improving parapets in Reserve Line. 2nd Party from 2nd Australian Field Coy. taken over work. Relief order issued. Arrangements made for relief of 1 Sect from the Bluffs for night 30/31.	
		12 noon		

N.M. Hodgkin. Capt. R.E.

Army Form C. 2118

WAR DIARY
or
INTELLIGENCE SUMMARY
(Erase heading not required.)

Instructions regarding War Diaries and Intelligence Summaries are contained in F. S. Regs., Part II. and the Staff Manual respectively. Title Pages will be prepared in manuscript.

Place	Date	Hour	Summary of Events and Information	Remarks and references to Appendices
HQ°s at T.20.c.4.1.	31/10		Works carried out. THAMES ST, 3o RESERVE, 3o SUPPORT Revetting, erecting trench frames & laying trench boards. DIAGONAL Trench boarding laid & Trench cleaned out & trench repaired where trench had been blown in. INTERNATIONAL & DRIVE Trench cleaned out Trench boards laid trench revetted. DEANSGATE Dug out frames made ready for erection & shown disposition. No infantry parties were available for work night of 30/31 st	

H M Hodgard
Capt R....
....FIELD REINFT....
FIELD COY R...

1875 Wt. W593/826 1,000,000 4/15 J.B.C. & A. A.D.S.S./Forms/C. 2118.

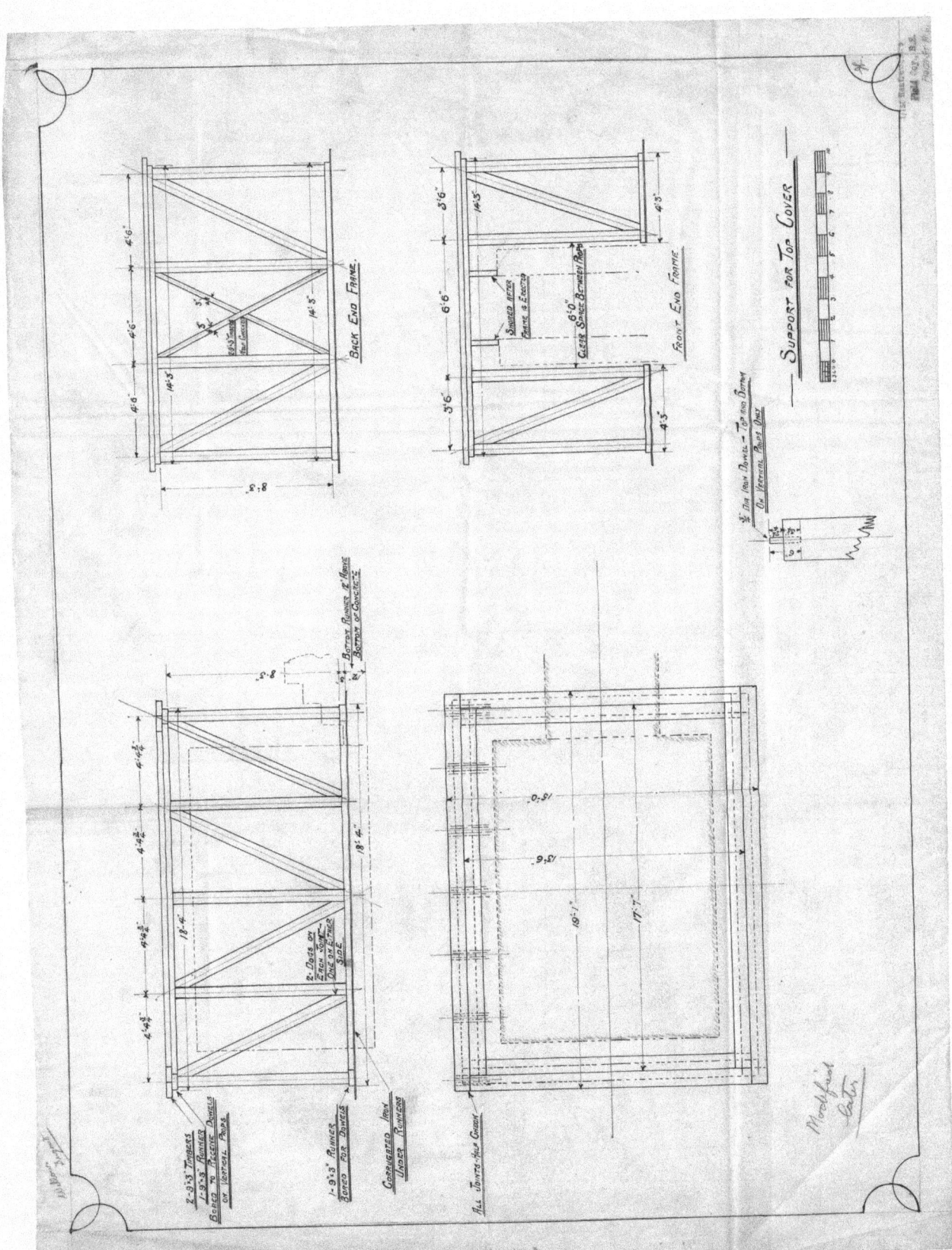

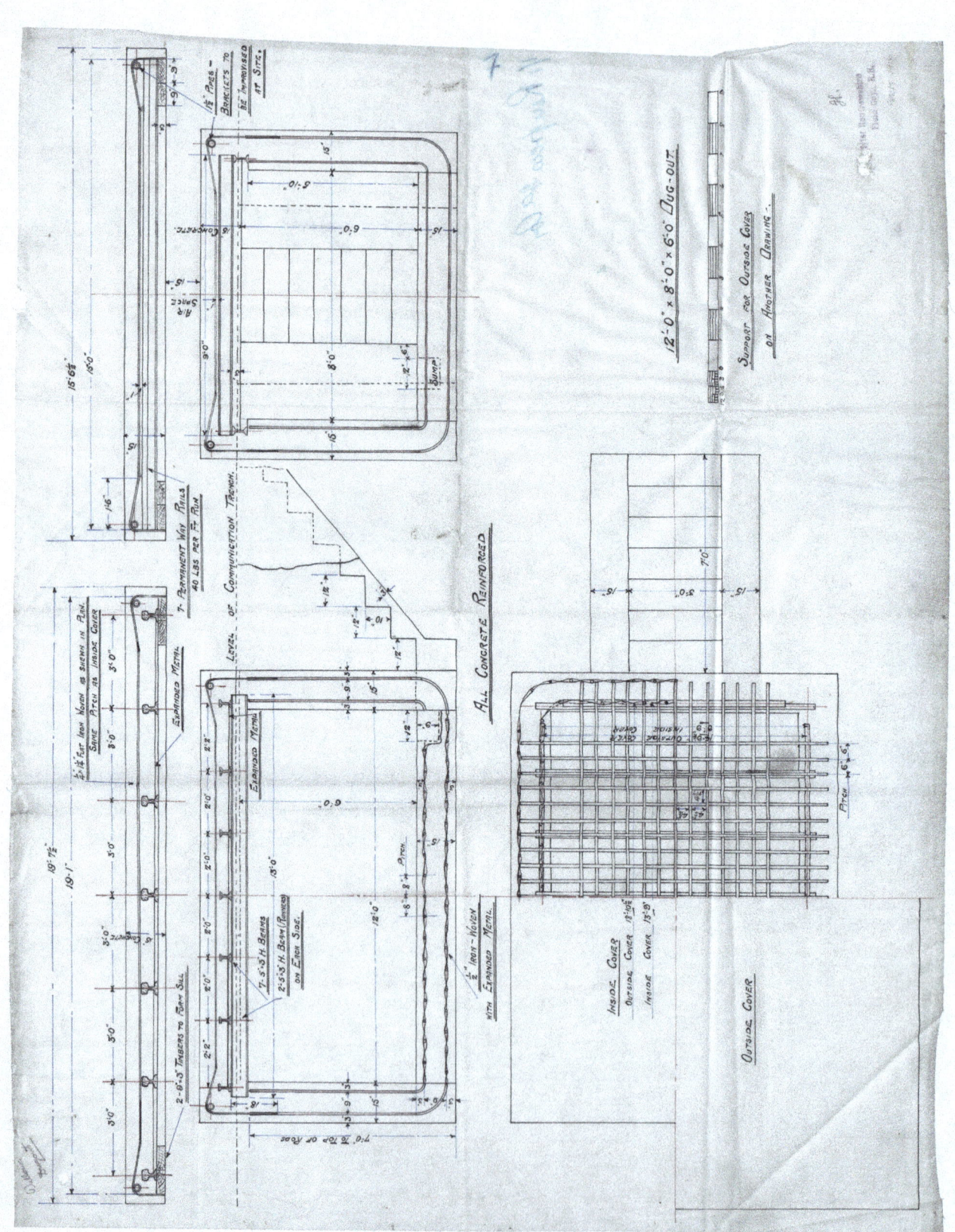

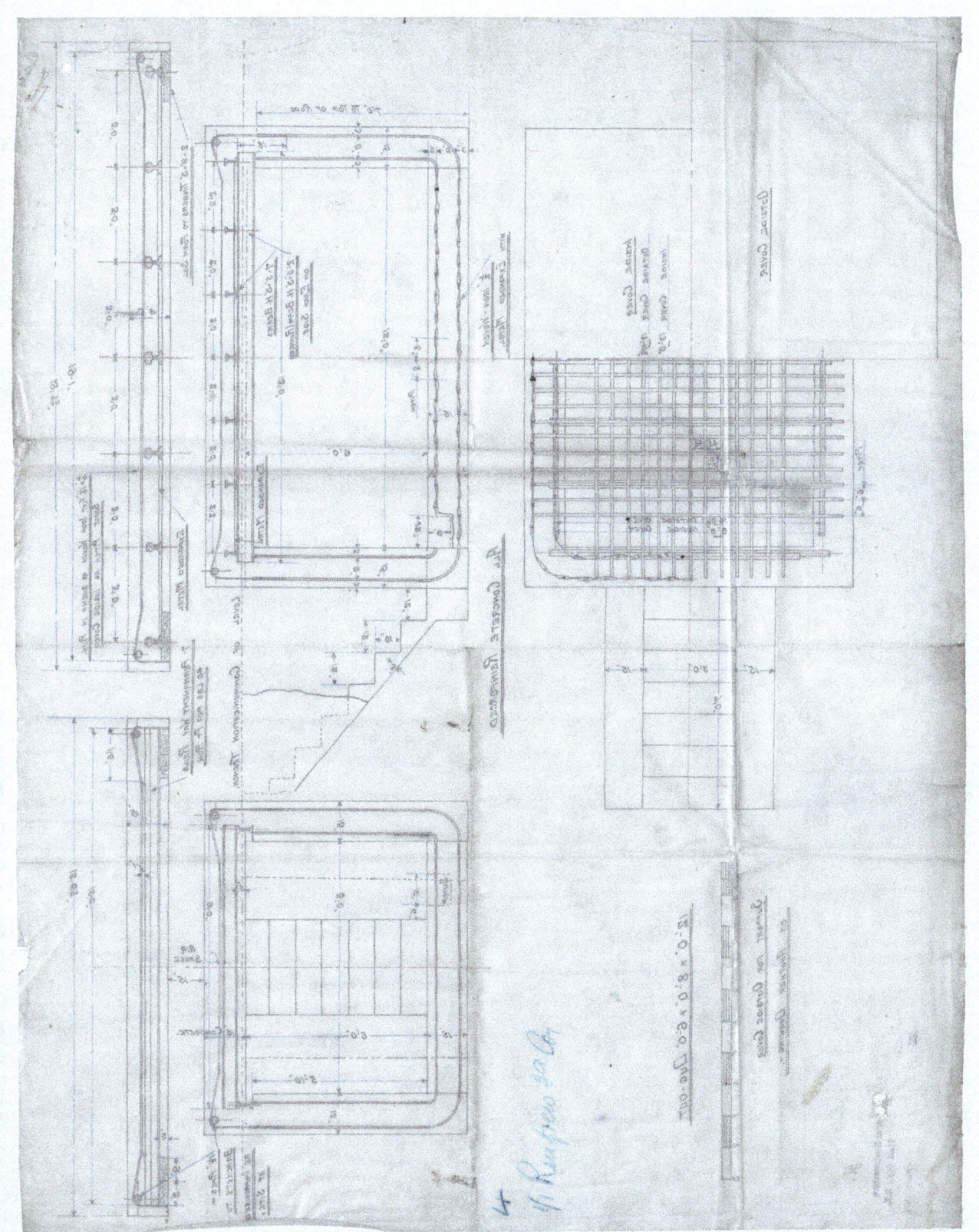

Army Form C. 2118

1/1 Renfrew ? CoRE
Vol 10

WAR DIARY
or
INTELLIGENCE SUMMARY
(Erase heading not required.)

Instructions regarding War Diaries and Intelligence Summaries are contained in F.S. Regs., Part II. and the Staff Manual respectively. Title Pages will be prepared in manuscript.

Place	Date	Hour	Summary of Events and Information	Remarks and references to Appendices
Hdqrs at I.20.c.4,1. Ref Map BELGIUM SHEET N°28 N.W.	1/6	1-0am 10-0pm	Hdqrs & N°1 Section. Relieved by 2nd Australian Field Coy. Engrs. proceeded to Camp C. at H.13. on VLAMERTINGHE-OUDERDOM Rd. 1 Section at H.33.a.3.5. continued work on Trenches. Erecting frames, laying floor boards & drainage of trenches. Section at H.33.a.3.5. relieved by 1 Section 2nd Australian Field Cy. All Matters & maps & correspondence handed over & relief completed at midnight. 1 N.C.O. & 2 sappers per letter remained attached to act as guides for relieving unit.	
Hdqrs at Camp C. H.13. Ref Map BELGIUM Sheet N°28 N.W.	2/6	2-0pm	Company employed erecting huts & harness room. Thinning of cook-house erected. Magazines at Ammunition Dump ventilated. Company inspected by O.C. Gas helmet inspection & Company drill. All animals inspected by Veterinary Officer & animals passed medical test.	

J.M.Hodgart
O.C., A.E. (T),
O.C., 1/1st RENFREWSHIRE
FIELD COY., R.E.

1875 Wt. W593/826 1,000,000 4/15 J.B.C. & A. A.D.S.S./Forms/C. 2118.

Army Form C. 2118

WAR DIARY
or
INTELLIGENCE SUMMARY

(Erase heading not required.)

Instructions regarding War Diaries and Intelligence Summaries are contained in F. S. Regs., Part II. and the Staff Manual respectively. Title Pages will be prepared in manuscript.

Place	Date	Hour	Summary of Events and Information	Remarks and references to Appendices
Hdqrs at CAMP C H.13. Ref Map BELGIUM Sheet No 27 NW.	3/9/16	10-0 A.M.	Company inspected by G.O.C. 4th Division. All work on huts completed, harness room & forage store completed. Grease dug around horse lines & framing of cook-house erected. Ventilation of magazines at ammunition dumps completed.	
Hdqrs at CAMP G.	4/9/16	9 A.M.	Advance party of 1 N.C.O. & Sapper per Ford proceeded to YPRES to take over billets. Whole parked ready to move.	
		1-30 pm	No 2 Sect & N party proceeded to VLAMERTINGHE to take over billets & standings for animals.	
		4-0 pm	Remainder of Coy left camp & marched to VLAMERTINGHE arriving at 7-0pm. No 1, 3 & 4 Sects proceeded to billets at Hdqrs. Mounted Sect billeted at H.2.C.6.5. Coy attached to 29th Division for work on YPRES defences in YPRES to be attached to 29th Division for work on YPRES defences.	

H.M.Hodgson.
CAPT. R.E. (T.)
O.C., 1/1st REN[...]
FIELD COY., R.E.

Army Form C. 2118

WAR DIARY
or
INTELLIGENCE SUMMARY
(Erase heading not required.)

Instructions regarding War Diaries and Intelligence Summaries are contained in F.S. Regs., Part II. and the Staff Manual respectively. Title Pages will be prepared in manuscript.

Place	Date	Hour	Summary of Events and Information	Remarks and references to Appendices
Hdqrs at H.8.A.4.B. Belgium Sheet N° 28 N.W. Ypres	5/9/16		Hdqrs v 1 Sect at H.9. Shaft made to dimensions HH feet stantings 5½ feet x 5½ feet. Framework & corrugated iron erected for 1 stantings 5½ feet long. Sections at YPRES. Start made on Strong Point at POTIJZE CHATEAU. Erecting tracks, frames & revetting with A.T. sheets. Drains dug to [?] wood. Tender out for Telephone Dugout. 1 Section employed on repairing cellar dug-outs in YPRES.	
Hdqrs at H.8.A.4.B.	6/9/16	9·0am	N°2. Sect left Hdqrs for VLAMERTINGHE with Section vehicle & 1 Pontoon wagon with equipment complete & proceeded to STAM TER BIEZEN to be attached to 4th Divisional Park for work on huts in Area.	
			Hdqrs Sect. employed on improving stables.	
			G.O.C. 4th Divn. inspected vehicles & animals of unit.	
		11pm	Sects at YPRES. POTIJZE CHATEAU. Placing French airmen revetting trench. Supports erected roof strengthened & drainage further improved of Telephone Dug-out.	
			Repairing & strengthening roofs of cellars in YPRES. Clearing and drying roads in ST JEAN. Horse drawn from forge Pack & 4 wagon loads conveyed to POTIJZE & ST JEAN. Draft of 1 N.C.O. & 10T arrived from Base	

N M Hodgat [?]
CAPT. R.E.
O.C. 175th F.[?]
FIELD COY

1875 Wt. W593/826 1,000,000 4/15 J.B.C. & A. A.D.S.S./Forms/C. 2118.

Army Form C. 2118

WAR DIARY
or
INTELLIGENCE SUMMARY
(Erase heading not required.)

Instructions regarding War Diaries and Intelligence Summaries are contained in F.S. Regs., Part II. and the Staff Manual respectively. Title Pages will be prepared in manuscript.

Place	Date	Hour	Summary of Events and Information	Remarks and references to Appendices
Hdqrs at H.S.M.&B. Pil Hoof Belgium Sheet 28 E N.W.	7/10		Hdqrs section. Erecting harness etc. & collecting bricks for paving stable. Sections at YPRES. POTIJZE CHATEAU. Clearing & revetting trench, erecting trench frames & revetting tiles. Clearing trees & doors replaced in front of sleeping quarters. Drying shed at ST JEAN. Roof propped, walls repaired & door erected. TELEPHONE Dug-out. Roof propped & centre supports erected. Cellars in YPRES strengthened. 4 waggon loads of stones conveyed to YPRES.	
Hdqrs at H.I.A.4.B	8/10		Hdqrs Sect. Floor laid in harness shop, framing completed. Stint work to brick floor in stables. Sect at YPRES. POTIJZE CHATEAU. Erecting trench frames, revetting & making up parapets. TELEPHONE Dug-out. Wood work complete & roof made proof. Drying room at ST JEAN. Doors propped & roof shored. Debris well rebuilt. 3 loads stone taken up to POTIJZE & ST JEAN.	

H.M.Hodgel
CAPT R.E.
O.C 174
FIELD C.

Army Form C. 2118

WAR DIARY
or
INTELLIGENCE SUMMARY
(Erase heading not required.)

Instructions regarding War Diaries and Intelligence Summaries are contained in F.S. Regs., Part II. and the Staff Manual respectively. Title Pages will be prepared in manuscript.

Place	Date	Hour	Summary of Events and Information	Remarks and references to Appendices
Hdqrs at H.S.A.H.8	9/16		Hqrs O.C. Erecting farriers shop & paving stables with bricks. Sects at YPRES. Erecting frames, revetting & laying timber boards.	
Ref Works Belgium Chat N° 27 HW			Repairing & strengthening dug-outs in YPRES.	
Hqrs at H.S.A.H.8	10/16		Hqrs O.C. Imovmt of farrier shop completed, laying brick floor in stables. Sects at YPRES. Repairing & strengthening cover of dug-outs in YPRES. 3 wagon loads stores conveyed to YPRES & POTIJZE.	
Hqrs at H.S.A.H.8	11/16		Hdg os Sect. Making Mining races for POTIJZE. Strong posts & laying floor in stables. Sects in YPRES. Fitting timber frames, enclosing trench, rebuilding parapet. Sheep bags dug & revetted drain bed sent to front. 3 wagon loads stores sent up to POTIJZE & ST JEAN.	
Hdg rs at H.S.A.H.8	12/16		Hqrs O.C. Making Mining races, brick floor completed in stable. Sects at YPRES. Erecting trench frames, rebuilding parapets, parapet revetted. 40 yds fire step equiptd. Excavation of tunnel for NE Empl started. 3 euris bird rev. Frames erected in communication trench & end of tunnel revetted. Stores drawn from Eng Park & sent up to POTIJZE. Draft of 4 O.R. arrived from Base.	

H M Hodwal

Army Form C. 2118

WAR DIARY
or
INTELLIGENCE SUMMARY
(Erase heading not required.)

Instructions regarding War Diaries and Intelligence Summaries are contained in F. S. Regs., Part II. and the Staff Manual respectively. Title Pages will be prepared in manuscript.

Place	Date	Hour	Summary of Events and Information	Remarks and references to Appendices
Hdqrs at H.P.A.4.S. By Maps. Belgium Sheet No.7 N.W.	13/10		Hdqrs Sect. Making trench frames for POTIJZE Strong point. Clearing roadways for stables. Sects at YPRES. Erecting frames & revetting trench. People's Nightstand & strong trench. Excavating tunnel for M.G.Empts. 3 mining frames fixed in. Panels revetted with timber. 4 wagon loads stores conveyed to POTIJZE.	
Hdqrs at H.P.A.4.S.	14/10		Hdqrs Sect. 20 trench frames made for POTIJZE CHATEAU. Clearing roads to stables. Sects at YPRES. Erecting frames & revetting trench. 40 yds fire-step revetted. Mining tunnel for M.G.Empts. 3 mining sizes erected. Revetting up parapet & revetting parados at Potijze Strong point. 4 wagon loads stores conveyed to POTIJZE.	
Hdqrs at H.P. A.4.C.	15/10		Hdqrs Sect. Making trench frames, setting drains for stables. Ground selected & site of new stables laid out. Sects at YPRES. Erecting frames in communication trench. Fixing steps completed. Revetting timber & filling in parapet. Excavation of tunnel to M.G. Empt. & mining pass somewhat timed. 3 wagon loads of stores conveyed to POTIJZE.	

J.H. Hodgsh, CAPT. R.E (T.)
O.C., 1/1st RENFREWSHIRE
FIELD COY., R.E.

WAR DIARY or INTELLIGENCE SUMMARY

Army Form C. 2118

(Erase heading not required.)

Instructions regarding War Diaries and Intelligence Summaries are contained in F.S. Regs., Part II. and the Staff Manual respectively. Title Pages will be prepared in manuscript.

Place	Date	Hour	Summary of Events and Information	Remarks and references to Appendices
Hqrs at H.2,17,4,8. Ord. Map Belgium Sheet 11 & 27 N.W.	16/6		Major Scott left after stables third and 9 completed floors of old stables completed. Scots at YPRES. Erecting tiered frames. Drainage of communication trench completed. Gallery to M.G. Emp¹ completed & enemy cases finished. Start made on excavation of M.G. Emp¹.	
		1 pm	Orders received for work to be concentrated & entrain at HOUPOUTRE at 8 pm. All vehicles packed ready to move. Letters recalled from YPRES.	
		5.0 pm	Orders from move cancelled for the 16th to entrain on the 17th instead.	
		5.15 pm	N°⁵ 1, 3 & 4 Sections arrived at Hqrs from YPRES.	
Hqrs at H.2,17,4,8.	17/6		Company inspection & drill. Gas helmet inspection.	
		9 pm	All vehicles left to entrain at HOUPOUTRE	
		9.30 pm	Personnel of Coy. left VLAMERTINGHE arrived at station troops	
		5.0 pm	Entrainment started & completed at 5.50 p.m.	
		6.45 pm	Train left HOUPOUTRE Station.	

W. M. Hodgson.
CAPT. R.E (T)
O.C., 1/1st R...
FIELD CO...

1875 Wt. W593/826 1,000,000 4/15 J.B.C. & A. A.D.S.S./Forms/C. 2118.

Army Form C. 2118

WAR DIARY
or
INTELLIGENCE SUMMARY
(Erase heading not required.)

Instructions regarding War Diaries and Intelligence Summaries are contained in F. S. Regs., Part II. and the Staff Manual respectively. Title Pages will be prepared in manuscript.

Place	Date	Hour	Summary of Events and Information	Remarks and references to Appendices
	18/9/16	6-30 a.m.	Horses arrived at SALEUX, detrainment started & completed at 4-50 a.m. Proceeded watered & fed. Breakfast served to Coy.	
		10-0 a.m.	Coy. coy. left SALEUX for LONGPRE route via AMIENS, arrived LONGPRE at 1 p.m. Troops billetted & animals provided for what Parade &c.	
LONGPRE	19/9/16		Company Drill. Gas helmet drill. Lectures to N.C.O's. Men by Lieut. Officers on construction of wires & construction of strong points.	
LONGPRE	20/9/16		Company Drill. Lectures on Field Works. Wiring strong points.	
LONGPRE	21/9/16		Company inspected by O.C. Foot Gear equipment checked & overcoats. Company drill. Gas helmet drill. Wiring and Field Works. Short parade on construction of panniers for carrying water by pack animals.	
		5 p.m.	Company parade. Lyell Lecture on Wiring and construction of Field Works.	

K. M. Stobart
Capt.
O.C. 1/1? ? ?
? FIELD Co. ?

Army Form 'C. 2118

WAR DIARY
or
INTELLIGENCE SUMMARY
(Erase heading not required.)

Instructions regarding War Diaries and Intelligence Summaries are contained in F.S. Regs., Part II. and the Staff Manual respectively. Title Pages will be prepared in manuscript.

Place	Date	Hour	Summary of Events and Information	Remarks and references to Appendices
LONGPRE	22/9/16		Company drill. Lecture by O.C. 4th on Field Engineering & Horny belt construction of defences.	
		8pm	Night parade of Company. Lectures of working parties & laying out field works. Work carried out on construction of pontoon.	
LONGPRE	23/9/16		Company drill. All N.C.O's were taken to site of the previous nights operations & lectured to by O.C. & O.C. Sections. A.D.S.S. inspected animals of Coy. Orders received for Coy. to proceed to ALLONVILLE on the 24th inst.	
LONGPRE	24/9/16		Company drill. All vehicles packed ready to move.	
		3pm	Company left LONGPRE & proceeded via PICQUIGNY to ALLONVILLE arriving there at 7 pm. Company billeted & animals stabled, vehicles parked.	
ALLONVILLE	25/9/16		Company drill. Lecture on construction by O.C. Readings of extracts from Hastings of a reference pamphlet handed out in accordance with "Divn." No. G.S.D./26/16. Work resumed on construction of pontoon.	

J.M. Hodgson
CAPT
O.C. 1/1 C.R.E.
1st FIELD COY., R.E.

Army Form C. 2118

WAR DIARY
or
INTELLIGENCE SUMMARY
(Erase heading not required.)

Instructions regarding War Diaries and Intelligence Summaries are contained in F.S. Regs., Part II. and the Staff Manual respectively. Title Pages will be prepared in manuscript.

Place	Date	Hour	Summary of Events and Information	Remarks and references to Appendices
	26/9/16	10-15 AM	Company left ALLONVILLE route via QUERRIEUX to CORBIE. Arrived at CORBIE. Company billeted in village. Animals & vehicles parked.	
		2-15 PM	Grass at 12.0.0 & Grass arrived from base.	
CORBIE	27/9/16		Company Drill. Instruction in Field Works. Mag Bodeny	
		5-0 pm	Company parade. Tracing out Field Works & extension of working party. Men received on pannier.	
CORBIE	28/9/16		Company Drill & Inspection of equipment. Working parties on Field Works. Party making tracing lines for 12th Bde. 20 mens made & handed over to Batt. 12 Panniers completed & delivered to D.A.D.O.S. 4 Div. Orders received to move to VAUX sur SOMME on the 29 inst.	

JHodgar.
Capt R.E. (T.)
O/C 1/1/W. LANCS SHIRE
FIELD COY, R.E.

1875 Wt. W593/826 1,000,000 4/15 J.B.C. & A. A.D.S.S./Forms/C. 2118.

Army Form C. 2118

WAR DIARY
or
INTELLIGENCE SUMMARY
(Erase heading not required.)

Instructions regarding War Diaries and Intelligence Summaries are contained in F.S. Regs., Part II. and the Staff Manual respectively. Title Pages will be prepared in manuscript.

Place	Date	Hour	Summary of Events and Information	Remarks and references to Appendices
CORBIE	29/10		Company Drill. All vehicles packed & ready to move.	
		12-0 Noon	Company left CORBIE & proceeded to VAUX sur SOMME. arrived at 2 p.m. Animals & vehicles parked. Stores drawn from Corps Park MERICOURT for making frames. 4 NCOs & 4 O.R. instructing 2nd Batt in mining & erection of mining frames.	
VAUX	30/10		Company Drill. Instruction in Field Works. Musketry. Working parties making mining frames for 12th Inf Brigade. 4 NCO & 4 OR instructing 2nd Batt in mining & erection of frames. Material drawn & work started on latrines in CORBIE.	

Signed

Lieut Colonel R.E.
O.C. 1/1 [illegible]

W.M. Hodgart
Capt
O.C. 1/1
Field Coy R.E.

1875 Wt. W593/826 1,000,000 4/15 J.B.C. & A. A.D.S.S./Forms/C. 2118.

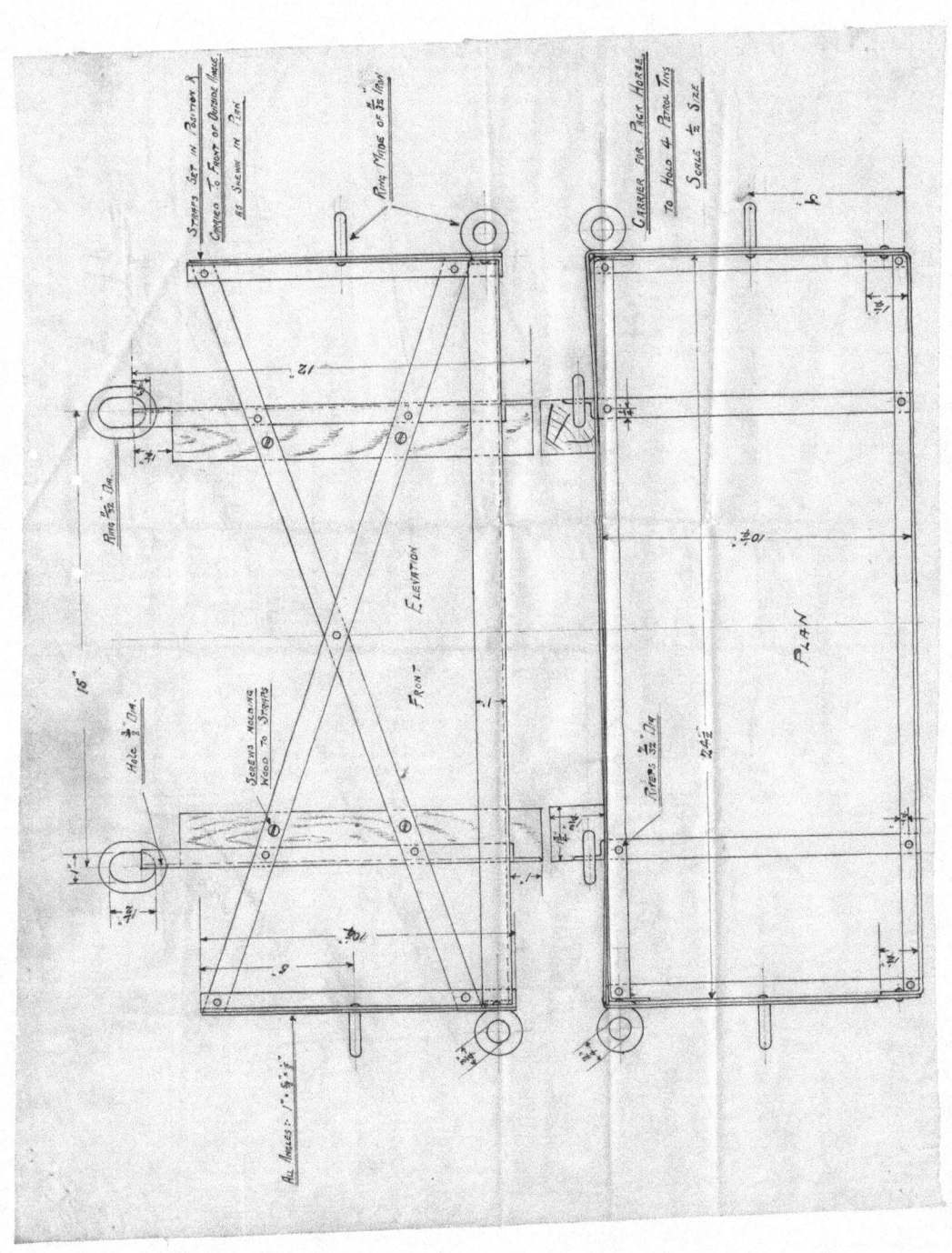

4th DIVISION.

1/IST RENFREW FIELD COMPANY.

ROYAL ENGINEERS.

OCTOBER 1916.

WAR DIARY
or
INTELLIGENCE SUMMARY

(Erase heading not required.)

Army Form C. 2118

1/1 Renfrew Coy RE

Instructions regarding War Diaries and Intelligence Summaries are contained in F.S. Regs., Part II. and the Staff Manual respectively. Title Pages will be prepared in manuscript.

Place	Date	Hour	Summary of Events and Information	Remarks and references to Appendices
VAUX sur SOMME	1/10/16		Church Parade. Party of 4 NCOs & 40 Sappers instructing 2 Beer Bns in mining & erecting mining cases.	
		8 pm	Company parade. Tracing strong points & extension of working parties. 7 Lieut. Atkinson, 7 Lieut. A. Kerr Abram. 7 Lieut. J.S. Stone joined units from Base.	
VAUX sur SOMME	2/10/16		Company drill. Lectures on Military Engineering (Field Works). Working parties erecting latrines in CORBIE. Parties NCOs & Sappers instructing 11th & 12th Brigade Inf. Battns. in mining & erection of mining cases.	
VAUX sur SOMME	3/10/16		Company drill. Tracing & laying out field works. Lectures by R.E. sections on Mining. Parties erecting latrines & cook houses in CORBIE. Parties of NCOs & Men instructing Inf. Battns. in mining & erection of mining frames. Party constructing panniers for carriage of water by pack animals. 7 Lieut. H.D. Dod joined unit from Base.	

H.W. Hodgart
CAPT. R.E. (T),
O.C., 1/1st RENFREWSHIRE
FIELD COY., R.E.

WAR DIARY
or
INTELLIGENCE SUMMARY

(Erase heading not required.)

Army Form C. 2118.

Place	Date	Hour	Summary of Events and Information	Remarks and references to Appendices
VAUX sur SOMME	4/10/16		Company Drill. Issue of Box respirators. Drill with same. Lecture on Gas Attack. Working parties constructing latrines & cook-houses in CARBIE. Work continued on fascines. Instructors supplied to 18th & 12th Bde Inf Bns for mining & excavation of mining faces.	
VAUX sur SOMME	5/10/16		Company Drill. Company practical work Box Respirators. Working party erecting latrines & cook houses in CARBIE, 12 Labourers & cook-houses completed. Work continued on construction of fascines & signboards made for Division. NCOs & men instructing 18th Bde Inf Bn HQ in mining & excavation of caves.	
VAUX sur SOMME	6/10/16		Working parties constructing fascines, erecting cook-houses in CARBIE. Erecting cook & blackhouses for Div HQrs. Marking & painting notice boards for Div. Remainder of unit on Drill & Route March. Instructional parties supplied to 11th & 12th Bdes for mining. Construction of fascines. Second period of Coy. Field Works & consolidation of trenches.	

R.M. Hodgson. CAPT., R.E.
O.C., 1/1st RENFREWSHIRE
FIELD COY., R.E.

WAR DIARY
or
INTELLIGENCE SUMMARY
(Erase heading not required.)

Army Form C. 2118

Instructions regarding War Diaries and Intelligence Summaries are contained in F.S. Regs., Part II. and the Staff Manual respectively. Title Pages will be prepared in manuscript.

Place	Date	Hour	Summary of Events and Information	Remarks and references to Appendices
VAUX sur SOMME	7/10/16		Working parties completing Latrines & wash-houses in tents. Water tanks, Easels & Blackboards completed & delivered at this H.Q. Remainder of unit on work details on Consolidation schemes. Below for unit to proceed to CITADEL CAMP at F.21.c. on the 8th inst.	
	8/10/16		Unit left VAUX at 10.15 am & marched to CITADEL CAMP under orders of 12th Inf Bde. Remained marched by cross country tracks. Transport by road via MEAULTE.	
		4-30pm	Unit & tanks arrived transport arrived at 5pm. Bivouac erected. Animals & vehicles parked at F.21.c. B1 amp ALBERT N500 1 P.M. & 1g V.R. left at CARRIE to complete construction of Pannions.	
Ref Map France Sheet N° 57c S.W.	9/10/16	7.0am	Company marched out CITADEL CAMP & proceeded by cross country tracks to Camp at S.29.C.6.2. Transport proceeded by road.	
		12.0 noon	Personnel of unit arrived at S.29.C.5.2 & relieved 9th London Field Coy R.E.	
		4.0pm	Transport arrived. Animals & vehicles parked at F.4.d.5.4. by Sergt Tolhurst. Pontoon Equipment dumped at CORNOY. Unit placed under orders of 4th Infantry Brigade.	

H.W. Hodgard
Lieut
OC 1st COY 1st Tunnelling Co.
(1) TUNNELLING R.E.

WAR DIARY
or
INTELLIGENCE SUMMARY

(Erase heading not required.)

Army Form C. 2118.

Instructions regarding War Diaries and Intelligence Summaries are contained in F. S. Regs., Part II. and the Staff Manual respectively. Title Pages will be prepared in manuscript.

Place	Date	Hour	Summary of Events and Information	Remarks and references to Appendices
H.Qrs. at S.29.c.6.2. Ref Map Sh.N57c S.W.	10/10		Company employed building shelters in camp. Cookhouse at R.E. Dump. Bench mocking boards made & delivered to the 10th & 12th Brigades. Parties of N.C.O's & men taken over roads & tracks leading to forward areas.	
H.Qrs at S.29.C.5.2	11/10		Working parties employed on improving trench shelters & building road to camp. 1 Section Cleaning & excavating old dug-out for HQrs. in BERNAFAY WOOD. Party surveying old wells in CURRLEMENT: eight wells being found & two cleared. Depth taken but no water was recorded owing to wells being partially filled with debris. 4th Div Egyptian Labs N°.14 arrived. Loads, stores & tools made up for 2 sections of unit to be held in reserve but ready to move forward at shortest notice.	
		6.0pm	Rehearsal parade, Parley N.C.O's & men taken over forward roads to GINCHY.	

A.M.Hodgart
Capt R.E.
Field Coy R.E.

Army Form C. 2118

WAR DIARY
or
INTELLIGENCE SUMMARY
(Erase heading not required.)

Instructions regarding War Diaries and Intelligence Summaries are contained in F.S. Regs., Part II. and the Staff Manual respectively. Title Pages will be prepared in manuscript.

Place	Date	Hour	Summary of Events and Information	Remarks and references to Appendices
Hérsat S.29.c.5.2 Ref Map Trônes Wood S.W.	12/10/16		Company employed erecting shelters & felling trees in BERNAFAY WOOD. Making log road at R.E.Dump Trônes Wood. Two sections standing by under orders of 11th Inf. Bde. 43 Pannier mules by detail at CORBIE delivered to D.A.D.O.S. 4th Div.	
	13/10/16		1 Sect employed roadmaking at R.E.Dump, TRÔNES WOOD. 1 Sect employing dug-out in BERNAFAY WOOD & making sign-boards. 2 Sects standing by under orders 11th Inf. Bde, employed felling & hauling timber for dug-outs, roads, etc.	
	14/10/16		Company employed erecting shelters & improving N.E. sign-post. Making log road at R.E. DUMP. Sites selected for dug-outs at T.O. Central Lines drawn to start work on TELEPHONE Dug-out on the 15th inst. Many cross roads & routes to sets. 43 pack panniers delivered to D.A.D.O.S. 4th Div. from detail at CORBIE.	

K.M.Hodgson. CAPT.
O.C., 1/1st [...]
FIELD CO[...]

1875 Wt. W5193/826 1,000,000 4/15 J.B.C. & A. A.D.S.S./Forms/C. 2118.

Army Form C. 2118

WAR DIARY
or
INTELLIGENCE SUMMARY
(Erase heading not required.)

Instructions regarding War Diaries and Intelligence Summaries are contained in F.S. Regs., Part II. and the Staff Manual respectively. Title Pages will be prepared in manuscript.

Place	Date	Hour	Summary of Events and Information	Remarks and references to Appendices
Hugo at S.29.C.5.2 Ref Map Albert 57.c.S.E. 3 M.	15/10/16		Company employed felling & hauling logs for dug-outs from BERNAFAY WOOD. excavating dug-out in BERNAFAY WOOD. Making mining cases for mineshafts erecting french shelters in O.R. opposite erected from CORBIE. 1 N.C.O. & 5 O.R. attached to MINDEN POST DUMP to complete pannieres.	
	16/10/16		Start made with TELEPHONE dug-out at T.P. Central. 1 N.C.O. & Sappers & 1 Sec. working in continuous 6 hour shifts. Sites selected for shelters at T.G.H.Q. Baby Elephant shelters drawn ads fitted & transported to site. 2 shelters erected during night. 1 Sect felling trees & making log roads at R.E. Dump in TROHES WOOD. Dug-out completed in BERNAFAY WOOD.	
	17/10/16		Work continued on TELEPHONE Dug-out and mining cases made for shafts. Elephant shelter crown & sides fitted & taken to site of dug-outs at T.G.H.Q. Road completed at R.E. Dump TROHES WOOD. 4 splinter proof shelters completed in BERNAFAY WOOD for accommodation of unit. Trees felled & uprights cut for dug-outs.	

A.M. Hodgart
CAPT, R.E. (T.)
O.C., 1/1st RENFREWSHIRE
FIELD COY., R.E.

WAR DIARY
or
INTELLIGENCE SUMMARY

(Erase heading not required.)

Army Form C. 2118

Instructions regarding War Diaries and Intelligence Summaries are contained in F.S. Regs., Part II. and the Staff Manual respectively. Title Pages will be prepared in manuscript.

Place	Date	Hour	Summary of Events and Information	Remarks and references to Appendices
HQrs at S.9.c.5.2. Of Map Sheet N° 57.c S.E.	18/10		1 Sect. assisted by working party of R.A.M.C. excavating pits for elephant shelters at T.9.A.9.1. 3 shelters completed & 4 pits excavated during night of 17th/18th. Work continued on TELEPHONE dug-outs, many saps made. Stores carted to sites. Logs trimmed & cut for props for dug-outs.	
	19/10		Work completed on R.A.M.C. shelters at T.9.A.9. 6 shelters erected. Parties of 1 NCO & 12 sappers on TELEPHONE dug-outs an extension which as no pit particularly available. Excavations for more Elephant shelters in BERNAFAY WOOD started. Reconnaissance of old trenches east of GINCHY - took LES-BŒUFS carried out.	
	20/10		Working parties on TELEPHONE dug-outs. Mining crews made for 2nd by-out. Party surveying wells in MONTAUBAN & GINCHY. Tops of wells cleaned but no water could be sounded owing to wells being filled with debris. Two fly-proof latrine boxes made. Excavation for Elephant shelters in BERNAFAY WOOD.	

H M Hodgart
CAPT, R.E. (T),
O.C., 1/1st REM(?)
FIELD COY

WAR DIARY or INTELLIGENCE SUMMARY

Army Form C. 2118

(Erase heading not required.)

Place	Date	Hour	Summary of Events and Information	Remarks and references to Appendices
Map 57c S.2.9, c.5.2.	21/10		Shafts made with new dug-out at T.I. Central, entrances to shafts revetted & shafts started, work carried on by continuous shifts. Work continued on TELEPHONE dug-out shafts completed & start made with entrance to chambers. Mining cases made, pit props cut, elevating prepared & carted to site. Erecting small elephant shelter at GUILLEMONT for "U" Inf Bde. Elephant shelter half erected at BERNAFAY WOOD.	
Ref. Map Sheet No 57c. S.M.	22/10		Work continued on Dug-out at T.I. Central. 40 Mining Cases made. Elephant shelter in BERNAFAY WOOD. Small elephant shelter completed in BERNAFAY WOOD. 2 Leteow digging shelter for assembling at SUNKEN Rd. LESBŒUFS. T.4.C. "Div Operation Order No 51 received. N°1034 G/Sergt McLaren. D. Wounded in Action (Remained at duty) " 1364 Corpl Cardwell. R. " 1164 Sapt Graham. R. Wounded in Action (To Hospital) } Shell splinters " 1142 " Jackson	

H.M. Hodge
Captain R.E.
O.C. 1/1st R.M. [illegible]
FIELD Co. R.E.

WAR DIARY or **INTELLIGENCE SUMMARY**

Army Form C. 2118

Place	Date	Hour	Summary of Events and Information	Remarks and references to Appendices
Hdqrs at S.29.c.5.2. Ref Map Sheet N° 57C SW	23/10/16		Work continued on Dug-outs at T.I. Central stores taken up. Latrines erected on GUILLEMONT Rd at S.29.c.5.2. & S.30.0.9.3. Elephant shelter completed in BERNAFAY WOOD. 2 Lts starting by under orders of the 11th Inf Bde. 1 Sect of 222nd Field Coy R.E. started to take over work on relief of unit. All work in hand & stores handed over.	
	24/10/16	10.15 am / 3.15 am	All vehicles, personnel & transport moved to SANDPITS at 8 am. Remainder of unit marched out on relief by 222nd Coy R.E. Move completed & Coy concentrated at F.19.c.9.3. Ref Map ALBERT Sheet 57000.	
Hdqrs at F.19.a.9.3. Ref Map ALBERT 1/10000	25/10/16		Company at Sandpits. Company Drill.	
	26/10/16		Company at Sandpits. Company Drill & inspection of kits.	

W M Hodgart
CAPT., R.E. (T)
O.C., 1/1st REN........
FIELD COY., R.E.

Army Form C. 2118

WAR DIARY
or
INTELLIGENCE SUMMARY
(Erase heading not required.)

Instructions regarding War Diaries and Intelligence Summaries are contained in F.S. Regs., Part II. and the Staff Manual respectively. Title Pages will be prepared in manuscript.

Place	Date	Hour	Summary of Events and Information	Remarks and references to Appendices
Hdqrs at F.19.c.9.3. Ref. Map ALBERT 1/40,000	27/10	12.15pm	Company moved from SANDPITS, for MEAULTE under orders of the 11th Inf. Bde.	
		3.15pm	Arrival in MEAULTE. Coy billeted. Animals & vehicles parked.	
	28/10		Company at MEAULTE. Coy inspection by O.C. & Company Drill. Orders received for Transport to proceed to new area on the 29th inst.	
	29/10	6.35am	1st line Transport & tool vehicles left MEAULTE with Transport 11th Brigade route via CORBIE, AMIENS to LONGPRE les AMIENS. Half march & Transport billeted at LONGPRE for the night at 4.30pm.	
		3.30pm	Church Parade. Remainder MEAULTE.	
	30/10	4am	1st line Transport & tool vehicles left LONGPRE route via PICQUIGNY, CROUY, HANGEST to MERELESSART. owing to the exhausted state of the animals, march was made for the right owing to the exhausted state of the animals.	
		11.15am	Remainder marches left MEAULTE & marched to HERICOURT.	
		1.30pm	Entrained at HERICOURT, train leaving at 2pm.	
		5.15pm	Detrained at AIRAINES, Company left marching via DREUIL, MERELESSART, CITERNE & FRUCOURT.	

H.W. Hodgart. Capt R.E. (TF)
O.C. 1/1st Renfrewshire
Field Coy R.E.

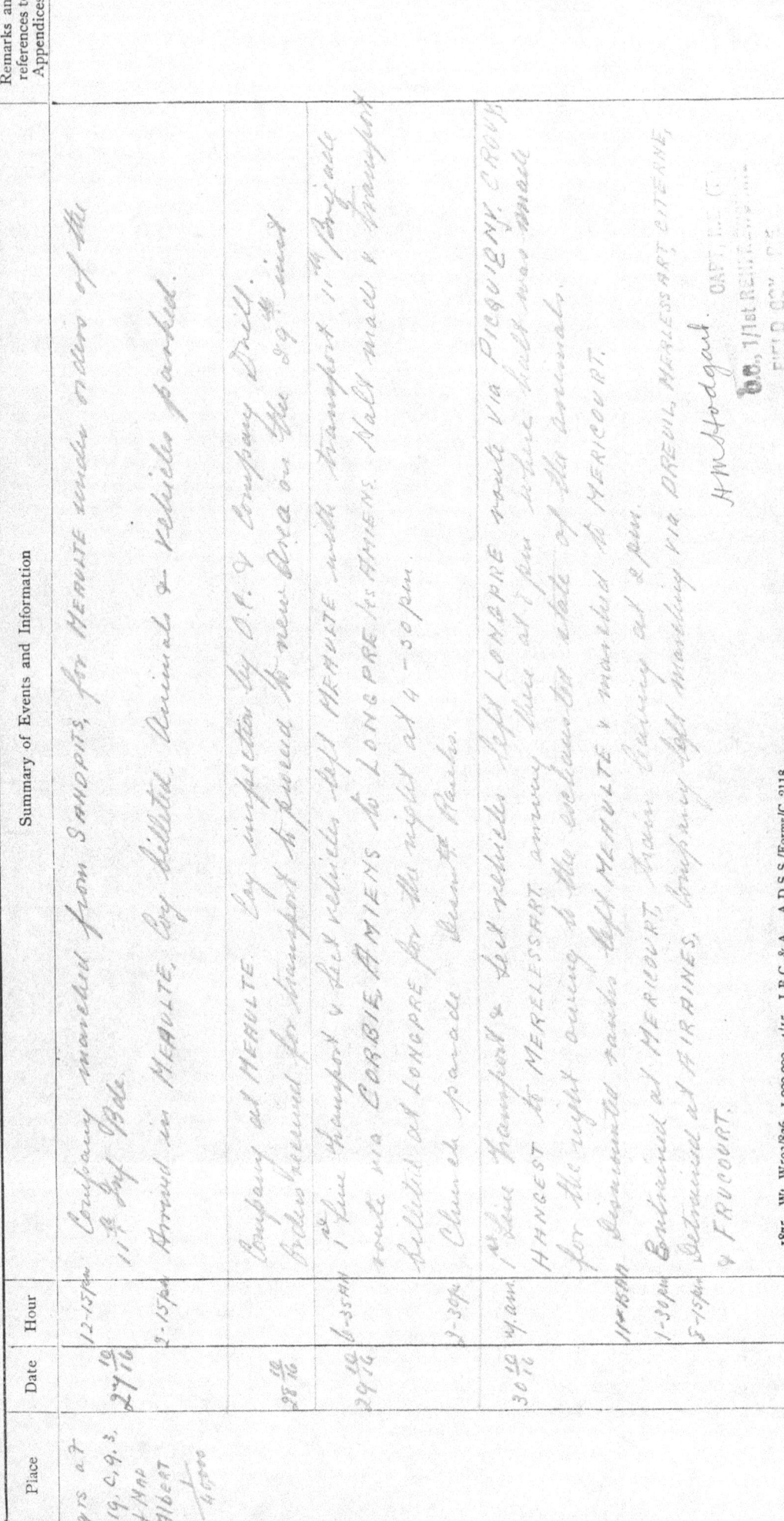

Army Form C. 2118

WAR DIARY
or
INTELLIGENCE SUMMARY

(Erase heading not required.)

Instructions regarding War Diaries and Intelligence Summaries are contained in F. S. Regs., Part II. and the Staff Manual respectively. Title Pages will be prepared in manuscript.

Place	Date	Hour	Summary of Events and Information	Remarks and references to Appendices
HdQrs. at DOUDELAINVILLE	31/1/16	12-45 AM	Dismounted parties arrived at DOUDELAINVILLE & billeted.	
		9 AM	Transport left MEREBESSART marched to DOUDELAINVILLE arrived at 12-15 pm animals stabled, vehicles parked by roadside in village.	

A.M. Hodgart Capt. A.S.C.
O.C. ....
FIELD COY. R.E.

4th DIVISION.

1/IST RENFREW FIELD COMPANY.

ROYAL ENGINEERS.

NOVEMBER 1916.

Army Form C. 2118.

WAR DIARY
or
INTELLIGENCE SUMMARY.
(Erase heading not required.)

Instructions regarding War Diaries and Intelligence
Summaries are contained in F. S. Regs., Part II
and the Staff Manual respectively. Title pages
will be prepared in manuscript.

Place	Date	Hour	Summary of Events and Information	Remarks and references to Appendices
Hdqrs at POUDEHIVILLE Ref Map N.W. EUROPE Sheet No. 3	1/4/16		Route March. Company Drill. 11 am Div Engr Operation Order No 42 dated 1st received. 11 pm Operation Order No 53 dated 1st received. Dinner Party of 1 Officer & 10 O.R. proceeded to VILLEROY.	
Hdqrs at POUDEHIVILLE	2/4/16	1-30pm 10-0pm	Company parade. All ranks present. Harness inspected. Company marched out to VILLEROY via FRESNE DISEMONT. Arrived at VILLEROY. Company billeted all animals stabled move completed.	
Hdqrs at VILLEROY Ref Map DIEPPE Sheet 18.16.	3/4/16		Company Drill. Washing vehicles & overhauling & cleaning Company Equipment. 6 O.R. joined unit from Base.	

H.M. Hodgart
CAPT, R.E. (T.)
O.C. 1/1st RENFREWSHIRE
FIELD COY, R.E.

WAR DIARY
or
INTELLIGENCE SUMMARY.
(Erase heading not required.)

Army Form C. 2118.

Place	Date	Hour	Summary of Events and Information	Remarks and references to Appendices
Hdqrs. of YILLEROY Ref Sheet DIEPPE M/16	4/4/16		Company Drill & route march. Inspection of Vincient by V.O. Lectures on Field Geometry. Working party at OISEMONT erecting huts for Hdqrs & their 1AR. general purpose — o.1 —	
do	5/4/16		Company inspection. Kit inspection. Church parade. Working party at OISEMONT on Hdqrs hut.	
do	6/4/16		Route March. Lectures on Maps Reading. Use of Prismatic Compass. Working parties erecting huts in OISEMONT. Returns in VILEROY.	
do	7/4/16		Drill "as am. Physical Drill "as am. Lectures on Heeds level & Field Geometry. " use of Explosives & testing Electrical Circuits. Working parties erecting Hqrs huts in OISEMONT & erecting partition in MAIRIE OISEMONT company stores.	

R.M. Hodgson
CAPT. R.E. (T).
O.C. 1/1st L_____
FIELD COY. R.E.

Army Form C. 2118.

WAR DIARY
or
INTELLIGENCE SUMMARY.
(Erase heading not required.)

Instructions regarding War Diaries and Intelligence Summaries are contained in F.S. Regs., Part II. and the Staff Manual respectively. Title pages will be prepared in manuscript.

Place	Date	Hour	Summary of Events and Information	Remarks and references to Appendices
Hdqrs at VILLEROY Ref Sheet N° 8 DIEPPE 16	8/10	10am 2-9pm	Rnd't March. Inspection of Unit & billets by G.O.C. 4 Div. Marching & fighting stations Open Trench in DISEMONT completed.	
		2pm	13 sent 1 Officer 35 O.R. left for FLEXICOURT for work at 4th Army School of Instruction. 2 O.R. proceeded to BLANCHY to run a deep Electric lighting installation at Chateau occupied by 12 Infantry.	
"	9/10		Working parties completing lines & laying pads for H Wire tests. Trenches in VILLEROY & MOUFLIERS. 2 Officers & 65 O.R. evacuated Hd Tpd 4 O.R. proceeded to Mons BLANCHY for work with 13th Fd Coy.	
"	10/10	8pm	Working parties overlay latrines in DISEMONT & repairs to Church DISEMONT. Remainder of unit on Company Drill & Field Works. Night parade of unit. Instruction in Field works & Enemy Trenches.	

R.M. Hodgson Capt RE
O.C. 7/131 REN...

Army Form C. 2118.

WAR DIARY
or
INTELLIGENCE SUMMARY.
(Erase heading not required.)

Instructions regarding War Diaries and Intelligence Summaries are contained in F. S. Regs., Part II. and the Staff Manual respectively. Title pages will be prepared in manuscript.

Place	Date	Hour	Summary of Events and Information	Remarks and references to Appendices
Hdqrs at VILLEROY Ref Map DIEPPE Sheet No. 16	11/7		Working parties repairing ground & erecting latrines in OISEMONT. Medical evening roun for 11th Brigade Hqr. Remainder of unit. Route March & Drill.	
do	12/7		Working parties erecting quarters for 4th Hfld & repairing ground in OISEMONT. 40 Shoring races made for 11th Brigade. Remainder of unit overhauling stores & Church Parade.	
do	13/7		Working parties erecting latrines in 11th Bde area. Bridge at Pon BLANCHY inspected & reported on. 2 sets Bayonet fighting Gallows erected for 11th Bde. Repairs to Convent (OISEMONT) completed.	
do	14/7		Erecting latrines in 13th Bde. Instructional party for several days out at LETRANSLAY & VILLEROY. Remainder of unit Route March. Lectures on Explosives & evening & testing electric circuits.	

H.W. Hodges, Capt., R.E.
O.C. 1/1st Dev.....
FIELD COY

Army Form C. 2118.

WAR DIARY
or
INTELLIGENCE SUMMARY.
(Erase heading not required.)

Instructions regarding War Diaries and Intelligence Summaries are contained in F. S. Regs., Part II. and the Staff Manual respectively. Title pages will be prepared in manuscript.

Place	Date	Hour	Summary of Events and Information	Remarks and references to Appendices
Hd.qrs. at VILLERS Ref. Map Sheet 1906 DIEPPE	15/4/16		Working parties erecting latrines for 13th Bru. Trench digg. & tests for Div. Gas School at ST MAXENT started. Remainder of until Road March Lectures on Field Works Instruction in Demolitions.	
do	16/4/16		Parties erecting latrines & repairing billets on 8th Bn. area. Instructional parties on munai dug-outs made 450 ft. Party cutting trenches with hand driven excavator seven men in Wörschach village. Hostile aeroplane flying low passed to MILLONVILLE.	
do	17/4/16	8 a.m.	Moved to BA for MILLONVILLE by Motor Transport for work under the 3 May R.F.C. Working parties erecting latrines in Bu. area. Antici trench for LICHENES & MOUFLIERS made a platoon. Instructional parties work 11 p.m. till an hour before sun rise. 2 P.O. received aunt from Base. Instructional dug outs & trenches completed for 4 Div. Gas School.	

H.B. Hodgart
CAPT. R.E. (T).
O.C., 1/1st RENFREWSHIRE
FIELD COY., R.E.

Army Form C. 2118.

WAR DIARY
or
INTELLIGENCE SUMMARY.
(Erase heading not required.)

Instructions regarding War Diaries and Intelligence Summaries are contained in F. S. Regs., Part II. and the Staff Manual respectively. Title pages will be prepared in manuscript.

Place	Date	Hour	Summary of Events and Information	Remarks and references to Appendices
Hdqrs at VILLEROY Ref Map DIEPPE Sheet No. 16	18/4		Working parties erecting latrines & repairing billets in Bn. area. Fatigue with in workshop for T.M.B. Instructional parties on trench dig-out at TRAMSLEY & VILLEROY. Preparing timber in workshop for latrines (sets).	
do	19/4		Sunday inspection & Church parade.	
do	20/4		Working parties erecting latrines in Bn. area. Making & fitting water screens for Hoods. Party erecting Bayonet gallows & digging trench for 4 Vicker's School of Instruction. Targets made for 11 of the Machine Gun Coy.	
do	21/4		Working parties erecting latrines & repairing billets in Bn. area & fields in farms used for 11 in 8th Divn. pictures. Butts frames made for trench Mortars MOUCHIERS & LIGNERES. Party overlay fellows & excavating & revetting trench for 4 Div. Redoubt. Instructional party with 8th Bn on trench dig out.	

H.P. Hodgson Capt.
O.C. 1/1st ...... Field Coy.

Army Form C. 2118.

WAR DIARY
or
INTELLIGENCE SUMMARY.
(Erase heading not required.)

Instructions regarding War Diaries and Intelligence Summaries are contained in F. S. Regs., Part II. and the Staff Manual respectively. Title pages will be prepared in manuscript.

Place	Date	Hour	Summary of Events and Information	Remarks and references to Appendices
Hdqrs at				
VILLEROY Ref Map DIEPPE Sh.11 N°6	22/6		Working parties erecting latrines etc. for Rue ave. Party excavating & revetting trench for Dugout Ey Hq ad + Rue Palant. Fatigue Party carries for Bomb Dug outs. Instructional party for several Regt outs.	
"	23/6		Working parties erecting latrines & cutting paths for recent dug outs. Instructional party at MILERY TRANSLAY & HAPPENCOURT on recent dug outs. Notice boards made & billets for outlets in Div Area. All amount of work required by HQRS.	
"	24/6		Working parties completing latrines in Rue ave. Trench Covers & revetting mats made for Dug- Outs. Notice boards for roads completed & delivered 9 11 P.M.	

A H Hodgard
CAPT., R.E. (T.),
O.C., 1/1st RENFREWSHIRE
FIELD COY., R.E.

Army Form C. 2118.

WAR DIARY
or
INTELLIGENCE SUMMARY.
(Erase heading not required.)

Instructions regarding War Diaries and Intelligence Summaries are contained in F. S. Regs., Part II. and the Staff Manual respectively. Title pages will be prepared in manuscript.

Place	Date	Hour	Summary of Events and Information	Remarks and references to Appendices
HQ o at				
VILLERS Aux BOIS DIEPPE Sheet No 16	25th		Instructional party on mud dug out at FULLAY TRENCH & MANNEQUIN. Party working on instructional trenches at 4 Elm Allee. Stores and payment parade and of Engineers.	
do	26th		Inspecting parade. Inspector Inspected. Church parade.	
do	27th		Working parties making Latrine seats & note boards. Procuring tools & equipment. Labor Exchange and 1pm Half parade of details or H.M.T.F.M. Reinforcement.	
do	28th		Working parties unloading stores, repairing roads & cutting paths. Instructional party on Mud dug outs. Making drawing notice boards. Tool & working equipment. Drill. Party building brick pillar for gate at supply depot Boumont.	

M.M. Hodgart
Capt. R.E.
O.O. 2nd Reinforcements
Field Coy., R.E.

2353 Wt. W2544/1454 700,000 5/15 D.D. & L. A.D.S.S. Forms/C. 2118.

WAR DIARY or INTELLIGENCE SUMMARY

(Erase heading not required.)

Army Form C. 2118.

1/1 Renfrews A&B Coy
Vol 12

Place	Date	Hour	Summary of Events and Information	Remarks and references to Appendices
Hqrs. at VILLEROY Ref Map DIEPPE Sheet No 16	29/7/16		All Entire Company drilled & arranged to HANGEST & to dismantle at XV Corps Park. Having VILLEROY at 10 am. Wagons to return to VILLEROY. Company stove constructed. Party by motor lorry brought toolchest for place BLANCHY. Brick pillar completed & gate hung at Supply Depot FRAMICOURT.	
do	30/7/16		Working parties making ladders for Store at BLANCHY. Mining crews drawn from day task. By party repelling trenches & Reps. Remnants of sand Drill & Somerfly were interchanged.	

W M Hodgard
O.C. 1/1 ...
FIELD COY RE

4th DIVISION

1/IST RENFREW FIELD COMPANY.

ROYAL ENGINEERS.

DECEMBER 1916.

Army Form C. 2118.

WAR DIARY
or
INTELLIGENCE SUMMARY.
(Erase heading not required.)

Instructions regarding War Diaries and Intelligence Summaries are contained in F. S. Regs., Part II and the Staff Manual respectively. Title pages will be prepared in manuscript.

Place	Date	Hour	Summary of Events and Information	Remarks and references to Appendices
VILLEROY Ref Map DIEPPE Sheet No. 16	1/12/16	1-45PM	Lent vehicles & 1st line transport left VILLEROY for WOIREL. Unit employs packing stores & company Mess.	
	9-15PM		No. 3 Sect. arrived & received lent from ALLONVILLE.	
do	2/12/16	4-40AM	Transport left WOIREL for LONGPRÉ at 4-0 am.	
	12-0 NOON		No 1 Sect received cent from 27 Heavy Island FIENCOURT. Company Rest March. Line escape Ladder erected & completed at Chateau BLANGY, occupied by the 12th Field Ambulance	N.H.
do	3/12/16	6-0AM	Transport left LONGPRÉ for Camp 112 arrived at 4-0 p.m.	
	5-0AM		Dismounted personnel left VILLEROY, marched to OISEMONT.	
	10-0NOON		Entrained OISEMONT, detrained at MERICOURT at 3-15 p.m. & marched to Camp 112 at L.S.A. arrived at 4-30 p.m.	

J M Hodgart
MAJOR, R.E.(T)
O.C. 1/1st RENFREWSHIRE
FIELD COY., R.E.

Army Form C. 2118.

WAR DIARY
or
INTELLIGENCE SUMMARY.
(Erase heading not required.)

Instructions regarding War Diaries and Intelligence Summaries are contained in F. S. Regs., Part II. and the Staff Manual respectively. Title pages will be prepared in manuscript.

Place	Date	Hour	Summary of Events and Information	Remarks and references to Appendices
CAMP 112. L.2A Ref. MAP ALBERT	4/12/16	11-0AM	Company left camp & marched via BRAY to camp at BRONFAY FARM A.25. Central arriving at 2-0 pm.	
CAMP at A.25. C	5/12/16		Company in camp at A.25. Central. O.C. & 1 officer visited the trenches in new sector.	
do	6/12/16		Company marched from Camp 112. to Camp at A.12. Central arriving at 2 pm. Parties of NCO's men taken over lines in new sector.	
Camp at A.12. Central Ref MAP ALBERT	7/12/16		Company in camp at A.12. Central. Inspection of gas appliances & drill. Party visited trenches & took over shelters in new sector.	

J.M. Hodgart
MAJOR, R.E.(T)
O.C. 1/1st RENFREWSHIRE
FIELD COY, R.E.

Army Form C. 2118.

WAR DIARY
or
INTELLIGENCE SUMMARY.
(Erase heading not required.)

Place	Date	Hour	Summary of Events and Information	Remarks and references to Appendices
CAMP at A.12.c.central	8/12/16	1.30 AM	Nos 2,3 & 4 Sections left camp & proceeded to FREGICOURT.	
Rd NAP			No 3 Sect to MOUCHOIR COPSE to relieve 20th Coy Tunnel Engineers.	
ALBERT Sheet		5.0 AM	Relief completed, 1st Line Transport & Limbers left camp & proceeded to Camp at B.14.v. MAUREPAS with No 1 Sect. ALBERT SHEET	
			R.E. Dump at U.19.d.1.3. taken over & checked.	
Nor at T.24.c.6.8 Rd Map 57c S.W.4. COMBLES.	9/12/16		Work started, cleaning communication trench, 5th N.Yn Dugout, & entrance dug-out accommodation for sect. Transport employed carrying stores from Coy dump to forward dump at U.19.M.1.3	
Do	10/12/16		Work continued on 6th N.Yn dug-out & Main communication trench Dug-outs for Right & Left Batt HQrs started. R.A.M.P. dug-out at U.19.a.2.6. started. Transport carrying stores to forward dump. Back sect employed taking R.E. stores at MAUREPAS.	

J.M.Hodgeph

Army Form C. 2118.

WAR DIARY
or
INTELLIGENCE SUMMARY.
(Erase heading not required.)

Instructions regarding War Diaries and Intelligence Summaries are contained in F. S. Regs., Part II. and the Staff Manual respectively. Title pages will be prepared in manuscript.

Place	Date	Hour	Summary of Events and Information	Remarks and references to Appendices
Hd Qrs 1/1st E.Y. R.E. Map Combles Sheet 57c S.W.4.	11/7/16		Work continued on 13th H.N. dug-out. Right & Left Batt. H.Q. dug-outs R.A.M.C. dug-out. Clearing main communication trench, work in sector very considerably hampered owing to searching parties being required to dig & hand over out of the mud, the troubles being in a bad state owing to heavy rains.	
do	12/7/16		Work carried on in all dug-outs. Main communication trench dug-out. Started & floored bottom dug-out. 200 yards trench board track laid down along communication trench. Transport employed carrying stores to forward dumps.	
do	13/7/16		Work carried on all dug-outs in sector. 100 yards trench board track laid down to left sector.	
do	14/7/16		Work carried on all dug-outs in sector. 100 yards trench board track laid down to left sector. Transport employed carrying stores to forward dumps.	

W.H. Hodgard Major, R.E. (T)
O.C. 1/1st Renfrewshire
Field Coy. R.E.

Army Form C. 2118.

WAR DIARY
or
INTELLIGENCE SUMMARY.
(Erase heading not required.)

Instructions regarding War Diaries and Intelligence Summaries are contained in F.S. Regs., Part II. and the Staff Manual respectively. Title pages will be prepared in manuscript.

Place	Date	Hour	Summary of Events and Information	Remarks and references to Appendices
HQr at				
T.24, O.V.F. Ref Map COMBLES Sheet 57cS.E.SW4	15/7/16		Work continued on all dug-outs in sector. Laying trench boards to Right & Left sub-sectors. Transport employed carrying stores to forward dumps. Own section employed making roadway through transport lines.	
Do	16/7/16		Work continued on dug-outs in sector. R.W.H.E. dug-out started at T.24, N.7.9. 200 yds trench board track laid & track leader to Right sub-sector. Own section employed building horse standing & making roadway at MINNEAPOLIS.	
Do	14/7/16		Work continued on dug-outs & trench board tracks in sector. & thickening of Head cover of Dug-outs dug-out at MOUNTAIN COPSE. Own section employed building horse standings & roads in transport lines. Transport employed carrying stores to forward dumps	

J M Hodgson
MAJOR, R.E. (T)
O.C. 1/1st RENFREWSHIRE
FIELD COY, R.E.

Army Form C. 2118.

WAR DIARY
or
INTELLIGENCE SUMMARY.
(Erase heading not required.)

Instructions regarding War Diaries and Intelligence Summaries are contained in F.S. Regs. Part II. and the Staff Manual respectively. Title pages will be prepared in manuscript.

Place	Date	Hour	Summary of Events and Information	Remarks and references to Appendices
HdQrs at T34.S.8.3. Ref Map 1957 Bethune S.W.4.	18/7/16		Work continued on dug-outs. 2nd Chamber started on BHQ dug-out, frames plumbed & traced in stairway, 150 ft* trench-boom track laid. Nore dug-out passage punched out between galleries & lower chamber started. Our section employed on dug-outs & improvements at Div HQ.	
do	19/7/16		Work continued on improving trench cover at HdQrs dug-out at Mercinghem Posts. Clearing down communication trench & laying trench board tracks. Our section employed finishing drying shed & Lois steeplechase. Transport carrying stores to forward dumps. 1109 "Meadow" " " " " No 1382 Lapr Dick D Wounded in action (evacuated) Passenger on lorry	
do	20/7/16		Work continued on all dug-outs & lightening trench cover at 8th HQ dug-out for Right Batt Hdqrs. Work on new communication trench started trench board trench laid from Neuchuor Copse to PHMPX & completion of drying shed at T.19.c.9.10. Our section employed on drying shed & PHMPX & those standings.	

Wm Hodgart MAJOR R.E.
O.C. 1/1st A. ... Renfrewshire
R.E.

WAR DIARY
or
INTELLIGENCE SUMMARY.
(Erase heading not required.)

Army Form C. 2118.

Place	Date	Hour	Summary of Events and Information	Remarks and references to Appendices
HQ¹ⁿᵈ T.2.4.5. b.i. Ref. Map Ghent NE 1/40000 Sh. 11	21/4/76		Work continued on dug-outs. Chamber at B upper Mag out lined strips set in & chamber completed. Blue Trench 120 yards avenue trench cut & floor strewed. Back cut erecting dogleg shed & making A frames. Transport employed carrying stores to forward dumps.	
do	22/4/76		Work continued on dug-outs. Down gallery to RHMG dug out completed. Further dug for Shew Right Battn¹. HQs, 40 yards blue trench avenue. Apsyth field levels & stores taken up to dogleg dump. Back section employed making A frames & erecting dogleg shed.	
do	23/4/76		Work continued on dug-outs. 40 yds. Blue Trench revetted & floored. Back section employed making A frames & erecting dogleg shed. Transport employed carrying stores to forward dumps.	

JMᵇHodgas
MAJOR, R.E.
O.C. 1/1st RENFREWSHIRE
FIELD COY., R.E.

Army Form C. 2118.

WAR DIARY
or
INTELLIGENCE SUMMARY
(Erase heading not required)

Place	Date	Hour	Summary of Events and Information	Remarks and references to Appendices
H¼th etc. T 24, c, 6, 2. Pct Map Sheet N°57 S.W.4	24/12/16		Work continued on dug-outs. R.A.M.C. dug-out entrance at N°1 gallery completed. Poultry & sleeping place framed. Pack Lot. Gantry slinging shed & Making A frames. Transport carrying stores to forward dumps.	
do.	25/12/16		Work continued on B & H dug-out. Lost carrying dug-out pier at Watkins about 4 ft. Work continued on New tunnel. No gyns excavated & concrete Pack out employed making trench crossing, trench crossing shed, workshops & making A frames. Transport employed carrying stores to forward dumps.	
do.	26/12/16		Work continued on dug-outs. Foundation started for Elephant shelter for M.O. & dressing station. Tunnel towed track completed & levelled at front lines. Pack out employed in dugging shed & making R.E. stores at MAUREPAS. Hut moved to quarters in Ravine MAUREPAS.	

J.M. Hodgeon MAJOR. R.E. (T)
O.C. 1/1st RENFREWSHIRE
FIELD COY. R.E.

Army Form C. 2118.

WAR DIARY
or
INTELLIGENCE SUMMARY.
(Erase heading not required.)

Instructions regarding War Diaries and Intelligence Summaries are contained in F. S. Regs., Part II. and the Staff Manual respectively. Title pages will be prepared in manuscript.

Place	Date	Hour	Summary of Events and Information	Remarks and references to Appendices
H⁴ᵈʳˢ at T24 C.6.2. Ref. Map Amiens Sheet N°57 S.W.2.	28/10		Work continued on dug-outs. Supports 9ᵗʰ dug out shelter completed to Munch, new steps fitted in gallery. Excavation & revetting Blair Trench Back shelter employed, enemy trench mortar area & cavalry dugg shelters.	
do	29/10		Work continued on dug-outs & shelters of Back area and 10ᵗʰ supporting units. New support 11ᵗʰ dug-out started 4 trench dugg shelter dug out in tunnel & tunnel from Bullet & Route El No.6. MRMK dug out at Touching chamber completed. Back and refuse dug-out in new area & revetting digging stack. Party of 1ˢᵗ Home Counties F/ by R.E. taken over works in sector.	
do	30/10	3-4pm	Work continued on dug outs Excavation of a new chamber at 8ᵗʰ H.Q. completed. Portion of 1ˢᵗ Home Counties Held by Stoke over work in sector. Company relieved by Home Counties Field Co R.E. left returned to billets at MAUREPAS RAVINE on relief.	

R. M. Hodgart
MAJOR, R.E. (?)
O.C. 1/1st RENFREWSHIRE
FIELD CO...

Army Form C. 2118.

WAR DIARY
or
INTELLIGENCE SUMMARY.
(Erase heading not required.)

Instructions regarding War Diaries and Intelligence summaries are contained in F. S. Regs., Part II. and the Staff Manual respectively. Title pages will be prepared in manuscript.

Place	Date	Hour	Summary of Events and Information	Remarks and references to Appendices
Hedanquartes Ref Map ALBERT Trenches Sheet	31/7/16		1 Sect employed mostly Elephant shelters in RAVINE MAUREPAS. Erection of drying sheds Latrines. 3 Sects at RAVINE improving SUETS & trying trench tram track. Transport employed carrying parts of Nissen huts from DOMINO DUMP to sites for erection.	

M M Hodgart.
O.C. 1/1st RENFREW
FIELD CO,

4th Division

War Diarie,

406th Field Coy R.E, LATE 1/1 Renfrew,

January, To December
1917

Feb. 1919

Army Form 2118.

WAR DIARY
or
INTELLIGENCE SUMMARY.
(Erase heading not required.)

Instructions regarding War Diaries and Intelligence Summaries are contained in F.S. Regs., Part II. and the Staff Manual respectively. Title pages will be prepared in manuscript.

1/1st RENFREW...

Place	Date	Hour	Summary of Events and Information	Remarks and references to Appendices
HdQrs at MAUREPAS B.10.d.5.4 Ref Map N°. 62° N.W.	1/7		Corps Line moved out from RONCOURT at C.1.a.5.3. to C.7.Central. Company working on shelters in MAUREPAS RAVINE. Working parties on Camp X.	
do	2/7		Corps Line traced out to C.13.d.5.5. Trench completely alphabeted during day. Working parties erecting shelters & digging shelter in MAUREPAS RAVINE. Start made to convey NISSEN HUTS from Divisional dump by rail at B.21.	
do	3/7		Start made to wire front of Corps Line, erected by working party of Canadian Pioneers. Clearing, revetting & erecting trench at Corps HdQrs. Making water tanks, erecting NISSEN HUTS. O.P. for Lewis Gun sited at RANCOURT.	
do	4/7		Wiring party on Corps Line. 24 long hoods extra covering roof at Corps HdQrs. Erecting shelters & latrines at C.1.c.6.5. Evening, revetting & clearing trench at Corps HdQrs. Erecting shelters & latrines in MAUREPAS RAVINE. Carrying party at Camp X. Pumps repaired at MAUREPAS water point. Work on survey O.P. at RANCOURT started.	

Col. Bruno [?]
for O.C. 1/1st RENFREWSHIRE FIELD COY., R.E.

MAJOR, R.E. (T)
1/1st RENFREWSHIRE
FIELD COY., R.E.

Army Form C. 2118.

WAR DIARY
or
INTELLIGENCE SUMMARY.
(Erase heading not required.)

Instructions regarding War Diaries and Intelligence Summaries are contained in F.S. Regs., Part II and the Staff Manual respectively. Title pages will be prepared in manuscript.

[STAMP: 1/1st RENFREWSHIRE F COY. R.E.]

Place	Date	Hour	Summary of Events and Information	Remarks and references to Appendices
HUTS AT MAUREPAS B.14.a.5.4. Ref Map M¹ 62° N.W.	5/14		Wiring bivys cover. Clearing, revetting & covering trench at Corps Right H.Qrs. Party on Survey O.P. at RANCOURT, framing made for O.P. & taken to site. Party clearing NISSEN HUTS from Domino Dump to new site at B.14 Central.	
do	6/14		Working parties wiring Corps Line, trench at Corps Right H.Qrs, erecting NISSEN HUTS at B.14. Central. Work on O.P. at RANCOURT stopped & new site selected.	
do	7/14		Working party covering bivys bivys. This party was heavily shelled during the day, the runs being cut in several places. Work on new site of O.P. at RANCOURT started, erecting NISSEN HUTS at B.14.C. Party repairing pumps & piping at water point MAUREPAS RAVINE.	
do	8/14		Working parties wiring bivys line, work on this line was considerably retarded owing to unceasing shelling of ridge. Erecting NISSEN HUTS at B.14.C. Work continued on O.P. at RANCOURT, camouflage completed.	

[Signature] Major R.E. (T)
O.C. 1/1st RENFREWSHIRE FIELD COY., R.E.

WAR DIARY
or
INTELLIGENCE SUMMARY.
(Erase heading not required.)

Army Form C. 2118.

Place	Date	Hour	Summary of Events and Information	Remarks and references to Appendices
H/qtrs at B14.C.5.4. Rf Map 62c N.W.	9/7/17		Working parties erecting NISSEN HUTS at B.14.C. Work continued on timber at Corps Hqrs. Roof for O.P. at RANCOURT prepared & taken to site.	
do	10/7/17		Working parties erecting NISSEN HUTS, slicing & roofing huts at Corps Hqrs Hdqrs. O.P at RANCOURT. Transport employed cleaning DUMP of NISSEN HUTS & conveying to new sites.	
do	11/7/17	8-10 am	All dismounted ranks left billets in RAVINE & took up quarters in HUTS at B.14. Central. Working parties completing NISSEN HUTS, erecting Cook House & Latrines. Trench boards laid through Camp. O.P at RANCOURT completed by night party. Pump repaired at water point in MOISLAINS RAVINE.	
do	12/7/17		Working parties erecting NISSEN HUTS & laying trench boards in CAMP. Huts at Corps Hqrs Hqrs completed. Party fixing & jumping off dug-outs at JUNCTION WOOD.	

(sgd)

MAJOR, R.E.
O.C. 1/1st RENFREWSHIRE
FIELD COY., R.E.

WAR DIARY
or
INTELLIGENCE SUMMARY
(Erase heading not required.)

Army Form C. 2118.

Place	Date	Hour	Summary of Events and Information	Remarks and references to Appendices
H^qrs 0/8 B.14.a.5.4. Ref Map 62c N.W.	13/7/17		Working parties erecting NISSEN HUTS. These party worked continuously until huts were completed for accommodation of incoming Infantry. Party repairing & lining out dug-outs at JUNCTION WOOD.	
do	14/7/17		Erecting NISSEN HUTS. Tunnel completed at Info Hq & 11 Hqs. Hutson crews of erection of B.14.c. are Shells & huts being destroyed. No 1078 Sap. Faulkner J. Killed in Action. 1121 Spr. Nasson W. Wounded in Action. 1074 Spr. Dunlop. Wounded in Action. 1095 Spr. Brown J. Wounded in Action. No 1484 Daniel returned to duty.	
do	15/7/17		Company in rest. Dugouts & Shelters taken over in New area at CUREU.	
do	16/7/17		Company moved to dug-outs & Shelters in new area at CUREU at 9.6.c.8.8. Working parties employed erecting tents in dug-outs. Working party on dug-outs at JUNCTION WOOD.	

John Edwards for
MAJOR, R.E. (T)
O.O. 1/1st RENFREWSHIRE
FIELD COY. R.E.

Army Form C. 2118.

WAR DIARY
or
INTELLIGENCE SUMMARY

(Erase heading not required.)

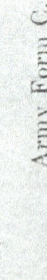

Place	Date	Hour	Summary of Events and Information	Remarks and references to Appendices
Maps ref S.G. G.P.P. Ref Map 62 N.W.	17/7/17		Working parties lining & flooring dug-outs at JUNCTION WOOD. Latrine trench in dug-outs at Hqrs erecting cook-house & latrines.	
do	18/7/17		Working parties lining & flooring dug-outs at JUNCTION WOOD. Start made on mined dug-outs at H.Qrs. on ascertaining trench scheme. Site laid out for new stabling & ration dumps. Cook-house erected at H.Qrs.	
do	19/7/17		Working parties lining & flooring dug-outs, erecting cook-house latrines at H.Q./Hqrs. at JUNCTION WOOD, work continued on mined dug-outs, frames cut & starting prepared.	
do	20/7/17		Dug-outs completed at JUNCTION WOOD. Framing erected for ration dumps. Party erecting stables in Quarry. Excavation for staff H.Qrs offices started at F.C.C.	

O.C. 1/1st Renfrewshire
MAJOR R.E.
FIELD COY.

Army Form C. 2118.

WAR DIARY
or
INTELLIGENCE SUMMARY.
(Erase heading not required.)

Instructions regarding War Diaries and Intelligence Summaries are contained in F.S. Regs., Part II. and the Staff Manual respectively. Title pages will be prepared in manuscript.

Place	Date	Hour	Summary of Events and Information	Remarks and references to Appendices
Hqrs est Q.6, S.1.9. Ref Map 51C N.W.	21/7/19		Working parties on Mural dug-outs at H/Qrs, erecting Patrol lamps, stables Lull House. Making frames for dug-outs.	
do	22/7/19		Working parties on Mural-dug outs, erecting tables in dug-outs. Erecting shelters for ration dumps. Drying Rums & NISSEN HUTS for 172nd M/G Coy.	
do	23/7/19		Working parties on mural-dug-outs & erecting huts. Erecting shelters for ration dumps, drying sheds, bath house & NISSEN HUTS at H/Qrs 172nd M/Gun Coy.	
do	24/7/19		Work stopped on Mural dug-outs at 12 noon & erecting huts, accommodation for 391 men much that. Erecting ration dumps, drying sheds, bath house, stort works with 3 formed shelters in Quarry, 3 stables completed in Quarry.	

O.C. 1/1st RENFREWSHIRE
FIELD COY., R.E.

Army Form C. 2118.

WAR DIARY
or
INTELLIGENCE SUMMARY

(Erase heading not required.)

Place	Date	Hour	Summary of Events and Information	Remarks and references to Appendices
Hapes at G.6.b.7.9. 1/1st Nyhmb E FC. N.W.	25/7/19		Parties erecting shelter & stables in Quarry. Digging stubs, bath house & Nissen Huts at 17.9.d.9.4pm. 3 Section thump shelters completed.	
do	26/7/19		Erecting shelter & stables in Quarry. Digging stubs, bath house & Nissen Huts. 3 NISSEN HUTS completed to date. 9 erected & 8 reported on 17.9.d.9.4pm & 17.9.d.9.4pm accommodation	
do	27/7/19		Erecting shelter & stables in Quarry. Bath house & Nissen Huts at 17.9.d.9.4pm. 3 digging stubs completed, erecting shelter for Return dumps.	
do	28/7/19		Working parties erecting shelter & stabling in Quarry, shelter for Return Dumps. Bath house & Nissen Huts at 17.9.d.9.4pm. Huts at 17.9.d.9.4pm demonstrapped.	
do	29/7/19		Working parties erecting shelter & stables in Quarry, accommodation for 2 horses completed. Erecting water dumps Queen huts & bath house. Stables towards completed for accommodation.	

O.C. 1/1st Renfrewshire
Field Coy, R.E.

Army Form C. 2118.

WAR DIARY
or
INTELLIGENCE SUMMARY.
(Erase heading not required.)

Instructions regarding War Diaries and Intelligence Summaries are contained in F. S. Regs., Part II and the Staff Manual respectively. Title pages will be prepared in manuscript.

Place	Date	Hour	Summary of Events and Information	Remarks and references to Appendices
Hqrs of 2/1 Fd Coy Roy Mons RE 1/2 RFR	30/7	9 pm	Working parties completing shelters in Queens. Hissett Hts at Pont Nieppe No 3 Sect Left to relieve sect of 9th Field by RE at B30 L. O.C. wanted overseen line with Nos 1 & 2.	
do	31/7	10 pm	Company inspection. No 1, 3 & 4 sect left to relieve 9th Field Coy on line at B30 L. Relief completed 5 PM.	

Colin Brown Lt Col
MAJOR, R.E.
O.C. 1/1st RENFREWSHIRE
FIELD COY R.E.

Army Form C. 2118.

WAR DIARY
or
INTELLIGENCE SUMMARY
(Erase heading not required.)

406TH (RENFREW) FIELD COMPANY, R.E.
No.......... Date..........

Vol 15

Place	Date	Hour	Summary of Events and Information	Remarks and references to Appendices
HOQRS at B.30.b.7.6. Ref Map M.62 NW 1/20,000	1/2/19		Working parties on Grenade stores at BRYAN MASSON & P.C. MADAME. Excavation of support line LOCUST TR. Support line started from point C.15.c.9.9. Sunk hoist track LONDON TR. Excavations for tunnel for Decauville track under PERONNE–BETHUNE Rd. 20 lengths Chev-de-Frise made & placed in position in line. Break in Decauville line repaired & line patrolled.	
do	2/19		Working parties on support lines at C.21.a.14. LOCUST TR. C.15.C.9.9. CROSS LADDER TR. Excavations for Grenade stores at BRYAN MASSON & P.C. MADAME. Excavation of dug-out at LOCK BARRACKS, repairing dug-outs at LANGTON BARRACKS, LEICESTER LOUNGE. Laying down board tracks LONDON TR & LADDER TR. Wired line post in Decauville track at B.31.A.9.9. Line patrolled day & night. Excavating tunnel PERONNE–BETHUNE Rd.	

J.N. Hodgart Major R.E.(T)
[O.C.] 406th (Renfrew) Field Company R.E.

WAR DIARY or INTELLIGENCE SUMMARY

Army Form C. 2118.

406TH (RENFREW) FIELD COMPANY, R.E.

Place	Date	Hour	Summary of Events and Information	Remarks and references to Appendices
11am 0st. B.30.b.7.6. Ref Map 1:62,500 N.W. 1/20,000	3/2/17		Working parties on Grenade Stores at BOYAU MASSON & P.C. MADAME. Excavation of dug-outs at LOW BARRIERS & RAMC. dug out at P.C. MADAME. Excavation of support line, work stopped at midnight owing to heavy front & persistent shelling of the trenches. Keiel Road track on LONDON & LADDER Tk New loop track started from BOUCHAVESNES to LADDER Tk at Dug-outs repaired at LEICESTER LOUNGER. LANGTON BARRIERS. Excavation of trench cradle PERONNE-BETHUNE Rd. Knife rest entanglements walks laid out. Deauville lines patrolled & section of line levelled.	
do	4/2/17	4-0am	Working parties on Grenade Stores at BOYAU MASSON & P.C. MADAME. French Grenade trench LONDON Tk & LADDER AVENUE. Repairing dug-outs at LANGTON BARRIERS & LEICESTER LOUNGE. Excavating dug-outs at LOW BARRIERS & P.C. MADAME. Entrances to old dug-outs closed in SUNKEN Rd. Excavating tunnel under PERONNE-BETHUNE Rd. Deauville lines patrolled. Break in line reported at 7-45pm. line repaired & abandon at 9-0pm. 1 Lieut. 526th (DURHAM) held by RE around this and attached to coy for work.	

H.M. Hodgart Major R E
Officer Comdg 406th (Renfrew) Field Coyps RE

Army Form C. 2118.

406TH (RENFREW) FIELD COMPANY, R.E.

WAR DIARY
or
INTELLIGENCE SUMMARY

(Erase heading not required.)

Place	Date	Hour	Summary of Events and Information	Remarks and references to Appendices
Hqrs at B.30.b.7.6. Ref Map 1162C NW 1/20,000	5/1/17		Working parties on General stores at BRYAN MASSON & P.C. MADAME. Artillery stations started at C.15.c.1.4 & C.15.c.2.1. Dug-outs at P.C. MADAME & LEE BARRACKS. P.B.I. dug-outs in SUNKEN Rd cleared. Front line trench LODGER Rd. Braceville tunnel under PERONNE - BETHUNE Rd. Dug-outs repaired at LEICESTER LOUNGE & LANGSTON B.H.Q. Braceville town patrolled. 1 French repaired.	
do	6/2/17		Working parties on General stores at BRYAN MASSON & P.C. MADAME. Dug-outs completed at LANGSTON B.H.Q. & LEICESTER LOUNGE. Trench tracks continued from LONDON Tr. v. LADDER AVENUE. French Issue Tracks continued. Start made with R.H.Q. Artillery Stations at C.15.c.1.4 & C.15.c.2.1. Small dug-outs for R.Y. Batt H.Q. at C.15.c.5.9½. Work continued on Braceville tunnel under PERONNE Rd. Braceville twn patrolled and found covered.	

H M Hodgart
Major R.E.
O C 406th (Renfrew) Field Coy R.E.

WAR DIARY or INTELLIGENCE SUMMARY

Army Form C. 2118.

406TH (RENFREW) FIELD COMPANY, R.E.

Place	Date	Hour	Summary of Events and Information	Remarks and references to Appendices
H'qrs at B.20.b.7.6. Bt Map E2 N.W. 1/5000	7/7/19		Work carried on at tunnel dug-outs for R.T.s LT. B.M.H. 19-97 R.A.M.C. Collecting station, trench head trucks LONDON AVE & LONDON AVE grenade stores at P.C. MADAME & BUYON MASSON. Derancourt tunnel into PERONNE RD. Shaft made with RD. Post at P.C. MADAME. Branch road to tunnel to MORRIS's WOOD. Horse trackway & standard G. tracks & glacis.	
do	8/7/19		Work carried on. Tunnel dug-outs for R.T.s LT. B.M.H. 19-97 R.A.M.C. Collecting station C.15.c.45, C.15.c.21, YLBER BARRACKS & P.C. MADAME. Trench tram tracks. LONDON AVE & LADDER AV. 400 yds Rwy laid over night. Grenade stores at P.C. MADAME & BUYON MASSON. Generators & tramway at Derancourt tunnel under PERONNE - BETHUNE RD. Crater of elephant shelter over RR. at C.30.a.3.9. BOUCHAVESNES. Erecting trainin dug-outs at B.21.7 B.20.6.5.55. A large quantity of nothing the enemy material turned up & brought to our support line at C.13.d.I.9. to facilitate work on forward line in between the trains activism.	

A.N.Hodgart Major R.E. F/
O.C. 406# (Renfrew) field Co. R.E.

WAR DIARY or INTELLIGENCE SUMMARY

(Erase heading not required.)

Army Form C.2118.

406TH (RENFREW) FIELD COMPANY, R.E.

Place	Date	Hour	Summary of Events and Information	Remarks and references to Appendices
HQrs at B.29.b.4.6. 51 MRP Sheet 66 e N.W. 1/20000	9/7/17		Working parties on minor dug-outs for R.I.L.T. Batt. H.Q. at Hdqrs Bn. B.15.a.4.0. & C.15.C.21. General stores at Bryan Mussen & P.t. Hudome Bromestey tunnel under Peronne Rd. Erecting timber in dug-outs at B.21.y. Holes moved up to forward dumps. Bouzancourt Line patrolled & broken right.	
do	10/7/17		Working parties on minor dug-outs for R.I.L.T. H.Qrs. Erecting plates at [illegible] C.15.C.1.4.3.Y C.15.a.2.1 & Rd. posts at Pt. Hudome Erecting timber at Hut. Bromestey tunnel under Peronne Rd. General stores at Pt. Hudome & Bryan Mussen. Repair telephoned shelter over well at C.20.a.5.7. Erecting [illegible] in dug-outs at B.21.y. Bouzancourt Line patrolled as trench in line.	
do	11/7/17		Work carried on R.I.L. Batt. H.Q. dug-outs. Rd. Post at 10/10/25 Pt.Hudome. Collecting station at [illegible] C.15.a.2.1. General stores at Bryan Mussen & Pt.Hudome. Bromestey tunnel over Wilson Rd. [illegible]. Erecting timber under Peronne Rd. Bois Italien track [illegible] Pk.	

H.N.Hodgart Major R.E.
O.C. 406th Renfrew Field Coy R.E.

Army Form C. 2118.

WAR DIARY
or
INTELLIGENCE SUMMARY
(Erase heading not required)

Instructions regarding War Diaries and Intelligence Summaries are contained in F. S. Regs., Part II. and the Staff Manual respectively. Title pages will be prepared in manuscript.

406TH (RENFREW) FIELD COMPANY. R.E.
No. ....
Date ....

Place	Date	Hour	Summary of Events and Information	Remarks and references to Appendices
HqrsdF.				
B.3.a.7.c. Ref Map Sheet 57C NW 1/20,000	12/7/19		Work carried on Batt H.Wn Wynnols, Billeting Station & dist. posts. Bn H.Q. & H.Q. MSG. Excavation of Stevensville tunnel PERONNE Rd. Finish new tracks Imper & London R.S. Guard note at PERONNE & BUSAN MSGN. Had men on Water Supply. Stevensville gave patrolled & a brade repair.	
do	13/7/19		Work carried on Bn H.Qn Wynnols, Billeting Station & Rd. party French Fatigs. Met directly of thus tracks prevented work, it was however started for water scheme new site Bn Hqrs the Erevannels with Excavation of tunnel under PERONNE Rd. Stevensville patrolled & maintained.	
do	14/7/19		Work carried on as Bn H.Qn Btgr Rds, Bulletting Stations & Rd. patrols. Heavy traffic IMPDEN & LONDON R.S. Excavation of tunnel PERONNE R.D. Excavation of tunnel Blevensville R.E. HQRDRE. Erevannels bus patrolled. Delivery of "JOIST SUPPORT 72" — Expectation of new Emmanuets sites & connecting of PERLEASE & LANGTON R.S., 9 O.R gimes unit from MS Test Bass.	

A.M.Hodgart Major R.E.
O.P. 406 (Renfrew) Field Coy R.E.

WAR DIARY
or
INTELLIGENCE SUMMARY

Army Form C. 2118.

406TH (RENFREW) FIELD COMPANY, R.E.

Place	Date	Hour	Summary of Events and Information	Remarks and references to Appendices
Hqrs at B.30.c.7.6. R/Mar 19/5/4 N/W	15/7/4		Working parties on Batt. H.Qrs dug outs. Excavation of dead parts R.A.M.P. dug-outs at P.I. MADAME, Colliery Station at IVER BARRACKS. Granville Tunnel under PERONNE Ft. Head trenches patrolled & 3 treks repaired in BOURNEMOUTH LINE. Excavation of Communication trench between ALPHA, LADDER & MARY Avenues.	
do	16/7/4		Working parties on Batt. H.Qrs dug-outs. Rest. Colliery Station & dug out for RIBLE. Excavation of Granville Tunnel. Work under to Hd. of 22.a.2.9. 130 yds. from head trench of LONDON Tr. laid. Excavation & survey of tunnels between ALPHA, LADDER & MARY Ave. Downwards were patrolled & 2 treks repaired at Pt. VIOLETTE.	
do	17/7/4		Working parties on Batt. H.Qrs dug outs continued. Excavation of Jumping trench over 1 Bay. Chamber completed in 1st Batt. H.Q. dug out & occupied by H.Q. Window etc. dug out handed over to 171st Tunnelling Coy R.E. Excavation of tunnel under PERONNE Rd. on Communication trench continued. Merry stop to this tunnel timeless patrolled & repln.	

A.M. Holgard
Major R.E.
O.C. 406 (Renfrew) Field Coy. R.E.

Army Form C. 2118.

WAR DIARY
or
INTELLIGENCE SUMMARY.
(Erase heading not required.)

Instructions regarding War Diaries and Intelligence Summaries are contained in F.S. Regs. Part II. and the Staff Manual respectively. Title pages will be prepared in manuscript.

406TH (RENFREW) FIELD COMPANY. R.E.
No. .... Date ....

Place	Date	Hour	Summary of Events and Information	Remarks and references to Appendices
110yr at B30 & 7.6. 1977 Bt Map 62° NW 1:10000	19/7/17		Work centred on Communication trenches. Landtapping of Mill at B30&.9. Excavation of tunnel under PERONNE RD BAIM dug out & air ports. Decauville track partially reused & reformed. Construction of other RE lines. 108 shims made complete. 1 opn. to dis. A.C. IV N° 3b. de-Im 118 recovered	
do	20/7/17	2-30pm 2-30pm	Dismounted Personnel marched from B30 & 7.6. to V'camp on relief in line by 490th (H.C) field Coy R.E. All Maps travel photos & correspondence handed over to relieving coy & guides supplied to relieving working parties. Relief complete. Dismounted personnel arrived at Bugt V. 142 at LINGER CAMP.	
do	21/7/17	10-0am 3-30pm	Company marched from LINGERCAMP to Camp 114. Arrived at Camp 114.	
110yr at LINGER CAMP	22/7/17	8-30am 11-30 A.M.	Company marched from Camps 114 to Camp 12. Arrived at Camp 12 at 11-30 A.M.	

A.M. Hodgart Major R.E.
O.C. 406th (Renfrew) Field Coy R.E.

2353 Wt. W3441/454 700,000 5/15 D. D. & L. A.D.S.S. Forms/C. 2118.

Army Form C. 2118.

WAR DIARY
or
INTELLIGENCE SUMMARY.
(Erase heading not required.)

Instructions regarding War Diaries and Intelligence Summaries are contained in F. S. Regs., Part II. and the Staff Manual respectively. Title pages will be prepared in manuscript.

406TH (RENFREW) FIELD COMPANY, R.E.
No. ....
Date ....

Place	Date	Hour	Summary of Events and Information	Remarks and references to Appendices
H.Q. at Camp 12	23/2/17		Company employed on changing equipment, arms (etc) Arms, ammunition & kits inspected by O.C. Coys.	
do	24/2/17		Company employed on Physical Drill, Rifle exercises & Squad Drill. Lecture to N.C.O. on trenty Revolutions by R.S.M. Blackburn R.E.	
do	25/2/17	10 am	Company parade. Inspection by O.C. 9 am Physical Drill. Church Parade. Read of Kilt Riflemen D.D. U.C.D. & Cois.	
do	26/2/17		Company employed on Physical Drill, Rifle exercises, Musketry & Squad Drill. Games & Football in afternoon. Lecture by Capt. M. Hargest on Organization of Working Parties.	
do	27/2/17 28/2/17		Company employed at Physical Drill, Rifle exercises & Squad drill. Lecture by O.C. on Organization & Training of Field Coys. Games & Football during afternoon. Coys visited by O.C. 243 H. Div.	

Major R.E. O.C.
406(Renfrew) Field Coy R.E.

2353 Wt. W2544/1454 700,000 5/15 D. D. & L. A.D.S.S.Forms/C. 2118.

Army Form C. 2118.

WAR DIARY
or
INTELLIGENCE SUMMARY.
(Erase heading not required.)

408TH (RENFREW) FIELD COMPANY, R.E.

No. .... Date ....

Instructions regarding War Diaries and Intelligence Summaries are contained in F. S. Regs., Part II. and the Staff Manual respectively. Title pages will be prepared in manuscript.

Place	Date	Hour	Summary of Events and Information	Remarks and references to Appendices
Apres et Camp 12.	28.7.19		Company employed overhauling dry tools & equipment & overhauling vehicles (etc).	

J.M. Hodgart Major R.E. (T)
O.C. 406 (Renfrew) Field Coy R.E.

Army Form C. 2118.

406TH (RENFREW) FIELD COMPANY, R.E.

WAR DIARY
or
INTELLIGENCE SUMMARY.
(Erase heading not required.)

Instructions regarding War Diaries and Intelligence Summaries are contained in F. S. Regs., Part II. and the Staff Manual respectively. Title pages will be prepared in manuscript.

Place	Date	Hour	Summary of Events and Information	Remarks and references to Appendices
Hqrs at CAMP 12 CHIPILLY H2 Ref.Map AMIENS 1/100000	1/14 3		Company employed on Physical Drill, Gas Drill & Rifle exercises. Lecture by O.C. on Organization & equipment of Field Coys.	
do	2/14 3		Company employed on Physical Drill & Infantry Drill. Lecture on Duties, Strength & Equipment. Small Arms Drill & Fire.	
do	3/14 3	4-0AM	4th Divisional Engr. Orders Beta 1089 received.	
		10-0AM	Company proceeded by Route March via BONNAY to LAHOUSSOYE. Company arrived & billeted at LAHOUSSOYE at 4 p.m.	
		5 pm	4th Divisional A.O. 1430 received.	
do	4/14 3	9-0AM	March continued via FRECHENCOURT, ST GRATIEN, MOLLIENS & VILLERS BOCAGE to TALMAS. Arrived & Company billeted at 4 p.m.	
do	5/14 3	5-30AM	March resumed via BEAUVAL to GEZAINCOURT, arrived at 2-0 p.m. & Company dismounted in shelter camp	

W Wedgwood Major R.E.
OC 406th (Renfrew) Field Cy R.E.

2353 Wt. W2544/1454 700,000 5/15 D. D. & L. A.D.S.S. Forms/C 2118.

Army Form C. 2118.

WAR DIARY
or
INTELLIGENCE SUMMARY.
(Erase heading not required.)

Instructions regarding War Diaries and Intelligence Summaries are contained in F. S. Regs., Part II. and the Staff Manual respectively. Title pages will be prepared in manuscript.

406TH (RENFREW) FIELD COMPANY, R.E.

Place	Date	Hour	Summary of Events and Information	Remarks and references to Appendices
	6/7/19	4-30 AM	Marched resumed route via DOULLERS, BOUQUE MAISON, REBREUVE to HOUVAL arrived at 1-15 pm. 9 Company billetted.	
		9-0 AM	4th Divisional Engr. O.O. N°.30 dated 5/7/19 received.	
	7/7/19	4-30 AM	March resumed route via MAZIERES, PENIN to SAVY arrived at 1-0 pm. Unit under orders of O.C. XVII Corps.	
Hrs at SAVY Rd Map LENS 11	8/7/19		Company employed on various Vehicles, Company Stores, Material on road setting at 7th D.S. Park taken over.	
do	9/7/19		1 Section employed on road setting at Corps Park. Remainder of unit on Spares Unit, Gas Alarm Shell & Rifle exercises. Work on Water supply taken over from 253rd A.T. Coy R.E.	

M J Holyard Lieut
Major RE
O.C. 406th Renfrew Field Coy R.E.

Army Form C. 2118.

WAR DIARY
or
INTELLIGENCE SUMMARY.
(Erase heading not required.)

408TH (RENFREW) FIELD COMPANY, R.E.

Place	Date	Hour	Summary of Events and Information	Remarks and references to Appendices
14pm at SAVY By HEALENS.11	10/3/17		1 Section employed setting rails for 50 metre curve, inside rails cut (60 cm lines). 1 Sect. employed on SAVY water supply. 2 Sections on Physical Drill, Bayonet Drill, & Field Engineering.	
do	11/3/17		1 Section employed assisting up rails & setting curves on 60cm rails. 1 Sect. on SAVY water supply. Track cut & Line til across railway at D.S.C. 2.4. 2 Sects on Physical drill, bayonet drill, bombing wiring & overhauling equipment.	
do	12/3/17		1 Sect. setting & cutting 60cm rails, 50 metre curve completed. 1 Sect on SAVY water supply, 34 Lengths, coupled up & on C line. 2 Sects. repairing overhangs & setting chains in BERLES. No. H.20131 Sgt LOGAN J. accidentally injured, admitted to No 2nd C.C.S. No.51544.	

M Hodgart Lieut
O.i/c 408 (Renfrew) Field Coy R.E.

Army Form C. 2118.

WAR DIARY
or
INTELLIGENCE SUMMARY.
(Erase heading not required.)

Instructions regarding War Diaries and Intelligence Summaries are contained in F. S. Regs., Part II. and the Staff Manual respectively. Title pages will be prepared in manuscript.

408TH (RENFREW) FIELD COMPANY R.E.

Place	Date	Hour	Summary of Events and Information	Remarks and references to Appendices
HQrs at SAVY.	13/8/17		1 Sect. all they can rack for 170 metre track, rack cut for curve. 1 Sect. on SAPP water supply. ARRAS road opened up & pipe led to watering point at D.H.Q.	
Ref HAPLINS 11.			Stores employed on Plymouth spearbill & field make tramway up & taking Electric current & transmission on Sapping & pump change	
-do-	14/8/17		1 Sect. employed on metre track tramway up & about the depôts. 2 Section Sappers supply pipe line across ARRAS Rd completed track exit & track across SAPP-AUBIGNY Rd completed tramway out for smoke paint. Sect. sapping & draining road in BERLES.	
-do-	15/8/17		1 Sect. mounting up along A Loop the tram rack. 2 Sect. C? SAP? water supply 10 length connected up or 12 new pipes laid & reservoir for connecting up main lengths. 1 Sect. cmetry stores & carefully all the on plans ARRAS-ST POL Rd at O.S.1.C.8.2.	

W A Holgate
for Major R.E. 77
O.C. 408 (Renfrew) Field Coy R.E.

WAR DIARY
or
INTELLIGENCE SUMMARY.
(Erase heading not required.)

Army Form C. 2118.

406TH
(GENERAL)
FIELD COMPANY, R.E.

Place	Date	Hour	Summary of Events and Information	Remarks and references to Appendices
Hqrs at — SAVY Bg Maj. LENS 14	16/3/17		1 Sect cutting & setting rails. 2/lt of 3000 metres of straight lengths completed. 2 Sects on Savypark supply. 3 Sect. ran to camp at Du. 2.1 completed with standpipe, cutting screws & sufficiency for supply at water point. Training completed for June & cartridge store.	
—do—	17/3/17		1 Sect. cutting & setting broom rods. 2 Sect on Savy water supply, cutting & running pipes to camp at Maroeuil & Écouvilles. Transit & horse drawn pattern at water point. 3 Sect. repairing roads & clearing stones in BERNETTE.	
—do—	18/3/17		1 Sect. come stopy up beyond 10 am sick. Church Parade for remainder of unit at AUBIGNY. Sports P.O. drawing afternoon.	

M.G. [signature] Major R.E.
O.C. 406 (Wessex) Field Coy R.E.

Army Form C. 2118.

WAR DIARY
or
INTELLIGENCE SUMMARY.
(Erase heading not required.)

Instructions regarding War Diaries and Intelligence Summaries are contained in F. S. Regs., Part II and the Staff Manual respectively. Title pages will be prepared in manuscript.

Place	Date	Hour	Summary of Events and Information	Remarks and references to Appendices
Hqrs at SAVY	19/3/14		1 Det employed setting & cementing up beam seats.	
Ref map 1EH 3 u.			Labor Savy water supply & water pumps on ARRAS Rd.	
			1 Det employed repairing billets in TILLOY.	
— do —	20/3/14		1 Det employed setting & cementing up beam seats.	
			2 Det on SAVY water supply & water pumps on ARRAS Rd.	
			1 Det repairing billets in TILLOY.	
— do —	21/3/14		1 Det employed cutting, setting & cementing up beam seats.	
			2 Rds on SAVY water supply, making framing for water tanks. Mains completed for same. 1 Det repairing billets in TILLOY.	
— do —	22/3/14		2 Det cementing up beam seats. 1 Det on Water supply, also on standpipes & branches completed on Blinf, erecting framing for tanks & stage tank. 1 Det boring rod & sides erecting loading platform at Railway station on ST Pol Rd.	

M Halyard Major
O.C. No 6 Company Field Coy RE

Army Form C. 2118.

WAR DIARY
or
INTELLIGENCE SUMMARY.
(Erase heading not required)

Instructions regarding War Diaries and Intelligence
Summaries are contained in F. S. Regs., Part II.
and the Staff Manual respectively. Title pages
will be prepared in manuscript.

406TH (RENFREW) FIELD COMPANY, R.E.

Place	Date	Hour	Summary of Events and Information	Remarks and references to Appendices
H^qr at SAVY Ref.Map. LENS 11.	23/3/17		Started connecting up loose ends of tube in Water supply, making roadway for water points on ARRAS Rd. Catridge store in St Pol R^d completed repairing fittigs in TUCAT. Latrine completed in SAVY.	
- do -	24/3/17		Started connecting up 60 c.m. rails of tub. in water supply, erecting frames for storage tanks on ARRAS Rd. making roadways at water points. Carbon equipment erected & dumped at HAUTE AVESNES.	
- do -	25/3/17		Lifting up of 60 c.m. rails at AK.PARK, Grouplea. Erecting frames for storage tanks, setting & setting poles for wires at SUBERIE, SAVY, making roadways at Water points on ARRAS Rd. Stores drawn from R.E. PARK & dumped at Divisional dump at HAUTE AVESNES.	
- do -	26/3/17		Lifting & setting 60 c.m. rails at R.E.dump, Connecting up mains water supply at SUBERIE, SAVK. Making framing for additional tanks at water points. Stones taken up to R.E. dump at HAUTE AVESNES.	

M Molyart p. 26/3/17
for O.C. 406th Renfrew Field Coy R.S.

Army Form C. 2118.

WAR DIARY
or
INTELLIGENCE SUMMARY.
(Erase heading not required.)

406TH (RENFREW) FIELD COMPANY, R.E.

Instructions regarding War Diaries and Intelligence Summaries are contained in F. S. Regs., Part II. and the Staff Manual respectively. Title pages will be prepared in manuscript.

Place	Date	Hour	Summary of Events and Information	Remarks and references to Appendices
SAVY	24/3/17		Working parties setting & cutting in on Poles at R.E. Park. Trench line put in for short overhang points. Making roadways at water point on ARRAS R.R. Stone drawn & stacked road to cross NISSEN Hut at ARRAS.	
Ref. Map SHTS 11.	28/3/14		Working parties connecting up along R.R. together to an road at R.E. Park. SAVY water supply. Making frames for internal tanks, above ration littera. wires at SUCERIE. SAVY. Making roadway at water point to ARRAS R^D for NISSEN HUT completed at TILLOY.	
do	29/3/14		Working of actions, putting, cutting & connecting up 6-in rails at R.E. Park. SAVY water supply. Canvas truck covered, new 14" trench lines laid to camp. making roadways at water points on ARRAS R^D.	
		1.45am	No. 144 Field marched out from SAVY to ARRAS. arrived at 9.15 am & billeted.	

M. Morgan Captain R.E. (?)
O.C. 406th (Renfrew) Field Co. R.E.

Army Form C. 2118.

406TH (RENFREW) FIELD COMPANY, R.E.
No. ....

WAR DIARY
or
INTELLIGENCE SUMMARY.
(Erase heading not required.)

Instructions regarding War Diaries and Intelligence Summaries are contained in F. S. Regs., Part II and the Staff Manual respectively. Title pages will be prepared in manuscript.

Place	Date	Hour	Summary of Events and Information	Remarks and references to Appendices
H'qrs at SAVY	30/3/19		Setting up & connecting up to 6" in mains at R.E. PARK. SAVY water supply. Excavation for cement tank completed and forming erected for additional tanks at motor pond on ARRAS Rd. 2" bored hole for additional demand. Store beam & NISSEN HUT started at TULLOY.	
Rd. NABLENS, 11.	31/3/19		Connecting up & strength together mains at R.E. PARK. SAVY water supply. Erecting forming & additional tank on ARRAS Rd. Preventing of line completed & water turned on pipes tested. NISSEN HUT completed at TULLOY.	

W. Arfut Captain
O.C. 406th (Renfrew) Field Coy. R.E.

WAR DIARY
or
INTELLIGENCE SUMMARY.

Army Form C. 2118.

406 (WEM) Field Company, R.E.

Month: Sept 17

Place	Date	Hour	Summary of Events and Information	Remarks and references to Appendices
Hqrs at SAVY. Ref Map LENS II.	1/9/17		Working parties employed cutting, setting & connecting up 60cm rails at Nº 1 R.E. Advanced Park. Main supply at SAVY. Cutting & reversing pipes line completed to tramway at junc of SAVY.	
			Sections at ARRAS. Plans prepared for widening of bridge over SCARPE at ST NICOLAS. River bottom prepared & stones for bridge drawn.	
—do—	2/9/17		Working parties employed connecting up 60cm rail at R.E. Park. Trestles framing for retained trunks at water point ARRAS Rd. Excavating landings for stone walls of bridge at ST NICOLAS stones brought to bridge site at night.	
—do—	3/9/17		Working parties cutting setting & connecting up 60cm rails at R.E. Park. All 1" standpipes removed from savy pipe line & 1½" reinstated. A frame hut in for extension of ST NICOLAS bridge parties milling timber & still finding party for rescued factures.	

M Hogart
Lt/Capt R.E.
O.C. 406 (W.Riding) Field Coy. R.E.

Army Form C. 2118.

406TH
(RENFREW)
FIELD COMPANY, R.E.

No.............
Date.............

WAR DIARY
or
INTELLIGENCE SUMMARY.

(Erase heading not required.)

Instructions regarding War Diaries and Intelligence Summaries are contained in F. S. Regs., Part II. and the Staff Manual respectively. Title pages will be prepared in manuscript.

Place	Date	Hour	Summary of Events and Information	Remarks and references to Appendices
H⁴ at SAVY Ref. MAP LENS 11.	4/7/17		Working parties setting & connecting up 6 cm rails at R.E. Park. Framing & netonal tanks erected for water front ARRAS R⁴. Erecting frames for St NICOLAS bridge. Parties relaying trusses & steel stringers made for trench bridges on BAILLEUL R⁴. girder.	
do.	5/7/17		Working parties connecting up 6 cm rails at R.E. Park. Cutting & receiving pipes for Tank connection at water point. Framing for St NICOLAS Bridge completed & stores drawn for same.	
		1.30pm	1ˢᵗ Line Transport left SAVY for ARRAS with kits & horse lines established at F.20.d.1.6. Ref Map sheet 51.B. N.E. 1/5000.	
		4.15pm	HQrs. No. 243 Bdes marched out from SAVY for ARRAS arrival at 9 p.m. Coy H. Qrs established at C.21.d.9.3. Ref Map ARRAS Sheet 1 & 3-1.L. N.W. 1/5000.	
H⁴ at C.21.d.9.3 Ref Map ARRAS Sheet 1 & 3.1B. N.W. 1/5000	6/7/17		Working parties on St NICOLAS Bridge where erection framing completed. Frames & strutted. Pipe made & frame terrerels laid on St NICOLAS - BAILLEUL R⁴ & trenches taken up for water.	

M. Strachan Lieut
R.H.O.⁴ 1 (Renfrew) Field Coy R.E.

Army Form C. 2118.

WAR DIARY
or
INTELLIGENCE SUMMARY.
(Erase heading not required.)

Instructions regarding War Diaries and Intelligence Summaries are contained in F. S. Regs., Part II. and the Staff Manual respectively. Title pages will be prepared in manuscript.

406TH (RENFREW) FIELD COMPANY, R.E.
No..........
Date..........

Place	Date	Hour	Summary of Events and Information	Remarks and references to Appendices
Hqrs at ARRAS C.21.d.9.2 Sub Depot B.18.M.W.	7/7/14		Working parties on tunnel at G.14, G.21, G.22, & G.19 & S.12. Tunnels framed, lined & completed. Excavation of St Nicolas bridge completed & started with Heavy Loads. Lorries. Nos 420133 Cpl. Miller H. & N.420298 Sapr McLean G. wounded in action.	
do	8/7/14		Working parties on tunnels. Trips for artillery at G.11.C.5.4 & G.11.d.9.6. 2 strengthening advance posts at St Nicolas. Store taken & dumps formed for roadstores & materials. Overhauling Coy equipment. Detail of work issued by O.C. for the repair & maintenance of St Nicolas - Bailleul R.d. in following schedules.	

W. Hague Major R.E. OC 406th (Renfrew) Field Coy R.E.

Army Form C. 2118.

WAR DIARY
or
INTELLIGENCE SUMMARY.
(Erase heading not required.)

Place	Date	Hour	Summary of Events and Information	Remarks and references to Appendices
Hqrs at ARRAS 51A.24.a. SIM.51B NW corner	9/4/17	5.30AM	ZERO HOUR Company standing by in dotors.	
		6.0AM	Company left billets in ARRAS & proceeded to rendezvous at ST NICOLAS.	
		7.0AM	Company left rendezvous & proceeded to ST NICOLAS - BAILLEUL Rd old tramlines. Filled in 4 bridged fascine tracks laid from 9.15 A.M. to 9.12.A.95. for field guns & pack animal tracks repair of road etc etc & where tracks commenced.	

N⁰ 420333 Cpl Smith R. 420079 Sgt Heywood J. (Killed in Action) (Shell)
N⁰ 420073 A/Cpl Hulse W.
  420064 " Dolan F.
  420003 Spr Anderson J.B.
  420019 " Burton F.
  106913 " Wilson A.E.   ⎫
  420336 " Cox J.   ⎪
  420309 " Moore G.   ⎬ Wounded in Action
  420185 " Newton J.   ⎪ (Shell Splinters)
  420010 " McKillop H.   ⎪
  420174 " Patterson W.   ⎭
  420199 " Roy A.
  420813 " White G.

M. Rodgers Capt R.E. 71st
OC No 6 (Highland) Field Cop R.E.

Army Form C. 2118.

WAR DIARY
or
INTELLIGENCE SUMMARY.
(Erase heading not required.)

Instructions regarding War Diaries and Intelligence Summaries are contained in F. S. Regs., Part II. and the Staff Manual respectively. Title pages will be prepared in manuscript.

406TH (RENFREW) FIELD COMPANY R.E.

Place	Date	Hour	Summary of Events and Information	Remarks and references to Appendices
W⁴⁴ at ARRAS C.21.d.9.2. Rd.Maps 1B MM Tren	10/7		Company employed on widening & repair of St NICHOLAS – BAILLEUL R⁴. This Coy opened & dealt with telephone. Horse transport enabled to move through from ST NICOLAS to G.6.A.3.5.	
-do-	11/7		Company employed on repair & maintenance of ST NICHOLAS – BAILLEUL R⁴. Log turning point laid & completed at G.12.a.1.4. for heavy motor transport.	
-do-	12/7		Company employed on the repair & maintenance of ST NICHOLAS – BAILLEUL R⁴. Log turning point laid at G.12.a.3.5. for Motor Ambulances. Widening of road continued. Shipment at G.12.c.10.10.	
-do-	13/7		Company employed on the repair & maintenance of ST NICHOLAS – BAILLEUL R⁴. Road bearers of ST NICHOLAS bridge re-packed & firmly wedged.	Authorized Capt H.H. W? Royal Engineers Field Coy 406

A5834 Wt.W4973/M687 750,000 8/16 D. D. & L. Ltd. Forms/C.2118/13.

Army Form C. 2118.

WAR DIARY
or
INTELLIGENCE SUMMARY.
(Erase heading not required.)

Instructions regarding War Diaries and Intelligence Summaries are contained in F. S. Regs., Part II. and the Staff Manual respectively. Title pages will be prepared in manuscript.

Place	Date	Hour	Summary of Events and Information	Remarks and references to Appendices
H.Q. at ARRAS C.21.d.9.2. Ref Map 51B NW 1/2000	14/7/19		Company employed on repair & maintenance of ST NICOLAS-BAILLEUL RR. Some track lifted to a point at G.C.d.2.2. & grouped spares for a lifter track.	
—do—	15/7/19		Company employed on repair & maintenance of ST NICOLAS-BAILLEUL RR. Shell shop of entrichment & track repaired at G.2.a.2.4. at the point the track metal road was damaged & shortly before the explosion.	
—do—	16/7/19		Company employed on the repair & maintenance of ST NICOLAS RR. Beams cut a log platform laid for unloading locomotives lorries at G.11.C.9.4. & G.11.C.5.1.	
—do—	17/7/19		Company employed on repair & maintenance of ST NICOLAS-BAILLEUL RD Widening of road & metal laid up to point at G.11.d.9.2. made available for double use for traffic.	

H.F. Sargeant. (Capt R.E.)
O.C. 406th Bangalore Field Coys R.E.

Army Form C. 2118.

WAR DIARY
or
INTELLIGENCE SUMMARY.
(Erase heading not required.)

406TH (RENFREW) FIELD COMPANY, R.E.

Instructions regarding War Diaries and Intelligence Summaries are contained in F.S. Regs., Part II. and the Staff Manual respectively. Title pages will be prepared in manuscript.

Place	Date	Hour	Summary of Events and Information	Remarks and references to Appendices
1400 at ARRAS Ref Map 57B M.W. 7500	18/4/19		Work continued on ST NICOLAS - BAILEUL RD. lay tracks tried & widening of road continued. Trench on south side of road filled in.	
– do –	19/4/19		Work continued on ST NICOLAS - BAILEUL RD. widening of road continued up to G.12.a.2.4.4. Log mat completed & fixed up from G.12.b.1.3.6. G.6.c.10.1.	
– do –	20/4/19	3.15 am	Orders received from O.C. XIII Corps R.E. XIII Corps to hand over work on ROUEN to 153rd Siam Coy R.E. work to be completed by 1 p.m. & unit to move under orders of 4 Div. at that hour. Work continued on ST NICOLAS RD. & work handed over to relieving Coy.	
		1 pm	Working parties withdrawn.	
		2.30 pm	Company left ARRAS & marched to MONTENESCOURT under orders of C.R.E. 4 Division	
		6 pm	Arrived at MONTENESCOURT & allotted rest as general reserve.	

W. Podmore Captn R.E.
O.C. 406 (Renfrew) Field Coy R.E.

Army Form C. 2118.

WAR DIARY
or
INTELLIGENCE SUMMARY.
(Erase heading not required.)

Instructions regarding War Diaries and Intelligence Summaries are contained in F.S. Regs., Part II. and the Staff Manual respectively. Title pages will be prepared in manuscript.

408TH (RENFREW) FIELD COMPANY. R.E.
No............... Date...............

Place	Date	Hour	Summary of Events and Information	Remarks and references to Appendices
HQrs at MONTIERES COURT Ref Map LENS. 11.	21/9/19	9.0am 2.30pm	Company inspection. Company left MONTIERES COURT & moved to LATTRE ST QUENTIN under orders of 13.Q.C. 12th Inf. Bde. arrived at 4 pm.	
HQrs at LATTRE ST QUENTIN Ref Map LENS. 11.	22/9/19	10.0am 2-3pm	Company employed on Drill & Rifle Exercises. Company Inspection. Orders received from B.Q.C. 12th Inf. Bde. to move on the 23rd inst. to ENTREE WATHUN area.	
Do —	23/9/19	10-11am 1-30pm	Company left LATTRE ST QUENTIN & marched to BERLEN COURT. Arrived in camp etc.	
HQrs at BERLEN COURT Ref Map LENS. 11.	24/9/19	9-0am	Letter to Officers N.C.O. by S.R.E.H. there on consolidation & points gained in the recent advance. Company found a limited system of trench sect & deep dug outs. These to be used for instructional purposes by pass.	

W. Nodgent Capt RE
O.C. 408 (Renfrew) Field Company R.E.

Army Form C. 2118.

WAR DIARY
or
INTELLIGENCE SUMMARY.
(Erase heading not required.)

Instructions regarding War Diaries and Intelligence Summaries are contained in F. S. Regs. Part II. and the Staff Manual respectively. Title pages will be prepared in manuscript.

405TH (DEERFIELD) FIELD COMPANY, R.E.
No.......... Title..........

Place	Date	Hour	Summary of Events and Information	Remarks and references to Appendices
BERLEN COURT	25/4/19		Company employed on Drill & rifle exercises lecture on strong points. * Rapid survey of ground.	
Pt Mn LENS. II	26/4/19		Company drill & rifle exercises. Company lecture. Overhauling company equipment & loading vehicles.	
- do -	27/4/19		Company drill overhaul of equipment completed. Parties of Officers & N.C.O. of 1st & 2nd Inf. Bde. lectured to & shewn over the new trench system & strong points. There were afterwards field in... upon shoot warned to be in readiness to move on the 28th inst. with the 1st Inf. Bde. Group.	

M.Holyot, Major R.E.
O.C. 405th (Deerfield) Field Coy R.E.

Army Form C. 2118.

WAR DIARY
or
INTELLIGENCE SUMMARY.
(Erase heading not required.)

Instructions regarding War Diaries and Intelligence Summaries are contained in F. S. Regs., Part II. and the Staff Manual respectively. Title pages will be prepared in manuscript.

Place	Date	Hour	Summary of Events and Information	Remarks and references to Appendices
Hames au Berlencourt Ref Map LENS.11.	28/7/14	9-11AM	Company left BERLENCOURT & marched to HAUTE AVESNES arriving at 3 p.m.	
		10.0pm	Orders received to march with 13th B.W. Group to a shelter camp at ST NICOLAS on the 29th inst.	
Hames at HAUTE AVESNES Ref Map LENS.11.	29th	4.15 pm	Company left HAUTE AVESNES & marched to ST NICOLAS arriving at 9.19.a.1.h.	
		11 AM	Shelter erected & HQrs established at 9.19.a.1.h.	
		4.0pm	Orders received for unit to relieve the 209 Field Coy R.E. on the 30th inst.	
Hqrs at G.19.a.1.6 1/40 Map FRANCE Sheet 51B NW 1/20000	30/7/14	9 AM	Dismounted parties left ST NICOLAS & marched to Railway embankment & relieved the 209 Field Coy R.E.	
		10-10.30 AM	Horse comp. estd. & HQrs established at 9.13.a.9.9.	
			Company employed erecting shelters for company O.C. & Lieut. officers reconnoitred ground & work to be taken in hand with C.R.E. 4th Division.	
			Night working parties sent out for work on strong point - trenches.	

M. Morgan (Capt R.E) (T.)
O.C. 406th (Renfrew) Field Coy R.E.

WAR DIARY or INTELLIGENCE SUMMARY

Army Form C. 2118.

406TH (RENFREW) FIELD COMPANY. R.E.
Date: May 1917

Place	Date	Hour	Summary of Events and Information	Remarks and references to Appendices
Huts at H13.a.9.9. West FRANCE 51B NW 1/10000	1/5/17		1 Section employed on clearing and repairing roads in FAMPOUX. 1 Section wiring in front of QUARRY STRONG POINT at I13.a.2.1. 1 section wiring EFFIE at H10.c.3.1. 1 Section excavating sites for dugout shelters for C.R.A. and C.R.E. on West side Railway Embankment at H13.d. 3 Reinforcements joined. Strength of unit at this date. Officers 7 = Other Ranks 194.	Wounded Batt RE 7/4 B.Hobbs (Received) 24.4.04
do.	2/5/17		Works continued on dugout shelters on Railway Embankment (H13.d) and clearing debris repairing streets in FAMPOUX. and completed to think at H19.a.5.8. No. 420332 Sapper Lean L. wounded by bullet.	
do.	3/5/17		Sections standing by during day awaiting orders. ZERO HOUR 3.45 am at 8.15 PM Sections moved forward to Quarry at I.13.a.2.1. in readiness to construct a ground unstable on CHEMICAL WORKS. This attack did not materialise and at 2 am on morning of 4/5 the Company moved back to billets. No. 420405 Sapper Maclean R. wounded. (Remained at duty) No. 420177 Sapper Nuttall R. wounded (shell) and evacuated.	

WAR DIARY
or
INTELLIGENCE SUMMARY

Army Form C. 2118.

406TH (RENFREW) FIELD COMPANY, R.E.
No. Date May 1917

Place	Date	Hour	Summary of Events and Information	Remarks and references to Appendices
Harbro at H.12.a.9.9. Sheet 51 N.W. FRANCE 1/20000	11/5/17		Work continued in Dugout shelters at Railway Embankment (H 13 a)/. 1 Section employed on construction of double raised concealed machine gun emplacement at H 18 a. 2.2. 1/3. Junction of CAWDOR, CAM, and CADIZ trenches (H 12 b 55.70) deepened and the approximate length for a strong point. Excavation commenced for erection of two shelters for Battalion Headqrs at H 18 b. 9.5.	
–Do–	5/17		Work continued on dugout shelters at Railway Embankment (H 13 d)/. Dugout for KRA completed. Work continued at Machine Gun Emplacement H 18 d. 22. 13. and small trench to emplacement completed. Excavation cleared & prepared for erection of frames for machine gun emplacement at 113 c 25. Work continues in relief at Battalion Headquarters at H 18 b. 9.5. One section improving STRONG POINT at junction of CAWDOR CAM and CADIZ trenches (H 12 b 55.70).	

W. Morgan Capt RE
O.C. 406th (Renfrew) Field Co. R.E.

Army Form C. 2118.

406TH
(RENFREW)
FIELD COMPANY, R.E.
Date: May/1917

WAR DIARY
or
INTELLIGENCE SUMMARY.
(Erase heading not required.)

Instructions regarding War Diaries and Intelligence Summaries are contained in F. S. Regs., Part II. and the Staff Manual respectively. Title pages will be prepared in manuscript.

Place	Date	Hour	Summary of Events and Information	Remarks and references to Appendices
Hyplus at H13a.9.9. Sheet FRANCE. 51B. N.W. 1/20000	16/5/17		Work continued on Dugout shelter at Railway Embankment (H13a) and on framed shelter coupled with elevation of revetment and headcover. Working party pumping water at Battalion Headquarters at I.13.a.2.1. Assembly trench traced from I.13.a.4.5 to I.13.a.3.6, in prolongation of CEYLON TRENCH.	
—Do—	17/5/17		Work continued on Dugout shelters at Railway Embankment (H13a) and also at Machine gun emplacement I.13.c.13.5 Pumping water at Battalion Headquarters (I.13.a.2.1) continued and measurements taken for reflooring same. 240 yards of new Assembly trench North of CANI TRENCH traced and infantry party started digging same. Working party clearing mined gallery and erecting frames at H.18.b.6.9. Excavation started for Elephant shelter in QUARRY at H.18a.2½.4.	No. 106 [illegible] (Ruyney) reclaims R.E. No. 106 [illegible] leave R.E.[?]

Army Form C. 2118.

WAR DIARY
or
INTELLIGENCE SUMMARY.
(Erase heading not required.)

406TH (RENFREW) FIELD COMPANY, R.E.
Date May 1917

Place	Date	Hour	Summary of Events and Information	Remarks and references to Appendices
Hugots at H.13.a.9.9. Sheet FRANCE 51BNW 1/10000.	8/5/17		Work continued on Dugouts at Railway Embankment (H13A) and one shelter completed. Excavation continued for Battalion Headquarters dugouts in QUARRY, at H.18 a.22 d. Two chambers sealed. Hewers inside in mined dugout at H.18 b.6.9. Work continued on machine gun emplacements at I.13.c.15.5.	
-do-	9/5/17		Work continued on Dugouts at Railway Embankment (H13A) and 2 shelters completed, for both. Framing for 3 in hut frames for Gnr Hut, prepared & erected for L.R.A. Work continued on machine gun emplacement at I.13.a.2.5. and party relaying floor of dugout in quarry at I.13.a.21. Stone taken to site. Work continued in mined dugout at H.18.b.6.9. and also at Battalion H'drs dugout at Battalion HQrs dugout many at H. 18 a 25. 4.	

Hodgart
O.C. 406th (Renfrew) Field Co RE.

WAR DIARY
INTELLIGENCE SUMMARY

Place	Date	Hour	Summary of Events and Information	Remarks and references to Appendices
Hqrs at H13d.9.9. Sheet FRANCE 51.B.N.W. 1/10000	10/5/17		At 7 am a direct hit was obtained on entrance to dugout at H 18 b.6.9. demolishing 5 frames of gallery. Work was stopped pending recce work but no casualties resulted. Work continued on dugouts for R.E.A at Railway Embankment (H13.d) and 2 completed. Communication trench from I13.a.8.5 to I13.b.0.7 cleared. New Assembly trench at I.y.c.3.5 dug through and cleaned and taken over by infantry before working party left. Two sections working by day. No 3 section (under Lieut Enor H. Brown) left Company Headquarters at 9 pm and moved forward to rendezvous at 11st. Infantry Bde Hqtrs in Quarry at I13.a.2.1 to take part in attack. No 186850 Sapper Wilken a splinter wound in leg and evacuated.	

M Halgarf Capt RE.
O.C. 406th (Renfrew) Field Co RE

WAR DIARY or INTELLIGENCE SUMMARY

Army Form C. 2118.

406TH (RENFREW) FIELD COMPANY, R.E.

Place	Date	Hour	Summary of Events and Information	Remarks and references to Appendices
Thiepval at H13a.9.9. sheet FRANCE 57 NW 1/20000	1/5/17		Work continued on dugouts at Railway Embankment H13A and work on machine gun emplacement at I.13.c.1.5. completed.	Wilson & Scott (Rollins) both 6.R. & not t(Rollins) 6.R
		ZERO HOUR 7.30 PM	No 3 Section moved forward in detached parties from magazines I.13.a.2.1. with parties of 11th Machine Gun Company to construct hasty machine emplacements. Emplacements were dug at I.13.b.7½.1½, I.13.a.6.4, I.13.a.4½.3½, I.19.b.3.9½, I.19.a.9.9. and guns got in position, ready for action at 9PM. The following Cavaliers wanted in one of the parties. No. 470177. Corpl Kyle W (killed) No 470238 Sapper Thomson R. (killed) and No 470015 Sapper Blair W (wounded). The remaining two Sapper Ho the R.E. party went forward and completed the whole task of the party and showed great devotion to duty, for which they were recommended for the Military Medal, in recognition of their good work. The other Cavaliers of the right recd No. 470002 Sgt Aincross P.S. and No. H50508 Sapper Walker J, both wounded by shell splinter	

WAR DIARY
or
INTELLIGENCE SUMMARY.
(Erase heading not required.)

Army Form C. 2118.

[Stamp: 408TH (RENFREW) FIELD COMPANY, R.E. No.... Date... May 1917]

Instructions regarding War Diaries and Intelligence Summaries are contained in F. S. Regs., Part II. and the Staff Manual respectively. Title pages will be prepared in manuscript.

Place	Date	Hour	Summary of Events and Information	Remarks and references to Appendices
HQrs at H.13.a.9 Sheet 51BNW France 1/20,000 51BNW	12/5/17		Working parties on Divisional accommodation at Railway Embankment. H.13.a.	
		4.30 P.M.	Headquarters Nos 1 and 3 sections left Railway Embankment H.13.a. and moved to shelter camp at ST NICHOLAS G.M.A. Company HQrs established there from 9.30 PM.	
		8 PM	Nos 1 & 4 sections moved forward to rendezvous at 11.45 P.M. but HQrs for consolidating in the line, but owing to the attack on the left not maturing that second returned to shelter camp at ST NICHOLAS G.M.A. arriving there 11 am 13/5/17. 4th Divisional RE operation order No 36 dated 14/5/17 received 11 PM notifying move to back area at TILLOY LES HERMAVILLE.	
HQrs at G.M.A. Sheet 51BNW 1/20,000 and France	13/5/17	1 AM	Divisional personnel marched to ROND PONT ARRAS and entrained there for TILLOY-LES-HERMAVILLE. Transport moved by road. Move completed 2.30 PM and completion reported to Divl Headquarters	
HENS 11. 1/100,000				

M.Adgers Capt R.E.
O.C. 408th(Renfrew)Field Co RE

WAR DIARY
or
INTELLIGENCE SUMMARY.
(Erase heading not required.)

Army Form C. 2118.

406TH (RENFREW) FIELD COMPANY R.E.
May 1917

Place	Date	Hour	Summary of Events and Information	Remarks and references to Appendices
HADON-LES-HERMAVILLE				
Shaw France 1/100,000				
— Do —	WENS 1 1/5/17		Company Parade and overhauling equipment. Nineteen reinforcements joined	
— Do —	15/5/17		Company Drill and Section Drill. Overhauling equipment	
— Do —	16/5/17		Company paraded and marched to DOFFINE FARM for inspection with 15th Brigade by Gen. Sir Edmund Allenby K.C.B. Commanding Third Army. Eight reinforcements joined	
— Do —	17/5/17		Working parties repairing wells and baths in MAIZIERES, PENIN and MONCHEAUX. Repairs carried out to wells and walls in HERMAVILLE	
— Do —	18/5/17		Working parties repairing wells in PENIN and MONCHEAUX. Repairing baths at MAZIERES and PENIN. Repairing walls and baths in HERMAVILLE	

Major OC 406th (Renfrew) Field Co. R.E.
O.C. 406th (Renfrew) Field Co. R.E.

WAR DIARY
or
INTELLIGENCE SUMMARY.

(Erase heading not required.)

Army Form C. 2118.

408TH (RENFREW) FIELD COMPANY, R.E.
May 1917

Places	Date	Hour	Summary of Events and Information	Remarks and references to Appendices
TILLOY-LES-HERMAVILLE Sheet 51aNW 1/100000	19/5/17		Working parties repairing wells in PENIN and MONCHEAUX. Repairing baths at MAZIERES and PENIN. Repairing wall and baths in HERMAVILLE.	
	20/5/17		Working parties on gates, jumps and horse troughs for Divisional Horse Show of G.H.Q. H.Q. Division in afternoon. Inspection of Company by G.H.Q. H.Q. Division in afternoon.	
Do.	21/5/17		Working parties on wells & baths at PENIN. Erecting horse troughs in MAGNICOURT. Repairing wall and wells in HERMAVILLE.	
Do.	22/5/17		Working parties on wells, baths at MAGNIERES and on wall and baths in HERMAVILLE. Horse troughs and gates for Divisional Show rehearsal.	
Do.	23/5/17		Working party erecting new horse standings in HERMAVILLE and sinking billets at TINCOY. One reinforcement joined.	

M Holgate Capt RE
O.C. 408th (Renfrew) Field Co RE

Army Form C. 2118.

WAR DIARY
or
INTELLIGENCE SUMMARY.
(Erase heading not required.)

Instructions regarding War Diaries and Intelligence Summaries are contained in F. S. Regs., Part II. and the Staff Manual respectively. Title pages will be prepared in manuscript.

405TH (GRENFREWD) FIELD COMPANY, R.E.
Date ... May 1917 ...

Place	Date	Hour	Summary of Events and Information	Remarks and references to Appendices
TILLOY –	24/4		Working parties employed on linking billets at TILLOY, repairing walls and wells at HERMAVILLE, wells at MONCHEAUX & PENIN	
HERMAVILLE				
Shell Sheene				
HENS.1 1/100 000	25/4		Working party in linking billets in TILLOY and making water troughs, gates and jumps for Horse Shows	
27D. –		5.30am	No 3 section transport moved to PENIN for work in 15th Bde Group.	
		2pm	No 1 section transport moved to MONCHEAUX for work in 10th Bde group.	
		3pm	No 4 section transport moved to MAGNICOURT for work in 11th Bde group.	
			Eight reinforcements joined	

No W5041 Sapper Campbell P & No W70398 Sapper Miller J, passed at DOFFIN FARM for permission to wear their Medal Ribbons by Corps Commander XVII th Corps.

M Stodart Lieut RE
O/c No 1 (Renfrew) Field Co RE

Army Form C. 2118.

WAR DIARY
or
INTELLIGENCE SUMMARY.
(Erase heading not required.)

Instructions regarding War Diaries and Intelligence Summaries are contained in F.S. Regs., Part II. and the Staff Manual respectively. Title pages will be prepared in manuscript.

Place	Date	Hour	Summary of Events and Information	Remarks and references to Appendices
MAGTO TILLOY LES- HERMAVILLE Sheet 51A/44	26/7		Working Parties repairing wells at MONCHEAUX, & HOUVIN Erecting staging for fallers at MONT EN-TERNOIS and altering position of water troughs at MAGNICOURT. Painting notice boards for Divisional Horse Shows	
HENS II 110000			Working Parties repairing wells at MONCHEAUX, HOUVIN and MAGNICOURT. Erecting sawing dam and forming place on River CANCHE at S.E end of MAGNICOURT and erecting single strand wire fence round source of water supply SE ext of village. Erecting seating in MONT-EN-TERNOIS for fellies.	
-DO-	27/7			
-DO-	28/7		Working parties repairing wells in PENIN and MONCHEAUX and HOUVIN Wood cut and made ready for enclosures for Divisional Horse show ground. Forming bathing place in River CANCHE south west of MAGNICOURT/. Constructing meat tables	

M.Morgan Capt RE
O.b. 403rd (Ruthen) Field Co. RE

WAR DIARY
or
INTELLIGENCE SUMMARY.
(Erase heading not required.)

Army Form C. 2118.

[Stamp: 406TH (RENFREW) FIELD COMPANY, R.E. — 7 May 1917]

Place	Date	Hour	Summary of Events and Information	Remarks and references to Appendices
MAGNICOURT	29/4/17		Working party repairing wells and erecting horse trough at BUNEVILLE. Repairing well at HOUVIN and bunks at MONCHEAUX.	
LES-HERMIN[?]			at MAIZIERES	
Sheet HENS II 50/4 1/100,000	30/4		Erecting latrines and jump stakes on Divisional Sports ground. Work continued such bathing pool in river CANCHE. Repairing latrines at GOUY-EN-TERNOIS and erecting two latrines at MAGNICOURT. Repairing wells at MONCHEAUX and baths at HOUVIN.	
-do-	31/5/17		Headquarters No. 2 Section and No. 4 Section moved to MONCHEAUX. Moved supplies 2.30pm. Erecting latrines, jumps, and cables on Divisional Sports ground. Strength Serve at this date = Officers 4 : Other ranks 230. O.C. 406th (Renfrew) Field Co. R.E.	M Holgart Capt. R.E.

Army Form C. 2118.

WAR DIARY
or
INTELLIGENCE SUMMARY.
(Erase heading not required.)

Instructions regarding War Diaries and Intelligence Summaries are contained in F.S. Regs, Part II. and the Staff Manual respectively. Title pages will be prepared in manuscript.

Place	Date	Hour	Summary of Events and Information	Remarks and references to Appendices
Roy Hoyds MONCHEAUX Trench Map. Sheet. LENS II. 1/100,000	1/6/17		Company in back area. Nos 1, 2 and 4 sections billeted at MONCHEAUX and No 3. section in detachment at PENIN. Remounts Ranks paraded and watched Co Divisional Horse show.	
-do-	2/6/17		Company employed on improving accommodation in back area. Making paths, repairing wells at HOUVIN MAIZIERES and GOUY-EN-TERNOIS. Erecting bunks in billets at MONCHEAUX and bath house at PENIN.	
-do-	3/6/17		Repairing paths, repairing wells at HOUVIN, MAIZIERES and GOUY-EN-TERNOIS. Erecting bunks in billets at HOUVIN and MONCHEAUX and erecting bath house at PENIN. Latrines erected at MONCHEAUX and HOUVIN.	

Samuel [?] Capt
A. No. 6th (Rupert's) Field Coy R.E.

WAR DIARY
or
INTELLIGENCE SUMMARY.
(Erase heading not required.)

Army Form C. 2118.

403RD (RENFREW) FIELD COMPANY, R.E.

Place	Date	Hour	Summary of Events and Information	Remarks and references to Appendices
Coy Hqrs at MONCHEAUX Map Ref. SHEET LENS II 1/100,000	4/6/17		Working parties repairing wells at HOUVIN MAIZIERES and GOUY-EN-TERNOIS; erecting bunking in billets at HOUVIN and MONCHEAUX. Latrines erected at MONCHEAUX and HOUVIN. Erecting trestles and repairing wall at PENIN.	
—do—	5/6/17		Working parties repairing wells at HOUVIN, MAIZIERES, and GOUY-EN-TERNOIS. Repairing bunking in billets and erecting horse troughs and latrines at MONCHEAUX. Erecting trestles and repairing wall at PENIN. Cutting wood for hedges.	
—do—	6/6/17		Working parties cleaning wells at HOUVIN MAIZIERES and GOUY-EN-TERNOIS. Cutting wood for targets and repairing bunking accommodation. Company instructed on rapid wiring strive entanglements and lecture given on map reading.	

JMWr Capt.
Ab Hobbs (Renfrew) Field Coy R.E.

WAR DIARY
or
INTELLIGENCE SUMMARY.
(Erase heading not required.)

Army Form C. 2118.

406TH (RENFREW) FIELD COMPANY.

Instructions regarding War Diaries and Intelligence Summaries are contained in F.S. Regs., Part II. and the Staff Manual respectively. Title pages will be prepared in manuscript.

Place	Date	Hour	Summary of Events and Information	Remarks and references to Appendices
Eng Hdqrs Our NONCHEAUX Ref map Sheet LENS 11. 1/100,000	7/6/17		Working parties improving billet accomodation, repairing wells &c at HOUVIN, MONCHEAUX, GOUY-EN-TERNOIS and PENIN. Infantry instructed in rapid wiring and laying out trenches and attacking tanks. One section H Company on square drill, cleaning equipment and repairing cycles.	
Do—	8/6/17		Working parties improving billet accomodation, repairing wells &c at HOUVIN, MONCHEAUX, GOUY-EN-TERNOIS and PENIN. Infantry instructed in rapid wiring and laying out trenches and attacking tanks, etc.— One section H Company, in square drill and musketry wiring and map reading.	

J.W. West Capt.
Eustace R.E.A.
O.b. 406th Renfrew Field Coy R.E.

Army Form C. 2118.

WAR DIARY
or
INTELLIGENCE SUMMARY.
(Erase heading not required.)

Instructions regarding War Diaries and Intelligence Summaries are contained in F.S. Regs., Part II. and the Staff Manual respectively. Title pages will be prepared in manuscript.

[Stamp: 406TH (RENFREW) FIELD COMPANY, R.E. No. ___ DATE 9 Jun 1917]

Place	Date	Hour	Summary of Events and Information	Remarks and references to Appendices
Coy Area at MONCHEAUX Sheet LENS II 1/100000	9/6/17		Working parties improving accomodation in billets and repairing wells etc at HOUVIN, MONCHEAUX, GOUY-EN-TERNOIS and PÉNIN. Infantry instructors in rapid wiring, laying out trenches and consolidating. One section of company instructed in wiring and lecture given on map reading.	
—do—	10/6/17		13th Inf Bde Operation Order No 45 dated 9th June 1917 received 8.30am 10/6/17, notifying move of units to ARRAS/. Dismounted ranks entrained at MONCHEAUX 9.30am and proceeded to ARRAS. Transport moved off separately. Move completed 6pm. Company Headquarters established at G.22.b.2.9. (Reference ARRAS, Sheet 51B NW 1/10000). 4th Divl Engineer Operation Order No 39 dated 10/6/17 received 11 pm, notifying move of units to BLANGY on 11th June 1917.	

JWDeu Gator
Major RE
O.C. 406th (Renfrew) Field Coy RE

Army Form C. 2118.

WAR DIARY
or
INTELLIGENCE SUMMARY.
(Erase heading not required.)

Instructions regarding War Diaries and Intelligence Summaries are contained in F.S. Regs., Part II. and the Staff Manual respectively. Title pages will be prepared in manuscript.

406TH (RENFREW) FIELD COMPANY, R.E.

Place	Date	Hour	Summary of Events and Information	Remarks and references to Appendices
Coy H.Qtrs at ARRAS. G.22.b.7.5. Refixer ARRAS Sheet 51B N.W. 1/10000.	11/6/17		Company moved to BLANGY and Headquarters established at G.14.a.8.6. (Ref ARRAS Sheet 51B.N.W. 1/10000). Transport moved to G.16.a.4.4. Move completed 9 p.m. 11/6/17. Working parties on dugout "A" between CAMBRIAN and CROOK on CINEMA TRENCH. (Ref PLOUVAIN SHEET 1/10000 = I.13.b.6.4.) and Dugout "B" between CROW and CONT on CINEMA TRENCH (I.13.b.5.5. PLOUVAIN SHEET 1/10000).	
Coy H.Qtrs at BLANGY. G.14.a.8.6. (Ref ARRAS Sheet 51B.N.W. 1/10000)	12/6/17		Dismounted tunnel moved to forward area at RAILWAY EMBANKMENT. H.13.d.9.0. and Headquarters established there. Move completed at 3 P.M. 12/6/17. Working parties on dugout A at I.13.b.6.4. and dugout "B" I.13.b.5.5. and dugout "C" in CORONA SUPPORT at I.14.b.5.8½.	
Coy H.Qtrs at RAILWAY EMBANKMENT H.13.d.9.0 (ARRAS Sheet 51B.N.W. 1/10000.	13/6/17		Work continued on Dugouts A, at I.13.b.6.4., "B" at I.13.b.5.5. and "C" at I.14.b.5.8½. 51> yards back row, (single tier four stands), erected at H.14.b. Working party improving company billets at Railway embankment.	

86 HOG't (Renfrew) Field Coy R.E.

WAR DIARY or INTELLIGENCE SUMMARY

Army Form C. 2118.

406TH (RENFREW) FIELD COMPANY, R.E.

Place	Date	Hour	Summary of Events and Information	Remarks and references to Appendices
On Hgts of Railway Embankment H13.b.9.0. Shut FRANCE 51B NW 1/10,000	14/6/17		Continuation of work on dugouts "A" (I.13.b.6.4.) "B" (I.13.b.5.5.) and "C" (I.14.b.3.8½). 180 yards of single apron wire erected from H.14.b.6.3. and completed to H.14.b.3.8. Trench traced and taped between CUPID and COCOA trenches through Railway. Working parties improving accommodation on Railway Embankment (H.13.b. and d).	
— Do —	15/6/17		Continuation of work on dugouts "A" (I.13.b.6.4.) "B" (I.13.b.5.5.) and "C" I.14.b.3.8½. Continuation of wiring on intermediate line, 200 yards single apron wire, completed from H.14.b.3.8. to H.14.b.4.5. Working parties excavating and erecting shelter huts at Railway Embankment (H.13.b. and d).	

J.M.Will Capt.
O.C. 406th (Renfrew) Field Cy. R.E.
Major R.E.

WAR DIARY or INTELLIGENCE SUMMARY
Army Form C. 2118.

408TH (RENFREW) FIELD COMPANY, R.E.
April 1917

Places	Date	Hour	Summary of Events and Information	Remarks and references to Appendices
Coy Hdqrs at Railway Embankment H13 b.9.0. Sheet FRANCE 51 B.N.W. 1/10,000	16/4/17		Continuation of work on dugouts "A" (I 13 b 6.4) and "C" (I 14 b.2.84). Continuation of wiring on intermediate line 230 yards of double apron fence entanglement started at H.14 b.4.5 and completed to H.14 b.4.1, and 150 yards continuation of same taped out. Working party digging trench between COCOA and CUPID. Working parties excavating and erecting shelter huts at Railway Embankment (H 13 b and d) — 30 yards wire entanglement erected in front CORONA TRENCH.	
—Do—	17/4/17		Continuation of work on Dugouts A (I 13 b.6.4) "B" (I 13 b.5.5) and "C" (I 14 b. 2. 84). Dugouts "A" and "B" completed. Continuation of wiring intermediate line — 230 yards of double apron fence entanglement half completed from H.14 b.4.1 to H14 d.1.9. Site for machine gun Dugout in COLOMBO TRENCH (I 14 c. 15.30.) marked out and stores taken to site. Working parties erecting shelter huts at Railway Embankment. (H 13 b and d)	

J.M.May Capt
major
O.C. 408th (Renfrew) Field Coy RE

WAR DIARY
or
INTELLIGENCE SUMMARY.
(Erase heading not required.)

Army Form C. 2118.

No. _June 1917_

405TH (RENFREW) FIELD COMPANY. R.E.

Place	Date	Hour	Summary of Events and Information	Remarks and references to Appendices
Coy HQrs at Railway Embankment A13 b. 9.0. Sheet FRANCE 51.B.N.W. 1/20,000	18/6/17		Continuation of work on Dugout "C" (I 14 b ½ 8½) in COLOMBO TRENCH (I 14 c 15.30). Continuation of wiring intermediate line. 230 yards of double apron fence entanglement (previous nights work) completed from H14 a 1.9. to H14 a ½ 9½. Total distance of double apron fence on Intermediate line, completed from H14 b ½ 8½, to H14 a 2. 9½. 30 yards of pickets to wiring line in front of CUPID TRENCH. Working parties excavating and erecting shelters at Railway Embankment (H 13 b and d).	
	19/6/17		Continuation of work on Dugout "C" (I 14 b ½ 8½) and Machine Gun dugout in COLOMBO TRENCH (I 14 c 15.30). Dugout "C" received a direct hit, which caused a fall in the roof. Working parties excavating and erecting shelter huts at Railway Embankment (H 13. b and d)	

J.W. Weir Capt
H.Ω.O.C. 405th (Renfrew) Field Coy R.E.

WAR DIARY
or
INTELLIGENCE SUMMARY
(Erase heading not required.)

406TH
RENFREW
FIELD COMPANY, R.E.
No. 2 June 1917

Place	Date	Hour	Summary of Events and Information	Remarks and references to Appendices
by Haro ad Railway Embankment H 13 b. 9.0. Sheet FRANCE 51B. N.W. 1/20, 0-0-0	30/4/17		Continuation of work on dugout "C" in CORONA (I 14 b ½, 8½) and machine gun dugout in COLOMBO (I 14 c 15.30). Materials for interior repairs to Battalion HQrs dugout in CRETE, carried up to site. Single span 11 feet wide made through Railway Bridge at H 18 d 2½, 1½. Gap in wire entanglement from CEMETRY H.14 d. 0.8. to point where double apron wire started H.14 d. ½, 9½ completed for a distance of 60 yards. 40 yards wire completed in front of CUPID TRENCH. 5 machine gun emplacements sited and traced ready for digging at H.14 b. 0.9. H.14 b. 1.8½, H.14 b. 3½. 5. H.14 b. 3.7. and H.14 d. 0.9. Working parties excavating and erecting shelters at Railway Embankment (H 13 b and d)	

Signed
O.C. 406 (Renfrew) Field Co. R.E.

Capt
406 Coy R.E.

WAR DIARY
or
INTELLIGENCE SUMMARY.
(Erase heading not required.)

Army Form C. 2118.

Place	Date	Hour	Summary of Events and Information	Remarks and references to Appendices
By HQrs at Railway Embankment H.13.b.9.0. SHEET FRANCE 51 B NW 1/20000	21/4/17		Continuation of work in Dugout "C" in CORONA (I 14 c 6 & 8) and machine gun dugout in COLOMBO (I 14 c 15.30.) Repairing Battalion HQrs dugout in CRETE and entrance to concrete dugout in CORONA SUPPORT. 30 yards apron wire were erected in front of "CORONA" and 10 yards in front of "CUPID". Excavation for three machine gun emplacements started at _____	
			Working parties excavating and erecting shelter huts at Railway Embankment (H 13 b and d)	
— do —	22/4/17		Continuation of work in Dugout "C" in CORONA (I 14 c 6, & 8.) and machine gun dugout in COLOMBO (I 14 c 15 30) Repairs to Battalion HQrs dugout in CRETE completed. Working parties excavating and erecting shelter huts at Railway Embankment (H 13 b and d). Notification received that the award of the Military Cross to Lieut. G. Roy H. Bethune, _____	

Lewis Capt.
for Major R.E.A.
No 406th (Renfrew) Field Coy R.E.

WAR DIARY
INTELLIGENCE SUMMARY

Army Form C. 2118.

406TH (RENFREW) FIELD COMPANY, R.E.
June 1917

Place	Date	Hour	Summary of Events and Information	Remarks and references to Appendices
Coy Hdqrs at Railway Embankment H13 b 9.0 Shere FRANCE 51 B.N.W. 1/20,000	23/6/17		Continuation of work on dugout "C" in CORONA (I 14 b 3 8½) and machine gun dugout in COLOMBO (I 14 c 15.30) Erecting machine gun emplacements at H14 b 3½ 5, H14 b 3.2 and H14 d 0.9. No work done on emplacements at H14 b 0.9 and H14 b 1 8½. Owing to heavy shelling / Working party camouflaging road from H16 d 6.3½ to H16 d 8.3½. Stores for wiring in front of CUPID carried to site but no wiring done owing to heavy shelling. Work continued on improving accommodation at Railway Embankment (H13 b and d)	
	24/6/17		Continuation of work on dugout "C" in CORONA (I4 b 3 8½) machine gun dugout in COLOMBO (I 14 c 15.30) and on machine gun emplacements at H14 b 3½ 5, H14 b 3.2 and H14 b 1 8½. Stores for wiring in front of CUPID and CORONA carried to site but no wiring done owing to shelling. Work continued on improving accommodation at Railway Embankment (H13 b and d)	

H.W.Weir Capt
comdg 406th (Renfrew) Field Coy RE
O.C. 406th (Renfrew) Field Coy RE

WAR DIARY
or
INTELLIGENCE SUMMARY
(Erase heading not required.)

Army Form C. 2118.

406TH (RENFREW) FIELD COMPANY, R.E.

Place	Date	Hour	Summary of Events and Information	Remarks and references to Appendices
Coy HQrs at Railway Embankment A13 b, 9.0. Sheet FRANCE 61BNW 1/20,000	25/9		Work continued on machine gun emplacements at H 14 b, 3, 5 (completed), H14 b, 3, 3, and H14 d, 0, 9 (completed); and work on dugout "C" in CORONA, I 14 b c, 15. 30, and machine gun dugout in COLOMBO, I 14, c. 15. 30. Work continued on improving accommodation at Railway Embankment (H 13 b and d).	
	26/9		Work on machine gun emplacements "August "C" in CORONA I 14 b, 3, and machine gun dugout in COLOMBO (I 14 c 15.30) handed over to 90th Field Coy R.E. 19th Division from 12 noon. Wire and pickets for wiring SCABBARD TRENCH taken up line and dumped at H 30 b 5.4. Work continued on improving accommodation at Railway Embankment (H 13 b and d) and work for Canada shelters ceased. Captain 2 H Weir (576th (Durham) Field Coy RE) took over command of Company from 6pm. 26th during the absence of Major M Hodgart on leave.	

Signed (Rufus) Field Coy RE
O.C. 406th (Renfrew) Field Coy RE

WAR DIARY
or
INTELLIGENCE SUMMARY.
(Erase heading not required.)

Army Form C. 2118.

Instructions regarding War Diaries and Intelligence Summaries are contained in F. S. Regs., Part II. and the Staff Manual respectively. Title pages will be prepared in manuscript.

406TH (RENFREW) FIELD COMPANY.
No. _____ June 1917

Place	Date	Hour	Summary of Events and Information	Remarks and references to Appendices
Ref Map Sheet FRANCE 51BNW. 1/20.000 at Railway Embankment A13 b.9.6	30/6/17		Continuation of work on improving accommodation on Railway Embankment (A. 13 b and d). - Rails salving material from Embankment. 150 yards wire entanglement erected in front of SCABBARD TRENCH and 40 yards out, commencing at ELBOW TRENCH and running round to the road	
— Do —	1/5/17		Continuation of work on improving accommodation on Railway Embankment (H 13 a and b). 150 yards widened to 3' and recessed to 4'6 in MUSKET TRENCH. Materials for wiring in front of SCABBARD TRENCH, taken up line and carried to end of JOHNSON TRENCH.	

J.W.W. Capt. R.E.

O.C. 406th (Renfrew) Field Coy. R.E.

WAR DIARY
or
INTELLIGENCE SUMMARY.
(Erase heading not required.)

Army Form C. 2118.

406TH (RENFREW) FIELD COMPANY, R.E.
June 1917

Place	Date	Hour	Summary of Events and Information	Remarks and references to Appendices
Coy Hdqrs at Railway Embankment H13.b.9.0. SHELL FRANCE	29/6/17		Continuation of work on improving accommodation on Railway Embankment (H13 b and d). 150 yards of MUSKET TRENCH widened to 4' and deepened to 5'. 130 yards double apron wire erected in front of SCABBARD TRENCH.	
51BNW 1/10,000	30th		Continuation of work on improving accommodation on Railway Embankment (H13 b and d). Working parties widening and deepening MUSKET TRENCH and material for wiring in front of SCABBARD TRENCH taken up. Excavations commenced for Machine Gun Dugout in FINGER TRENCH, and two trench shelters in HALIFAX TRENCH, and Elephant shelter at H32.d.Y.2.	
-30-			Strength of Company at this date — Officers 6. Other Ranks 228.	

James Carr R.E.A.
(?) Hobbs (Lieut.) Field Coy R.E.

Army Form C. 2118.

WAR DIARY
or
INTELLIGENCE SUMMARY
(Erase heading not required.)

406TH (RENFREW) FIELD COMPANY R.E.
No. 1
Date: 1-3/Sep/17

Place	Date	Hour	Summary of Events and Information	Remarks and references to Appendices
NHP References SHEET 51B NW H.13.d.81	1/9/17		Strength N.in 6 Officers 220 other ranks. Working parties employed erecting shelters on RAILWAY EMBANKMENT. H.13.C. Erecting shelters in HALIFAX TRENCH. Excavation of M.G. dug out in FINGER TR. Excavation of MUSKET TRENCH dug parties employed on improving & widening same. 120 y'ds double apron fence completed in front of SEABOARD TR. Work started on Elephant shelter at H.30.d.2.7.	
do	2/9/17		Company employed erecting shelters on RAILWAY EMBKT. H.13.C. Shelter for dressing station completed in HALIFAX TR. 60 yds entanglement erected on WRIST LANE. Excavation for Elephant shelter at H.30.d.2.7. Completed. Excavating dug out in FINGER TR. Firing steps erected in H. Strong Point.	
do	3/9/17		Company employed erecting shelters in RAILWAY EMBKT & HALIFAX TR. Excavation for dug out at H.31.d.77. started. Excavation of M.G. dug-out in CHAIN & ELBOW TR. in FINGER TR. Erecting small trench shelters in CHAIN & MUSKET TR. Day parties employed improving H. Strong Point & Musket TR. Night parties employed on extension of MUSKET TR.	

W.Modgwick Major R.E.
O.C. 406 (RENFREW) Field Coy RE.

Army Form C. 2118.

WAR DIARY
of
INTELLIGENCE SUMMARY.
(Erase heading not required.)

Instructions regarding War Diaries and Intelligence Summaries are contained in F. S. Regs., Part II. and the Staff Manual respectively. Title pages will be prepared in manuscript.

406TH (GREENFIELD) FIELD COMPANY.
Month: ....
Date: 6-7-17.............

Place	Date	Hour	Summary of Events and Information	Remarks and references to Appendices
Hdqrs at H.13.C.2.1. Sheet N° 51.B N.W.	4/7		Working parties employed on Erecting shelters in HALIFAX TR. Dressing station completed. Excavation of M.G. Dug-out in FINGER TR. Lunging Bay H⁰⁰ Dug out in SCABBARD. Widening & deepening SCABBARD TR. Artillery bridge erected over BAYONET TR.	
-do-	5/7		Working parties improving 10th Bttn Hdqrs at H.13.C.D.O. RAILWAY EMBKMT. Widening & deepening MUSKET TR. Improving fire steps in H strong point. Elephant shelter completed at H.30.A.2.7. Shelter excavated in CHAIN TR. Excavations for M.G. Dug-out in FINGER TR. & SCABBARD TR. Excavations for Lying H⁰⁰ in SCABBARD	
-do-	6/7		Working parties on excavation of Dug-outs in FINGER & SCABBARD TRs. Excavation of Coy H⁰⁰ shelter in SCABBARD. Excavating MUSKET TR. Dug parties deepening & widening same. Erecting shelters in HALIFAX TR. & erecting small tunnel shelters in CHAIN & CURB TR. N° 203162 Sapper Cove J.Y. (Wounded in Action) Hospital.	

W. Hodgart. Major R.E.(T)
O.C. 406th Brigham Field Coy R.E.

Army Form C. 2118.

WAR DIARY
or
INTELLIGENCE SUMMARY.
(Erase heading not required.)

406TH (RENFREW) FIELD COMPANY, R.E.

No. 3.   Date 9-7-17

Place	Date	Hour	Summary of Events and Information	Remarks and references to Appendices
Hqrs at H13.6.8,1 Sheet Nr.51.B N.W.	7/17	2	Working parties erecting shelters in HALIFAX Tr., excavating dug-outs in FINGER Tr. & SCABBARD Tr. Erecting small trench shelters in CHAIN & HELBERO Tr. Revetting & deepening strong point at M.36.W.R.9.B. Deepening & widening MUSKET Tr., night parties working in continuation of trench to CURB LANE.	
-Do-	8/7/17		Company employed erecting shelters in HALIFAX Tr., excavation of mined dug-outs in FINGER Tr. & SCABBARD Tr. Excavation of MUSKET Tr. continued. Improving & deepening H.Strong point. Erecting shelters in CHAIN & HELBERO Tr. Dug-house completed for 18 H.Q'rs.	
-Do-	9/7/17		Company employed on erecting shelters in HALIFAX Tr. Excavating mined-dug-outs in FINGER Tr & SCABBARD Tr. 12 trench shelters erected in ELGAR Tr. Excavation of MUSKET Tr. Trench shelters erected in CHAIN Tr. Revetting & erecting fire steps in H. strong point. Revetting & repairing SCABBARD Tr. Shelters erected in SCABBARD Tr.	

W. Stafford Major R.E.(T)
O.C. 406th (Renfrew) Field Coy R.E.

Army Form C. 2118.

WAR DIARY
or
INTELLIGENCE SUMMARY.
(Erase heading not required.)

Instructions regarding War Diaries and Intelligence Summaries are contained in F. S. Regs., Part II. and the Staff Manual respectively. Title pages will be prepared in manuscript.

[Stamp: CHESTER FIELD COMPANY No. 4 .... 1917]

Place	Date	Hour	Summary of Events and Information	Remarks and references to Appendices
Hope at H.13.c.5.1. Sheet N.51.B. N.W. 1/20000	10/4/17		Company employed erecting shelters in HALIFAX Tr., BOW N90 & cook-house completed. Excavation of MUSKET Tr. carried through to CURB LANE. Erecting trench shelters in HELBERD, CHAIN, & SCABBARD Tr. Mined dug-out in FINGER Tr. completed. Excavation of mined dug-out in SCABBARD. Excavation of site for English shelter at H.30.d.1.4.	
- do -	11/4/17		Company employed erecting shelters in HALIFAX Tr., excavation of mined dug-out in SCABBARD Tr. Deepening & widening of MUSKET Tr. Company H90 completed in SCABBARD Tr. Revetting & recovering fire-steps in strongpoint at H.36.a.4.9.4. Excavating & erecting trench shelters in ELBOW, HELBERD & SCABBARD Trs. Excavation of site for E.S. at H.30.d.1.4.	
- do -	12/4/17		Company employed erecting shelters in HALIFAX Tr. Company N90 completed. Excavation of mined dug-out in SCABBARD Tr & site for English shelter at H.30.d.1.4. Lining trench shelters in SCABBARD, CHAIN, ELBOW & HELBERD Tr. Deepening & improving trench at H strong point H.36.a.4.9.4. Repairing & revetting SCABBARD Tr.	

M. Hodgart Major R.E.
O.C. 206th (Cheshire) Field Coy R.E.

Army Form C. 2118.

406TH
(RENFREW)
FIELD COMPANY, R.E.
No. 5
Date 15.7.17

WAR DIARY
or
INTELLIGENCE SUMMARY.
(Erase heading not required.)

Instructions regarding War Diaries and Intelligence Summaries are contained in F. S. Regs., Part II. and the Staff Manual respectively. Title pages will be prepared in manuscript.

Place	Date	Hour	Summary of Events and Information	Remarks and references to Appendices
Hypr cat H13.b.6.1 Sheet 51B NW	13/7/17		Company employed sinking shelters in HALIFAX T?. Excavation of mined dug-out in SCABBARD T?. second shaft started. Marking mule track & tunnelling Battery bridge over CURB T?. Erection of English shelter at H.30.d.14. completed. Lobby dug-outs in FINGER T?. & CURB LANE. Sinking trench shelters in ELBOW & NEW ST.	
—do—	14/7/17		Company employed erecting shelters in HALIFAX T?. Excavation of site for Brit. Bomb store at W.03 SIDING started. Marking of mule track from LANCER LANE to CURB LANE completed. Excavation for mined dug-out in SCABBARD T?. Parties repairing & revetting SCABBARD & CHAIN T?. Erecting & lining trench shelters in ELBOW & CHAIN T?. Revetting & erecting steel covers on B.S. at H.30.d.10.	
—do—	15/7/17		Company employed excavating & making framework of Lee Bond Store at H.34. a.9.4. Shelters in HALIFAX T?. Excavation of mined dug-out in SCABBARD T?. Revetting work & face of B.S. at H.30.d.44. Revetting & repairing SCABBARD ELBOW WRIST trenches. Erecting trench shelters in CURB, ELBOW & CHAIN T?.	

W. Hodgart Major R.E.(T)
O.C. 406 th (Renfrew) Field Coy R.E.

A 3834 Wt.W4973/M687 750,000 8/16 D. D. & L. Ltd. Forms/C.2118/13.

Army Form C. 2118.

WAR DIARY
or
INTELLIGENCE SUMMARY.
(Erase heading not required.)

Instructions regarding War Diaries and Intelligence Summaries are contained in F. S. Regs., Part II. and the Staff Manual respectively. Title pages will be prepared in manuscript.

406TH (RENFREW) FIELD COMPANY, R.E.
No. 6
Date 1.5.17

Place	Date	Hour	Summary of Events and Information	Remarks and references to Appendices
Map ref: H.13. & B.1. Sheet 51B NW	16/4/17		Company employed erecting shelters in HALIFAX TR. 3 shelters completed. Excavation of site for Dimick Brick Stores. Excavation of M.G. dug-out in SCABBARD TR. Erecting shelters in HELBEARD, CHAIN & MUSKET TR. Fitting interior & completing Head cover of expired shelters at H.30.L.14. Deepening & widening communication to H.Strong point.	
—do—	17/4/17		Company employed, erecting shelters in HALIFAX TR. excavation of Dick Bond Stores at N.403 Lithorn. Excavation of M.G dug-out in SCABBARD TR. Erecting trench shelters in MUSKET, HELBEARD & CHAIN TRS. Elephant shelter at H.30.B.44 completed. Improving fire steps & deepening trench in H.Post.	
—do—	18/4/17		Company employed, erecting fraining & revetment for Div Boundaries in country trench shelters in HALIFAX TR. Erecting fittings in Cpy 147th SCABBARD TR 2 CHAIN TR. Wire entanglement erected in front of RIFLE TR. Improving trench in H.Post & MEN ST. Excavation of dug-out in SCABBARD TR. Infantry trench shelters in CHAIN & HELBEARD TR. Charges laid in camouflets No 750 at H.36.B.54 & fired at 2.05 a.m. shelters & report attached.	

W. Forsyth
Major R.E.
O.C. 406th Renfrew Field Cy R.E.

Army Form C. 2118.

WAR DIARY
or
INTELLIGENCE SUMMARY
(Erase heading not required.)

406th (RENFREW) FIELD COMPANY, R.E.
No. 4
Date 21/7

Place	Date	Hour	Summary of Events and Information	Remarks and references to Appendices
H.Qrs of H.13.R.2.1. Sheet M.51.B N.W. trans	19/1/17		Parties working on shelters in HALIFAX Tr. Dug-Bomb stores at 403 Lithgr. Excavation of mined dug-out in SCABBARD Tr. Lacing trench shelters in CURB & HELBERD Tr. Erecting wire entanglement in front of RIFLE Tr. Revetting & repairing SCABBARD, CROSS BOW & WAIST Trs. Shelters erected in by N9m dug-out in CURB & N.E.	
— Do —	20/1/17		Working parties completed work on shelters in HALIFAX Tr. excavating at 18 shelters to shell & mm soil, 1 dressing station, 2 lg N9m & Butt N9m men & cook-house. Erecting frames & excavating for Dug-Bomb stores. Excavation of mined dug-out in SCABBARD Tr. In 706 more entanglement erected in front of RIFLE Tr. Erecting trench shelters in HELBERD & CHAIN Trs.	
— Do —	21/1/17		Working parties completed mined dug-out in SCABBARD Tr. Repairing revetting in SCABBARD, CROSS BOW & WAIST Trs. Erecting wire entanglement in front of RIFLE Tr. Erecting trench shelters in HELBERD & MUSKET Trs. Night parties carrying & deepening WELFORD Tr. & H. Strong point. Charges laid on dugouts of trench No720 demolished.	

L. Arkcoll Major R.E.
O.C. No 6 (Renfrew) Field Coy R.E.

Army Form C. 2118.

WAR DIARY
or
INTELLIGENCE SUMMARY.
(Erase heading not required.)

Instructions regarding War Diaries and Intelligence Summaries are contained in F.S. Regs., Part II. and the Staff Manual respectively. Title pages will be prepared in manuscript.

406TH (RENFREW) FIELD COMPANY, R.E.
No. 5
Date 24.7.17

Place	Date	Hour	Summary of Events and Information	Remarks and references to Appendices
Hqrs at H.13.b.5.1. Sheet No 51B N.W. 1/20,000	22/7/17		Working parties employed erecting bomb stores at 403 siding. Riveting & deepening SCABBARD, WRIST & CROSSBOW and MUSKET TRS. & of Q.M. MELFORD TR. cleared. 100 yds new entanglement erected between NEW TR. & HARNESS TR. Erecting & lining French shelters in ELBOW & SCABBARD TRS. erecting knife rests for gap.	
– do –	23/7/17		Working parties employed erecting Dead Bomb store. Rivetting & deepening SCABBARD, NEW ST. WRIST TRS. Erecting French shelters in ELBOW, BAYONET & MUSKET TRS. Clearing MELFORD & erecting platform & emplacement in O.P. erecting new entanglement RIFLE TR. Rivetting fire steps & parapet of H.Stony point. Telegraph pole at I.13.d.5½.1. blown down with a view of erecting a dummy stump for the purpose of an O.P.	
– do –	24/7/17		Working parties erecting bomb store at 403 siding. Repairing & revetting SCABBARD, NEW ST, WRIST TRS. Erecting trench shelters in ELBOW & SCABBARD TRS. Improving fire step & deepening trench in H.Stony point. Erecting wire entanglements in front of CHAIN TR. TANK No 730. Bottom plates removed, debris buried & camouflaged.	

W. Wyant Major R.E.(T)
O.P. No 406 (Renfrew) Field Coy R.E.

A5834 Wt.W4973/M687 750,000 8/16 D.D.&L. Ltd. Forms/C.2118/13.

WAR DIARY
or
INTELLIGENCE SUMMARY.
(Erase heading not required.)

Army Form C. 2118.

406TH (RENFREW) FIELD COMPANY, R.E.

Place	Date	Hour	Summary of Events and Information	Remarks and references to Appendices
H/Qrs at H13.d.2.1. SHEET N° 51B NW	25/7/17		Working parties employed excavating & erecting framing on Divl Bomb stores. Erecting steel shelters in ELBOW MUSKET TR. O.P. in MELFORD TR. Repairing & deepening MAIST, NELSON MUSKET & RIFLE TR. Completing wire entanglement in front of CHAIN TR. Party clearing Both H'Qrs in HALIFAX TR. which had been blown in by a direct hit.	
— do —	26/7/17		No 1 Bomb store at No 3 siding completed. Excavation & frames completed for new Batt H'Qrs in HIMALAYA TR. Repairing SCABBARD TR & erecting shelters in ELBOW & MUSKET TRS, connecting up wire entanglement between CHAIN & RIFLE TR. Artillery bridge erected over LANCER LANE at H.36.a.24.	
— do —	27/7/17		Steel covers on No 1 Bomb store erected by Electr. framing erected for No 2 store. Batt H'Qrs in HIMALAYA TR completed, erecting trench shelters in ELBOW TR. Sapping traverses & erecting RIFLE TR. Excavation of H S26 at J.13.c. 6&.7 started. Two galleries started in RIFLE TR for O.P. at Telegraph pole I.13.a. 8&.1. Repairing SCABBARD TR.	

W.Holgate Major RE
OC 406 (Renfrew) Field Cy RE

WAR DIARY or INTELLIGENCE SUMMARY

Army Form C. 2118.

(RENFREW) FIELD COMPANY, R.E.
No. 10 Date 30/7/17

Place	Date	Hour	Summary of Events and Information	Remarks and references to Appendices
N9 a 9 H.13.c.7.1 SHEET M. 51.B. N.W.	28/7/17		Working parties revetting ELBOW & SCABBARD Tr. & Artillery Bridges erected over WELFORD Tr. & JOHNSON LANE. Excavation of Safe at I.13.2.Ch.9. Erecting frames for O.P. in RIFLE Tr. Widening revetting & traversing RIFLE Tr. Preparing accomodation for beds in HAPPY VALLEY. Work stopped on M.G. Bomb store owing to two shell bits which completely destroyed framework erected.	
— No —	29/7/17		Preparing mushroom for M.G. Bomb Store. Erecting shelter in HAPPY VALLEY. Camouflage screen erected at H.36.a.3.2. Revetting & refixing SCABBARD Tr. Erecting hurdle shelter in SCABBARD & ELBOW Tr. Filling in shell holes on Artillery track. Filling irrigation ditch at H.13.d.2. for 18 pdr Guns.	M.42005 Sapr. AITKEN M (Wounded in Action)
— No —	30/7/17		Working parties employed clearing debris from site of M.G. Bomb store. Erecting trench shelters in SCABBARD & ELBOW Tr. Excavation of Y hsp. Erecting camouflage screen in VALLEY at H.36.a.3.2. Clearing HARNESS Tr. & traversing RIFLE Tr. Erecting wire entanglement of CHAIN Tr. 40 large dump carts erected for 18 Pdr.	

M. Polgard Major R.E.
O.C. 405th (Renfrew) Field Company R.E.

WAR DIARY

INTELLIGENCE SUMMARY

(Erase heading not required.)

Army Form C. 2118.

Place	Date	Hour	Summary of Events and Information	Remarks and references to Appendices
Nrgrs at H13.b.8.1 SHEET N°51 B. N.W. Ypres	31/7		Company employed in revetting & repair of shelters in HARNESS & SCABBARD TR. Excavation of info at Y POST. Revetting & traversing RIFLE TR. Camouflage screen completed at H.36.a.32. Hastily trenched watercut from H.36.a.33. to LONE LANE & DRAGON TR. filled in. Erecting shelters in ESSEX TR. Erecting framing & clarting of N°2 Bomb Store. Excavation of dug-out at Les Bidets in HAPPY VALLEY. Through no Senior Officer 220th ranks.	W/Sgnd. Major R. O'Hare O.C. 406 (Renfrew) Field Coy R.E

Demolition of Tank No 480

On the Night 16/17 July charges were laid in tank according to diagram attached.

Charges (a & b) were similar consisting of slabs guncotton on top, under girder and slabs on floor on top of girder.

At each of the upright angles on forward end a 20·25 cm German shell was placed with slabs of guncotton and were placed thus:—

[sketch of shell with slabs]

On the after end two more German shells were placed with their bases underneath the cross shafts running from differential casing. These had slabs placed as in above sketch.

A Charge (c) was placed on left hand side (port) of slabs running continuously along angle iron to acute angle in front. It then passed across the whole front angle.

A Charge (d) was run along the floor on STARBOARD side from base of shell back to angle and then right across back along angle iron.

Detonators No 13 were placed at the points marked on diagram and were connected in series as shown.

Leads were run to a dug-out 250 yds distant and continuity tested.

Charge was fired at 2.45 a.m.

Effect (a)

The side girders were laid over on their flat. Gun turrets were blown clear. Differential casing was blown clear in two pieces. Radiator was blown clear in rear. Forward floor plate (b) bent

(2)

at right angles. Engine bed and 14'0" of floor plating remained intact, except where differential casing was blown off. Engine was practically intact, but all rivets in floor plating were loosened. Floor plating simply bent over with engine bed on top. (see sketch).

Two of the German shells did not detonate. Cause of this was due to the fact that the work was done in the dark, no keys for loosening fuzes were at hand. It is not certain which shells they were. One was probably the forward shell on STARBOARD side.

Total charge used for this was 14 slabs and 4. 20.25 cms German shells.

To remove the engine bedplate from floor plating a further charge was laid on the night 20/21 and fired at 2.45 a.m.

This was made up as follows; (see diagram II)

Charge (a)
Plate mentioned in para (6) had three slabs guncotton placed on front side for the purpose of carrying away this prop.

Charge (b) consisting of 6 slabs was placed on STARBOARD side of mild steel engine bedplate commencing in front of point where differential casing had been, and extending forward.

Charge (c) consisting of another 6 slabs was placed forward of this with a gap of about 1'0" between (b & c).

Charge (d) consisting of 6 slabs was placed on Cast Iron Engine Frame at centre of Engine.

All these charges were tamped with Sandbags and fired electrically. Detonators were connected in series.

Effect

The Engine Frame & bed were blown clear of floor plating and the whole landed between side girders.

(3)

The 3/8" plate forward which was shoring up bed was not removed but cut clear.

The 14'0" of floor plating was not removed but loosened and sprung slightly upwards when the weight of engine bed was removed.

All these plates were quite loose, but a further charge of 18 slabs was required to cut these away.

This reduced the general level of debris to 2'0" above ground level. The parts were covered with earth and camouflage.

(Sgd) M Hodgart Major RE
O.C. 406th (Renfrew) Field Co RE

Nº 3.

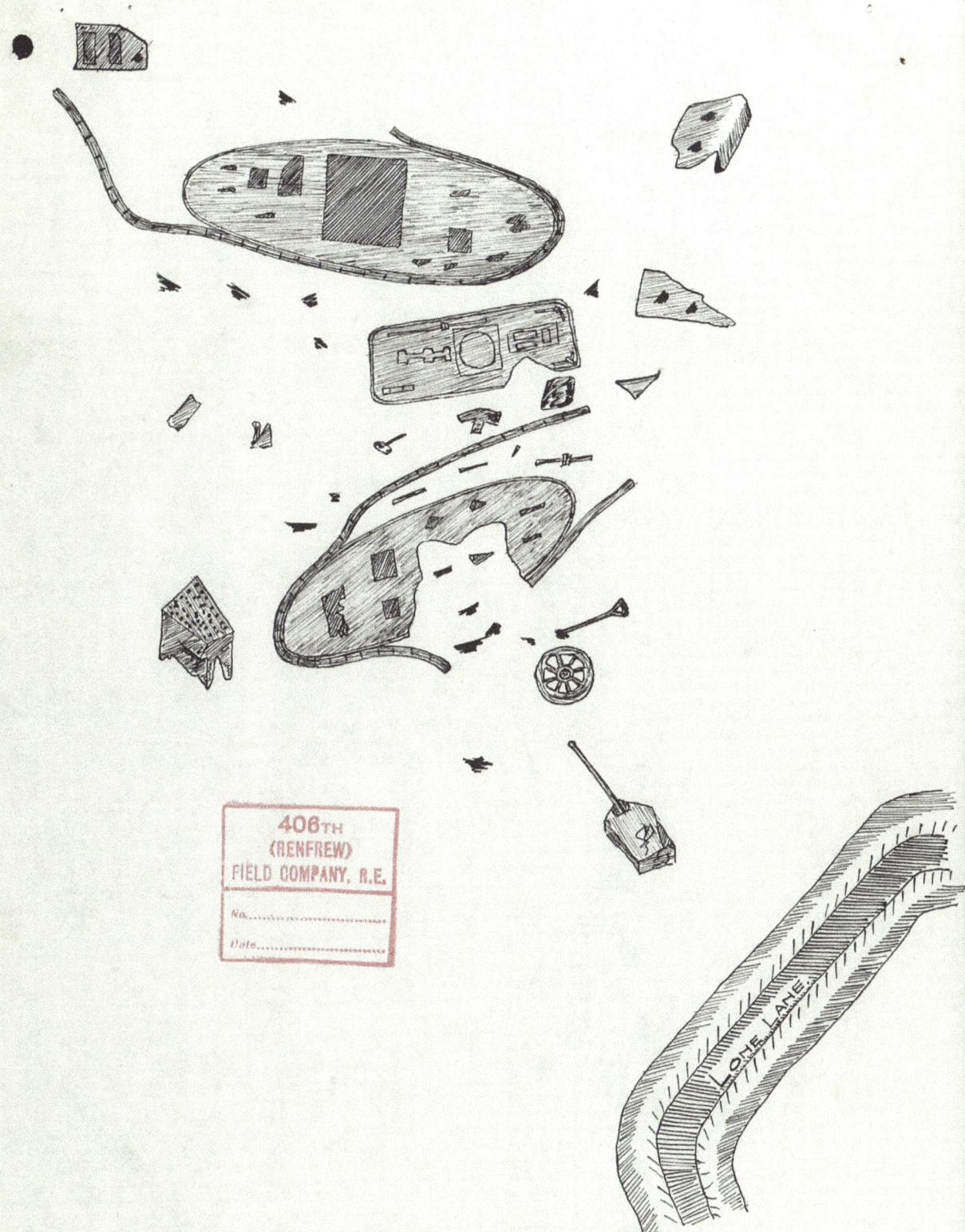

Nº 2.

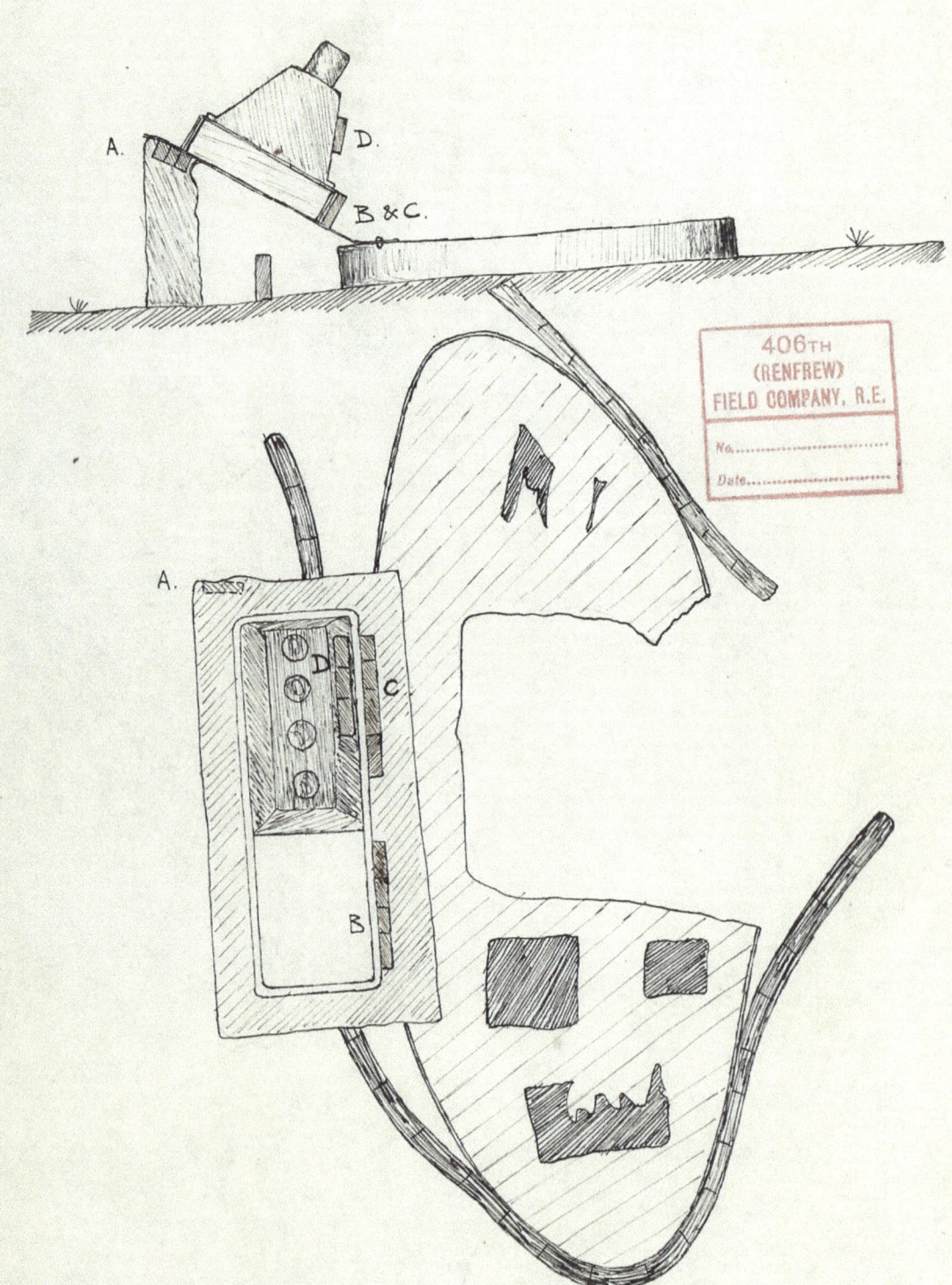

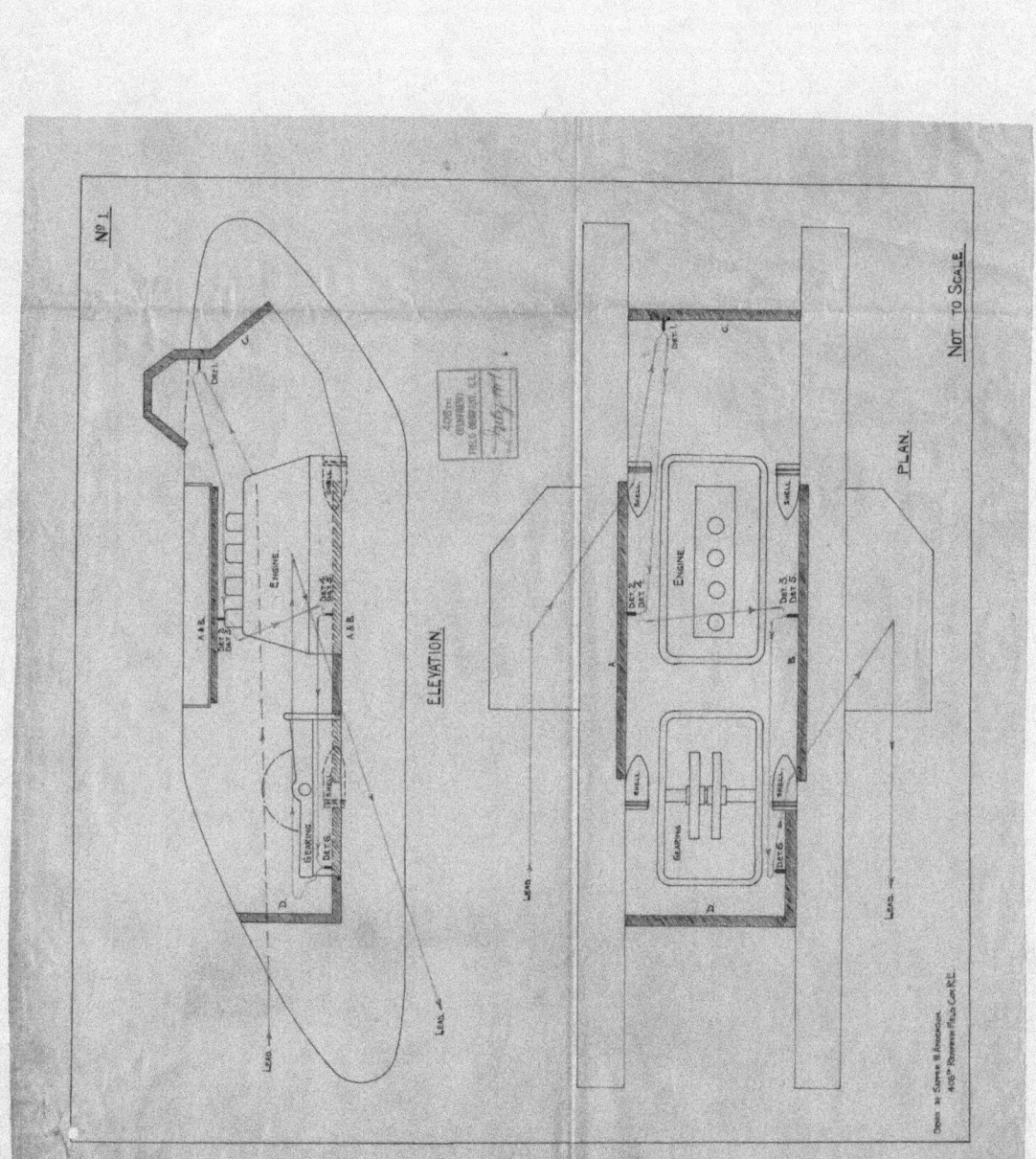

Army Form C. 2118.

406 2n Coy RE
4 Vol 21

WAR DIARY
or
INTELLIGENCE SUMMARY.
(Erase heading not required.)

Instructions regarding War Diaries and Intelligence Summaries are contained in F.S. Regs., Part II. and the Staff Manual respectively. Title pages will be prepared in manuscript.

Place	Date	Hour	Summary of Events and Information	Remarks and references to Appendices
HQrs at H.13.d.9.0. 1/40 Maps 51B NW 20/20	1/5/17		Company employed erecting Bomb store, excavation of dug-out at Y Sap. Excavation of dug-out HAPPY VALLEY. Making Hotchkiss stands, traversing & loop-way RIFLE TR. Clearing & revetting SCABBARD, ELBOW & RIFLE SUPPORT. Company Strength. 6 Officers 230 Other ranks.	
-do-	2/5/17		Company employed erecting Bomb store, excavation of Y Sap, erecting entanglement on CHAIN TR. Clearing & revetting SCABBARD, ELBOW & RIFLE SUPPORT. Traversing & revetting RIFLE TR. Shelters erected for revetting at R4 FMENT.	
-do-	3/5/17		Company employed on excavation of Y Sap, erecting entanglements on CHAIN TR. Excavation of dug-out in HAPPY VALLEY. Erecting Head-cover on Bomb stores. Clearing & revetting RIFLE, SCABBARD & CHAIN TR.	
-do-	4/5/17		Company employed on excavations for Y Sap, erecting Hotchkiss wipes & making track, improving Head-cover on Bomb stores, erecting entanglement on CHAIN TR. Excavation of dug-out in HAPPY VALLEY. Clearing, revetting RIFLE, RIFLE SUPPORT & SCABBARD TR.	

W Holgate
Major R.E.
O.C. 406th Highlnd Field Coy R.E.

WAR DIARY or INTELLIGENCE SUMMARY.

(Erase heading not required.)

Army Form C. 2118.

Instructions regarding War Diaries and Intelligence Summaries are contained in F.S. Regs., Part II. and the Staff Manual respectively. Title pages will be prepared in manuscript.

Place	Date	Hour	Summary of Events and Information	Remarks and references to Appendices
Hqrs at H.13.c.9.0. Map Ref. No. 51.B. N.W.	5/8/17		Company employed on excavation of dug-out & V Posts, erecting french shelters in MUSKET Tr., erecting wire entanglement on CHAIN Tr., excavation of dug-out in HAPPY VALLEY. Excavation of site for B.H.Q. accommodation at H.23.d. 4.8.1.R. Erecting A.A. cover on Bomb store. Clearing & resetting SCABBARD RIFLE & CHAIN Tr.	
-do-	6/8/17		Company employed on excavation of dug-out & V Posts, excavation of B.H.Q. accommodation at H.23.d., excavation of dug-out & V Post, erecting trench shelters in MUSKET Tr., erecting wire entanglement on CHAIN Tr., Ratcliffe bridge carried at H.23.d. 1.3. Erecting dagos of dug-outs over Bomb stores. Clearing & resetting CHAIN, RIFLE & SCABBARD Tr.	
-do-	7/8/17		Company employed on excavation of V Post dug-out in HAPPY VALLEY & B.H. site at H.23.d., erecting entanglement on CHAIN Tr. Erecting trench shelters in MUSKET Tr. Company employed on CHAIN, RIFLE & SCABBARD Tr. Erecting frames for roads on B.H. Posit.IV.	
-do-	8/8/17		Bomb stores at H.Q.S. SIDING completed. Excavation of site for B.H. accommodation at H.23.d. - dug-out dug HAPPY VALLEY. Making road of Somersue wire, excavation of M.G. Obsy. dug-out dug HAPPY VALLEY H.3.6.7.2. erecting & resetting frames for B.H. Obsy. Road-way at O.P. Emket & dug-outs.	

W. Hodgson. Major R.E.
O.C. 406 (Renfrew) Field Coy. R.E.

WAR DIARY
or
INTELLIGENCE SUMMARY.

Army Form C. 2118.

406TH (RENFREW)
FIELD COY. R.E.
Volume 3

Place	Date	Hour	Summary of Events and Information	Remarks and references to Appendices
Maps at H.13.c.9.o. Ref MAP No 51.B. NW	9/17		Company employed on excavation of R.E. Hqs - also in HAPPY VALLEY. Erecting wire entanglements on CHAIN T.P. Machine gun dug-out started. Clearing & wiring SCABBARD RIFLE & RIFLE SUPPORT T.P. 20 coils concertina have now made up.	
-do-	10/17		Company employed on excavation of R.E. & M.G. Hqs - also HAPPY VALLEY. Excavating dug out for 8th Bn HQrs accommodation. No wiring parties for night of 9/10. Bumps to functions.	
-do-	11/17		Company employed on excavation of R.E. & M.G. Hqs - on the HAPPY VALLEY must entanglement on CHAIN T.P. erecting up coils of concertina wire for entanglements. Clearing & wiring CHAIN SCABBARD NEW ST & RIFLE T.P.S.	
-do-	12/17		Company excavating R.E. & M.G. Dug-outs in HAPPY VALLEY. Excavation of 10 ft & 9ft completed & flooring taken to coils erected. Erecting new shelter in MUSKET T.P. erecting & frames fire steps & laying trench boards in SCABBARD. Clearing trench & erecting traverses in RIFLE.	

M.Adjutant Major R.E. W.
O.C. 406 (Renfrew) Field Coy R.E.

Army Form C. 2118.

WAR DIARY
or
INTELLIGENCE SUMMARY.
(Erase heading not required.)

Instructions regarding War Diaries and Intelligence Summaries are contained in F. S. Regs., Part II. and the Staff Manual respectively. Title pages will be prepared in manuscript.

406TH (RENFREW) FIELD COMPANY
No. 6.
Date ....

Place	Date	Hour	Summary of Events and Information	Remarks and references to Appendices
H.Qrs. at H.13.b.9.0. Ref Map N.&.5.f.B NW	13/7/17		Company employed on excavation of R.E. & M.G. dug-outs HAPPY VALLEY. Framing a roof completed for B.P. M.G. LANCER LANE. erecting tunnel shelter on CURB T.R. Clearing & revetting SEABOARD & CHAIN T.R. 300 yds wire entanglement erected on CHAIN T.R.	
-do-	14/7/17		Company employed on excavation of dug-outs LANCER LANE. erecting wire entanglement on CHAIN T.R. erecting tunnel shelter on MUSKET T.R. Clearing & revetting SEABOARD, CHAIN & RIFLE T.Rs. Framing sheets for B.P. MUSKET T.R. & tunnel trace. excavating sites for huts at STIRLING CAMP H.13.a.	
-do-	15/7/17		Company employed on excavation of framing dug-outs in HAPPY VALLEY erecting tunnel shelter on MUSKET T.R. Clearing & laying tunnel boards in CHAIN SUPPORT & framing RIFLE T.R. erecting wire entanglement on CHAIN T.R. Camouflage found to side of Pineapple Cockon in YPRES. excavation of sites continued.	
-do-	16/7/17		Excavation of M.G. dug and HAPPY VALLEY completed. Laying tunnel boards & clearing CHAIN SUPPORT. erecting tunnel shelter in MUSKET T.R. excavation of YPRES continued. Clearing, revetting & erecting tunnel shelters on SEABOARD SUPPORT & RIFLE T.R. Framing for huts erected in STIRLING CAMP.	

h. Holgart
O.C. and 406th/Renfrew field Coy R.E.

A5834 Wt. W4973/M687 750,000 8/16 D. D. & L. Ltd. Forms/C.2118/13.

Army Form C. 2118.

WAR DIARY
or
INTELLIGENCE SUMMARY.
(Erase heading not required.)

Instructions regarding War Diaries and Intelligence Summaries are contained in F.S. Regs., Part II. and the Staff Manual respectively. Title pages will be prepared in manuscript.

403rd (RENFREW) FIELD COMPANY, R.E.
No. 5
Date: 5/17

Place	Date	Hour	Summary of Events and Information	Remarks and references to Appendices
HdQrs at H.13.d.9.0 Ref. Map M⁰ 51B 2/20 N.W.	18/5/17		Company employed on excavation & framing of R.E. dug out HAPPY VALLEY. Framing & laying of R.E. dug out completed and setting out and entrenchment CAHIN Tr. setting trench shelter in MUSKET Tr. and laying frames & trench boards in SCABBARD Tr. R.E. Support, Kits for O.P. MUSKET Tr. Camouflages & cup started on day and night, also at R.E. dug out well at 18/4 Mayer Trestles Kits & carrying into for huts at R.E. dug out.	
- do -	19/5/17		Company employed excavating R.E. dug out and HAPPY VALLEY excavation of dug-outs for CAHIN Tr. setting trench shelter in CAHIN Tr. setting lined, completed of BILAINE tree-cover works at CAHIN Tr. TIMBER LINE completed, setting gas-curtains on day-outs, but most accommodation for 60 men completed at Implement. Work on under from DUGOUT to SCABBARD ALLEY handed over to 506th Durham L.I. Fd. Coy. R.E.	
- do -	19/5/17		Work on English shelter for R.A.M.C. at H.30.d.49. started & camouflage erected over cover for O.P. MUSKET Tr. excavation of R.E. dug out and HAPPY VALLEY continued. Laying trench boards in SCABBARD Tr. setting trench shelter in SCABBARD, erecting frames & laying trench boards in SABBARD SUPPORT & etc. dug outs & excavation of huts at R.E. dug out.	
- do -	20/5/17		Company employed on excavation for O.P. MUSKET Tr. R.A.M.C. shelter at H.30.d.9.4. R.E. dug out and in HAPPY VALLEY. 100 ft. double upon frame erected on CAHIN Tr. setting CHAIN SUPPORT & NEW St., Laying trench boards in RIFLE SUPPORT. Cleaning & erecting signal cabin for Div Bde completed at R.E. dug out H.13.d.9.0	

W. Wolpert Major R.E. (?)
O.C. 403rd (Renfrew) Field Coy. R.E.

Army Form C. 2118.

WAR DIARY
or
INTELLIGENCE SUMMARY.
(Erase heading not required.)

406TH (RENFREW) FIELD COMPANY, R.E.
No. 6
Date 7.4.17

Instructions regarding War Diaries and Intelligence Summaries are contained in F.S. Regs., Part II and the Staff Manual respectively. Title pages will be prepared in manuscript.

Place	Date	Hour	Summary of Events and Information	Remarks and references to Appendices
Hqrs at H13.b.9.0. Ret Map Sheet M51.B type NW	21/5/17		Company employed on excavation of Hqrs and HAPPY VALLEY, excavation of site for O.P. MUSKET T⁰, excavation of chamber for periscope at Y Sap, excavating site of Rd post at H.38.C.3.1. Clearing & revetting CHAIN T⁰, RIFLE NEW & RIFLE SUPPORT. Excavating site for hut on Railway Embkt.	
- do -	22/5/17		Company employed on excavation & tramming of O.P. MUSKET T⁰, organisation of dug out at H.30.C.8.1. Excavation of dug & chamber for periscope at Y Sap, excavating & tramming Hqrs out in HAPPY VALLEY. Level lines & revetting for steps on RIFLE SUPPORT. Clearing CHAIN T⁰ & NEW S⁰. and there were entanglements CHAIN T⁰. Continuous level works in Rd Embkt	
- do -	23/5/17		Tramming of O.P. MUSKET T⁰ & dug down through on MUSKET T⁰ excavation of Y Sap & chamber for periscope. Wiring was employed in CHAIN T⁰. Clearing & fitting and digging in MUSKET T⁰, excavation of pit for L.S. dugout at H.38.C.3.1. Stepping in RIFLE NEW Sergeants RIFLE. Continuing tramway CHAIN T⁰ laying down RD Embkt	
- do -	24/5/17		Tramming on MUSKET T⁰. Hut on RD Embkt excavation of chambers for Lagging & Clearing places on O.P. MUSKET T⁰. one excavation of chamber for water aft Y Sap completed, 3 of shafts adapted for R.E. Hqrs out in HAPPY VALLEY. Level lines & fixing steps in RIFLE T⁰. Clearing & laying beside trench boards were RIFLE SUPPORT & HALBRO T⁰ wiring wire entanglement on CHAIN T⁰ excavation of site for hutting on Rd Embkt.	

W. Holgate. Major. RE
Off. g.o.c. (Relieved) Field Company.

WAR DIARY or INTELLIGENCE SUMMARY

Army Form C. 2118.

406TH (RENFREW) FIELD COMPANY, R.E.
No. 7
Date 29-7-17

Place	Date	Hour	Summary of Events and Information	Remarks and references to Appendices
H.Qrs at H.13.b.9.0 Ref Map Sheet M.51.B 2000 NW.	26/7/17		Excavating & framing dug-out in HAPPYVALLEY sinking well for periscope in chamber at V. Sap. placing ladders on sides of O.P. MUSKET TR. Clearing & revetting HELGARD TR. Erecting A frames & erecting fire steps in RIFLE TR.	
-do-	27/7/17		Company employed sinking shaft for periscope well at V. Sap. Lining O.P. MUSKET TR with ladders, excavation of ext. for Old R.E. LINE H.30.a.3.1. Laying trench boards & clearing CABIN RIFLE SUPPORT & HARNESS TR. Two framed banks Made for footbridge across RIVER SCARPE at H.13.b.9.3. MR 572322 Sap SAUNDERS E. (Wounded in Action Bullet L. Hand Remained at Duty)	
-do-	28/7/17		Widening shaft at V Sap. Overhead cover erected on O.P. MUSKET TR. Excavation of Old Post at H.30.a.3.1 & R.E. Dug-out HAPPY VALLEY. Chamber of a T.M. dug-out HARNESS TR. partly. Revetting LEMON TR. LEMON AVE. and through to INNER LANE. Repairing & revetting HARNESS TR. Hut completed on R. Bank TR. with accommodation for 60 men.	
-do-	29/7/17		Revetting O.P. in MUSKET TR. sinking shaft for periscope in V. Sap. excavation of exts. for Roll Post at H.30.a.3.1. Clearing HELGARD TR. Battery Entrance LEMON TR. LEMON LANE. Laid exting fire steps in RIFLE TR. All night working parties for Tunnelers cancelled. Excavating exts. for 3" cm fuel on R.P. Post.	
-do-	30/7/17		Well in O.P. V Sap. completed & Final chamber prepared for exhaust. Tunnel extras immediate & LEMON TR. completed. Excavation of exts. for Roll Post at H.30.a.3.1. Framing R.E. dug-out of Happy Valley. Erecting Munich frames & fire step in RIFLE TR. clearing & revetting & repair travels tracks on CABIN RIFLE SUPPORT & HARNESS TR. where platform erected for Lewis gun at H.13.d.9.3. R.E. excavator on loan for work on Lochford Line for night of 29/30.	

M. Hodgart Major R.E
O.C. 406 Renfrew Field Coy R.E

Army Form C. 2118.

WAR DIARY
or
INTELLIGENCE SUMMARY

(Erase heading not required.)

Instructions regarding War Diaries and Intelligence Summaries are contained in F. S. Regs., Part II. and the Staff Manual respectively. Title Pages will be prepared in manuscript.

Place	Date	Hour	Summary of Events and Information	Remarks and references to Appendices
H.Qrs at H13.6.9.0 Ret Map No 51 B.N.W. 2000	30/1/17		Company employed, excavating & framing R.E. dugout in HAPPY VALLEY. Excavation of R.E. dugout at H.30.d.3.1. nearing completion. Erecting new entanglement on support line, erecting flies strip & erecting M frames in RIFLE 7th, repping traverses in RIFLE SUPPORT, & laying French & laying french boards in CHAIN & LEMON 7th cutting new trench between CHAIN & BRIDOON 7°.	
Do	31/1/17		Company employed mounting I Sap. & infantry & placing concertina-type wire, excavating & framing R.E. Dug-out HAPPY VALLEY. Excavators for R.S. at H.30.c.3.1 completed trenches & also level & shelter enlarged. Deepened between CHAIN & BRIDOON. Erecting M frames in RIFLE 7th. Laying trench boards in RIFLE SUPPORT. Frames erected & posns fitted for footbridge across River SCARPE at H.13.d.9.3. Attached Officers 6 O.R. 219. Attached Officers 2 O.R. 4.	

W Wodgate Major R.E. O/C
A.P. 206th Brigade Field Coy R.E.

2449 Wt. W14957/M90 750,000 1/16 J.B.C. & A. Forms/C.2118/12

Army Form C. 2118.

WAR DIARY
or
INTELLIGENCE SUMMARY
(Erase heading not required.)

Instructions regarding War Diaries and Intelligence Summaries are contained in F.S. Regs., Part II. and the Staff Manual respectively. Title Pages will be prepared in manuscript.

400.. (RENFREW) FIELD COMPANY, R.E.
No. 1
Date 2-16

Place	Date	Hour	Summary of Events and Information	Remarks and references to Appendices
Hqrs at H.13.6.9.0. Rt MHR No 51 B NW	1/9/17		Company Strength Officers 6 O.R. 211. 12 O.R. transferred to No 2 Company and Coy as supplies to Estat Both Dis. O letter. C.R.N° 51306/106 D. 25/7. 1 OR rejoined unit from Base.	
— do —	2/9/17		Company employed every afternoon on Rd. post at H.30.C.31 & B.N.44 at STANCERLANE. Coy for present [unclear] on 1 Shift. This work could not be carried out every 4 teamen at night. Making & digging HARNESS RIFLE SUPPORT. Laying my track to to couch at — [unclear] at H.13 S.P.Q. Loads in CHAIN RIFLE LEMON T.R.	
— do —			Company employed every afternoon & his afternoon in RIFLE T.R. every N. corner on Rd Post at H.30.C.31. Excavation of R.E. dug-out & TM position in HARNESS. Mckery & laying trench boards in CHAIN, HARNESS & RIFLE SUPPORT.	
— do —	3/9/17		Every bed room on Rd post H.30.C.31 & B.N Nd.gn. in LANCERLANE. Every fine steps & laying trench boards in RIFLE T.R. deepening between CHAIN, BRIDOON & LINK & laying trench boards excavation of R.E. dug out in HAPPY VALLEY. Footbridge over River SCARPE completed for infantry in file with 25' span & 12' above maximum W.L. Old footbridge taken down.	

M.Aegan
Major R.E.
OC 400 [unclear] Field Coy R.E.

Army Form C. 2118.

WAR DIARY
or
INTELLIGENCE SUMMARY

(Erase heading not required.)

Instructions regarding War Diaries and Intelligence Summaries are contained in F.S. Regs., Part II. and the Staff Manual respectively. Title Pages will be prepared in manuscript.

406TH (RENFREW) FIELD COMPANY, R.E.

No. 2 Date F 2/17

Place	Date	Hour	Summary of Events and Information	Remarks and references to Appendices
H'qrs at H.13.c.4.0. Ref Map No 51 B N.W.	4/2/17		Working parties employed on excavation of R.A.M.C. dug-out & R.E. dug-out in HAPPY VALLEY. Clearing snow & further laying French trench in RIFLE BRIDOON LINK. RIFLE SUPPORT & CURB SWITCH. Working on R.S. Embankment.	
-do-	5/2/17		Company employed on excavation of R.E. dug-out & shafts of R.A.M.C. Dressing Station in HAPPY VALLEY. Revetting & erecting partitions in RIFLE SUPPORT BRIDOON & HARNESS TR. Erecting hut on R.S. Embank.	
-do-	6/2/17		Company employed on excavation of R.A.M.C. dug-out at H.3.D.C.3.1. Erecting Armour revetting & laying French trench boards in RIFLE SUPPORT, RIFLE LEMON & HARNESS TR. Refilling & laying French trench boards in RIFLE LEMON & HARNESS TR. Parties of Officers N.C.O. & men of the 73rd Field R.E. taken over work on HETON in view of relief.	
-do-	7/2/17		All night working parties employed on support line trenches. Work handed over to 73rd Field Coy R.E. & returns delivered. N.C.A. had been completed on Railway Embankment accommodation for 60 men.	
-do-	8/2/17		Our whole company moved from R.S. Embankment to RAWSART Camp at X.14.a.2.5 Ref Map No 51 C 5000 in accordance with CR52 & See OO No 2 D 2/2/17 9.
		12.0 noon	Whole Coy arrived	

W. Hodgart
Major R.E.(T)
O.C. 406th Renfrew Field Coy R.E.

Army Form C. 2118.

WAR DIARY
or
INTELLIGENCE SUMMARY
(Erase heading not required.)

Instructions regarding War Diaries and Intelligence Summaries are contained in F. S. Regs., Part II and the Staff Manual respectively. Title Pages will be prepared in manuscript.

Place	Date	Hour	Summary of Events and Information	Remarks and references to Appendices
H4 at RANSART Ref Map N°51E	9/9/17		Company inspection by O.C. Kit inspection & church parade. Company Pack & extra cape Keeves.	
-do-	10/9/17		Company in training at RANSART. Company employed on Drill. Rifle exercises & gas drill. Lecture to Officers & N.C.O. by C.O. & then on acting tender to Officers & N.C.O. by O.C.S. Practical work on acting tender to Officers & N.C.O. by O.C.S. Recruits squad instructed on Rorley drill & during drill by R.S.M. Blackburn D.S.	
-do-	11/9/17		Company in training, squad & physical drill. Gas drill. 15 by on Rapid Waving 15 by on preparing company position, trotting & tasking. Lecture by O.R.S. on organisation of a defensible position. Officers & N.C.O.'s on Rorley & during drill.	
-do-	12/9/17		Company in training, squad & physical drill. Company drill. 15 by on Rapid Waving 15 by on preparing chapes & tasking. Lecture & practical instruction to Officers & N.C.O. on storey parade by O.R.S. Recruits Litten Riding & during drill by R.S.M.	
-do-	13/9/17		Company in training squad drill rifle exercises, musketry, Rorley, trotting & tasking & overhauling equipment. Afternoon. Company Sports.	

W. Hodgart.
Major PS(?)
2nd (Burp..) Field Cy RE

OP 06

Army Form C. 2118.

WAR DIARY
or
INTELLIGENCE SUMMARY.
(Erase heading not required.)

Instructions regarding War Diaries and Intelligence Summaries are contained in F. S. Regs., Part II. and the Staff Manual respectively. Title pages will be prepared in manuscript.

Place	Date	Hour	Summary of Events and Information	Remarks and references to Appendices
N'age at RANSART R&Map 51C 1/4000	14/9/17		Company completed course of Musketry on RANSART ranges.	✓
-do-	15/9/17		Company employed on Rifle exercises, company drill & gas drill. 4 Company on Rapier wiring & by overhauling equipment afternoon company sports.	
-do-	16/9/17		Church parade & inspection by O.C. Coy.	
-do-	17/9/17		Company training. Company drill & gas drill. Practical demonstration to company by O.C. on strong points. Overhauling equipment & loading wagons.	
-do-	18/9/17	6.0 am	Camp struck & wagon loading completed.	
		9.0 am	Company left RANSART for march to PAS. in accordance with C.R.O. 80. M.O. No 23 @ 1.15 & 11th Bde S.C.I. No 111/5-55.	
		1.30 pm	Company arrived at PAS. & billeted	

Adjutant Major R+E
Ol+06 (?Stephens) 2nd in Coy R.E.

Army Form C. 2118.

WAR DIARY
or
INTELLIGENCE SUMMARY.
(Erase heading not required.)

Instructions regarding War Diaries and Intelligence Summaries are contained in F. S. Regs, Part II and the Staff Manual respectively. Title pages will be prepared in manuscript.

406TH (RENFREW) FIELD COMPANY R.E.

Place	Date	Hour	Summary of Events and Information	Remarks and references to Appendices
Hdqrs at PAS Ref Map LENS. II. F.S.	1917 19/9		Company in training. Company drill & gas drill. Trenching & loading wagons preparing for entrainment	
- do -	20/9	4.15PM 6.30AM	Transport left Pas for Mondicourt Station for entrainment. Dismounted units left arrive Mondicourt at 7.30AM entrainment completed at 9.0AM. left Mondicourt for Tilques Camp area at 9.10AM.	
		5.30pm	Arrived at Houpoutre detrained by 6.0pm.	
		6.15pm	Company left by road route for SALEM CAMP arrived at 8.0pm.	
		9pm	Main dinners completed on arrival camp site 11Ref 19MSCI 11/5555 @ 1817	
Hdqrs at SALEM CAMP X 39 c 3.4 Ref Map Sheet 19 S.E.	21/9/17		Company training. Squad & gas drill, knotting & lashing. Company parade & meeting latrines. Night marching for NCOs by compass	
- do -	22/9/17		Company in training. Physical, Squad & gas drill. Lecture on Lewis Mortar, trench hedging, knotting & splicing. Lecture on Maps reading night marching by compass for officers & NCOs.	

M.S. Hodyjh Major R.E. O/C. 0/c 406 (Renfrew) Field Coy R.E.

Army Form C. 2118.

406th Perform Field Cy RE
No 6
367

WAR DIARY
or
INTELLIGENCE SUMMARY.
(Erase heading not required.)

Instructions regarding War Diaries and Intelligence Summaries are contained in F.S. Regs., Part II. and the Staff Manual respectively. Title pages will be prepared in manuscript.

Place	Date	Hour	Summary of Events and Information	Remarks and references to Appendices
Hdqrs at SALEM CAMP X.39.C.2.4. Sheet N19 SE 1/40	23/9/17		Church Parade. Kit inspection. Lecture on map reading. Officers & NCOs night marching by permanent compass.	
—do—	24/9/17	2 pm	Company training. Including stores & equipment. Company inspected by Major Gen O.S.W. Matheson comdg 4th Div.	
—do—	25/9/17	3 pm	Company in training. Rifle exercises & bayonet drill. Company inspected in Marching order, arms & vehicles by Mr C.F. Freeman CRE 4th Div. 2 Officers & 100 O.R. attached to sent for work from 12th to Sep 18th. An average of tools & stores required for Strong points.	
—do—	26/9/17		Company training. Rifle exercises 500 drill, section guides instructed in use of prismatic compass. Flight made for Reston NCOs & Sappers. Attached infantry parties instructed in execution of wiring parties. Tracing trenches & strong points. O.C. & Section of NCOs near Loretto the time & work in progress as in the D3rd Field Coy RE.	

W. Hodgson
Major RE
OC 406th Perform field Cy RE

Army Form C. 2118.

WAR DIARY
or
INTELLIGENCE SUMMARY

(Erase heading not required.)

Instructions regarding War Diaries and Intelligence Summaries are contained in F.S. Regs., Part II. and the Staff Manual respectively. Title Pages will be prepared in manuscript.

Place	Date	Hour	Summary of Events and Information	Remarks and references to Appendices
H.Qrs at SALEM CAMP X29.C.24	24/7/17	7.30 AM	Dismounted personnel marched to INTERNATIONAL CORNER & entrained for ELVERDINGHE at 10.0 AM & marched to shelter camp at B.21.A.57.	
		8.30 AM	Mounted personnel left Salem Camp for shelter camp at B.21.A.57.	
		2.0 PM	No 9 Section proceeded to CANAL BANK for work in the night 24/25 with 4th Aust. Infantry.	
—do—	25/7/17	1.40 PM	No 4 Offrs 304 Other Ranks left Camp & marched to CANAL BANK at B.26.B.95. Old work taken over & relief completed by 7th Field By H.Q. Work started on repair of log track & trestle bridge across the STEENBEEK.	
H.Qrs at CANAL BANK B.26.B.95.	29/7/17		Working parties on log track over STEENBEEK Tramway track traced out & bridged. N°142019 Cpl Bryn J Wounded (Gassed) N°40397 Pte W Haslam Wounded (Gassed) N°42008 2nd Cpl Carlton J Wounded (Arm) Remained at duty.	
—do—	30/7/17		Working parties on Tramway Track to B.A.R. position E of STEENBEEK. 2 Sects repaired & patrolled. Repairing trestle bridge over STEENBEEK. Erecting hut baths on CANAL BANK. Repairing & removing shelters for Dressing station on CANAL BANK. Strength of Unit Officers 9 Other Ranks 311.	

McDougall Major R.E.
O.C. 4001th Brigade Field Coy R.E.

Army Form C. 2118.

WAR DIARY
or
INTELLIGENCE SUMMARY.
(Erase heading not required.)

Instructions regarding War Diaries and Intelligence Summaries are contained in F. S. Regs., Part II. and the Staff Manual respectively. Title pages will be prepared in manuscript.

A 06 / 7th Coy R.E.
V.II 23

Place	Date	Hour	Summary of Events and Information	Remarks and references to Appendices
HQrs at B.24.c.9.5. Ref. Map Sheet 28. NW	1/10/17		Strength of Unit Officers 211. Men employed on completion of tramways to battery positions on STEENBECK & WEEDON DUMP. Track cut from WEEDON DUMP to bivalve-type positions. Repair of trestle bridge over STEENBECK completion. Stones taken up for the repair of 60 pntr. bridge. Work on repair of aid post & erection of D.S. on CANAL BANK.	
-do-	2/10/17		Tramways completed to Howitzer battery. Shelters completed on the CANAL BANK. Aid post completed. Party erecting Dust Baths on CANAL BANK.	
-do-	3/10/17		Bridge for 60 pntr. completed over the STEENBECK. Excavating sites for Elephant shelters on CANAL BANK, erecting hunting accommodation in shelters on CANAL BANK.	
-do-	4/10/17		Erection of cubicles... completed on CANAL BANK. Excavation of sites & erecting Elephant shelters, erecting shelters in CANDLE TR. Erecting NISSEN HUTS & transport lines in SIEGE CAMP.	

J. M. Lee Capt R.E.(T)
for O.C. 406 (Wessex) Field Coy R.E.

Army Form C. 2118.

WAR DIARY
or
INTELLIGENCE SUMMARY

(Erase heading not required.)

405TH (RENFREW) FIELD COMPANY R.E.
No. 2
9.17

Instructions regarding War Diaries and Intelligence Summaries are contained in F.S. Regs., Part II. and the Staff Manual respectively. Title pages will be prepared in manuscript.

Place	Date	Hour	Summary of Events and Information	Remarks and references to Appendices
Hqrs at Bu.Eg. 5 Ref Map Sht N°2 8 N.W.	5/9/17		Company employed erecting shelters in PANDLE TR. & CANAL BANK. laying concrete floor in Scut Battles, erecting Nissen Huts & latrine standings at SIEGE CORNER.	
-do-	6/9/17		Erecting Elephant shelters in CANAL BANK. 6 shelters completed on PANDLE TR. Erecting NISSEN HUTS on CANAL BANK & transport lines.	
Hqrs at PANDLE TR	7/9/17		Working parties erecting NISSEN HUTS for Divl. H.Qrs on CANAL BANK, & Elephant shelters erected on CANAL BANK. Honoured work on extension & maintenance of B.TRACK taken over from 526 (Aberdeen) Field Coy R.E. 8 Elephant shelters erected in PANDLE TR. N°202012 Sapr M°Milliam Wm Killed in Action "430036" Laing D.T. G. Action Killed & buried at V24.C.7.7 Ref Map Sheet N°28. S.W.	
		2.0 pm	Major M°L. 194 Scots proceeded to live in PANDLE TR. Assembly line drawn and marked for 10th Bn.	
-do-	8/9/17		Working parties extending & maintaining B.TRACK. 4 Elephant shelters completed in PANDLE TR, erecting NISSEN HUTS & elephant shelters on CANAL BANK. N°497187 Sapr FINLAY Wounded in Action	
-do-	9/9/17		Working parties employed on extension & marking out B.TRACK. erection of NISSEN HUTS completed on CANAL BANK. excavating sites for P.S. on CANAL BANK. MAJOR. M. HODGART Killed in Action (Shell) at V.24.B.6.0. Buried at B.26.6.74. MAP NR 28. BELGIUM No. 420405 Sapr MOULTRIE.R.J Wounded (Shell) 430359 " SPIERS.A.J Action 420371 " CRAIG.D. Shell Shock (Evacuated)	

A5834 Wt.W4973/M687 750,000 8/16 D.D.&L.Ltd. Forms/C.2118/13.

J.R. [signature] Capt. R.E.(T)
for OC 405th (Renfrew) Field Cy R.E.

Army Form C. 2118.

WAR DIARY
or
INTELLIGENCE SUMMARY
(Erase heading not required.)

Instructions regarding War Diaries and Intelligence Summaries are contained in F.S. Regs., Part II. and the Staff Manual respectively. Title Pages will be prepared in manuscript.

406th (RENFREW) FIELD COMPANY, R.E.
No. 3
Date 17.17

Place	Date	Hour	Summary of Events and Information	Remarks and references to Appendices
Hqrs at CANDLE TR C.9.a.1.4. Ref Map Sheet 28 N.W.	10/10/17		Working parties employed erecting shelters on CANAL BANK, erecting NISSEN HUTS & horse standings at SIEGE CAMP, ELVERDINGHE. Covered section employed on maintenance & extension of B TRACK. No. 420242 Serjt STEWART J. Wounded in Action. (Shell)	
-do-	11/10/17		Working parties employed on repair & maintenance of TRACK B. erecting elephant shelters on CANAL BANK, erecting NISSEN HUTS & horse standings at SIEGE CAMP.	
-do-	12/10/17	5.0 pm	Working parties employed on repair & maintenance of TRACK B. French-horsed track laspes and & pankers to FERDAN HOUSE, erecting NISSEN HUTS & horse standings at SIEGE CAMP, erecting elephant shelters on CANAL BANK. No.3 S.et personnel from CANAL BANK to SIEGE CAMP.	
-do-	13/10/17		Parties employed on extension & repair of B TRACK. Dirt baths completed on CANAL BANK, erecting shelters on CANAL BANK & NISSEN HUTS in SIEGE CAMP. Parties of Officers N.C.O.s & Men of the 309th Field Coy R.E. taken over work in progress	
-do-	14/10/17	9.0 am 2.0 pm	All work in progress handed over to 309th Field Coy R.E. Relief completed. Dismounted personnel left PRINGLE 7.09 marched to ELVERDINGHE. Company entrained & detrained at PROVEN & marched to PORTSDOWN CAMP. Transport arrived & company concentrated at PORTSDOWN CAMP.	

J.W. Bell, Major R.E.
O.C. 406th Renfrew Field Coy R.E.

Army Form C. 2118.

WAR DIARY
or
INTELLIGENCE SUMMARY
(Erase heading not required.)

Instructions regarding War Diaries and Intelligence Summaries are contained in F. S. Regs., Part II. and the Staff Manual respectively. Title Pages will be prepared in manuscript.

Place	Date	Hour	Summary of Events and Information	Remarks and references to Appendices
Hdqrs at PROVEN PORTSDOWN CAMP	15/10/17		Company at Portsdown Camp. Company drill & overhauling stores & equipment.	
HAZEBROUK SHEET N°5	16/10/17	9.0 AM	Company marched from Portsdown Camp by march route for St Jan ter Biezen	
- do -		1-0 PM	Arrived at St Jan ter Biezen & billeted in Road Camp.	
HDQRS AT ROAD CAMP HAZEBROUK SHEET N° 5	17/10/17		Company in training. Squad drill & gas drill. Company needs & digging drains on Camp Brigade transport lines.	
- do -	18/10/17	7.30 PM	Company in training. Squad drill & gas drill. Transport left camp by route march moved to Peselhoek Station.	
		8.30 PM	Dismounted personnel left camp & marched to " "	
		11.0 PM	Company at Peselhoek. to entrain for XVII Corps area.	
	19/10/17	3.30 AM	Company entrained vehicles ready to move at 5-30 AM.	
		6.0 AM	Train left Peselhoek Station for Margeuil arrived at 2-15 PM. company detrained & marched to Bouvres.	
		5-3 PM	More Company killed.	
			N° 220295 Sapper McLaughlin J. accidentally injured whilst loading wagons.	

John Bell. Capt R.E.
O.C. ......Company Field Cycle

2449 Wt. W14957/M90 750,000 1/16 J.B.C. & A. Forms/C.2118/12.

Army Form C. 2118.

WAR DIARY
or
INTELLIGENCE SUMMARY

(Erase heading not required.)

Instructions regarding War Diaries and Intelligence Summaries are contained in F. S. Regs., Part II. and the Staff Manual respectively. Title Pages will be prepared in manuscript.

406TH (SCOTTISH) FIELD COMPANY. R.E.

Date 23/10/17

Place	Date	Hour	Summary of Events and Information	Remarks and references to Appendices
H.Qrs at GOUPES Ref Map LENS.II.	20/10/17		Company in training. Company drill & gas drill. Working vehicles, equipment & instructing stores. No. 534461 Sapr GARDNER W.J. (Wd auxiliary) Recvd in B.C. HARBARC.	
- do -	21/10/17		Company inspection. Church parade. Sports during afternoon.	
- do -	22/10/17		Company in training. Company & squad drill. Lectures & demonstration on gas. Rugby sports.	
- do -	23/10/17		Company in training. Company drill, musketry & lashings. Lectures by R.C. Officers on demolitions. Parties of Officers & N.C.O's men proceeded to line in MONCHY Sector to take over work of the 70th Field Coy R.E. Capt J.S. CRAMHALL R.E. took over command of unit.	

J.S.Hunter Capt R.E.
O/C 406 (Scottish) Field Coy R.E.

WAR DIARY
or
INTELLIGENCE SUMMARY.

(Erase heading not required.)

Army Form C. 2118.

406TH (RENFREW) FIELD COMPANY, R.E.
No. 6
Date 27.4.47

Place	Date	Hour	Summary of Events and Information	Remarks and references to Appendices
H'qrs at GOUVES Ref Map LENS, 11.	24/10/17	7:30AM	Company left GOUVES by March route to new area, H.qrs M⁰⁵ 2,3 & 4 Sections to forward area at N.3.c.4.6. N⁰ 1 Sect & transport to G.28.a.6.6. Ref Map 51.B. 5000. to relieve the 90th Field Coy R.E.	
		3.0PM	Move completed. 3 O.R. joined unit from Base.	
H'qrs at N.3.c.4.6. Ref Map 51.B 1/10000	25/10/17		Working parties employed on erecting A frames & revetting front line trenches with XPM panels, erecting A frames, revetting trenches, & forming fire steps in PAYMISTER T.? Parties employed carrying stores up to forward dumps.	
-do-	26/10/17		Night & Day working parties employed deepening & widening front line trenches & erecting A frames & revetting with XPM panels. Erecting A frames & revetting CAYMISTER & PIER AVES. Enemy action enemy trench mortaring hors d'oeuvres & lents on Langford lines.	
-do-	27/10/17		Working parties continued work erecting A frames & revetting CAYMISTER & PIER AVES. Erecting A frames revetting deepening & widening front line trenches. Enemy action employed erecting horse standings & lents on Pathfinding lines. Hissen huts completed at PEC & J. ADRIAN huts started. 19th H.10020 Sapper BROWN. T. ? removed to 93571 PIONEER ROSS W. ? Sec. (Sick)	
-do-	28/10/17		Working parties employed erecting frames & revetting front line trenches, & laying trench boards. Deepening & widening trench, erecting A frames revetting panels & Laying trench boards on front line trenches. Enemy action erecting horse standings & lents on Pathfinding lines, 1 ADRIAN hut completed.	

J. Carshill Capt R.E.
O.C. 406th (Renfrew) Field Coy R.E.

WAR DIARY
or
INTELLIGENCE SUMMARY.
(Erase heading not required.)

Army Form C. 2118.

Place	Date	Hour	Summary of Events and Information	Remarks and references to Appendices
H⁰⁰ʳˢ ᵃᵗ N₂L.H.S. 84 Map 57B 1/40000	29/7/17		Working parties continued work erecting A frames 9 P.M. revetting in front line trenches, erecting A frames & revetting in BANNISTER AVE & ROAAVE. Trench shelter completed for MONCKY DUMP. Men either employed erecting tents & horse standings on transport lines. 2ⁿᵈ ADRIAN hut completed.	
- do -	30/7/17		Work on erecting frames, revetting & trench boards laid in front line trenches. Revetting & clearing out PIKAAVE. Erecting frames, revetting & laying trench boards in BANNISTER AVE. New line of duckwalk toped out from junction of DALE TR & BANNISTER AVE to HIGHLAND SUPPORT in left sub sector. Men not employed erecting horse standings & huts on transport lines.	
- do -	31/7/17		Working parties employed erecting A frames revetting frames & laying trench boards in front of line trenches. Deepening & widening & revetting PIER AVE. Erecting frames revetting, clearing & drawing BANNISTER AVE. New line of DALE TR excavated and for 200 yards to a depth of 3'.	
	31/7/17		Strength of Unit 9 Officers 202 other ranks.	

J. R. Marshall
Capt R.E.
O.C. 406 (Renfrew) Field Coy R.E.

C.R.E.
4th Division

Herewith War
Diary for the
month of November
1914

J F Crawshall

Major R.E.

406TH
(RENFREW)
FIELD COMPANY, R.E.
No.
Date

3/12/17

WAR DIARY
OCTOBER 1917
Nov

408TH (RENFREW)
FIELD COMPANY, R.E.

Army Form C. 2118.

WAR DIARY
or
INTELLIGENCE SUMMARY
(Erase heading not required.)

Instructions regarding War Diaries and Intelligence Summaries are contained in F.S. Regs., Part II. and the Staff Manual respectively. Title pages will be prepared in manuscript.

406TH (RENFREW) FIELD COMPANY, R.E.
No ...... Date 10/7/1917

Place	Date	Hour	Summary of Events and Information	Remarks and references to Appendices
H'qrs at N.2.c.2.3. Ref Map 51.B.2/40	1/7/17		Strength of Unit. 7 Officers 202 Other Ranks. Working parties employed revetting CANISTER AVE & PEAR ALLEY, erecting revetting frames & revetting trenches in front line trenches. NEW DALE TR. Excavation completed for 200 yds. Pier section employed sorting duck/sawings & huts on Divl Transport lines.	
- do -	2/7/17		Working parties employed revetting NEW DALE TR., Repairing & revetting front line & communication trenches. Building & laying trench boards in CANISTER TR. & PEAR AVE. No 490915 T/Cpl Newman D. J. wounded in action. 546662 Sgt Mathie W. } (Shell Splinter) 533140 " Lullabor H. } wounded in action, remained at duty.	
- do -	3/7/17		Working parties employed on excavation of DALE TR. Revetting PAAR & PANISTER AVE. Deepening & widening & revetting front line trenches, Building & laying trench boards in NEW DALE TR. 1 D.R. reported unit from Base.	
- do -	4/7/17		Excavation of NEW DALE TR. completed, parties revetting & clearing PAAR & CANISTER TRS. Erecting frames & revetting front line trenches, revetting & laying trench boards in NEW DALE TR. 9 O.R. joined unit from Base.	
- do -	5/7/17		Working parties employed revetting & tanklaying NEW DALE TR. Deepening & revetting PAAR, CANISTER & front line trenches. Work started on improving & revetting sapes at N-12. Pier section employed erecting horse standings & huts on Divl Transport lines.	
- do -	6/7/17		Company employed on revetting & tanklaying & tank bordering front line trenches, sapes & PEAR CANISTER TRS. Building & travel dressing NEW DALE TR. Pier section employed making roads laying brick floors & stalls in Divl Transport Lines.	

J Marshall
Major R.E.
Officer i/c (Renfrew) Field Coy RE.

WAR DIARY or INTELLIGENCE SUMMARY

Army Form C. 2118.

Instructions regarding War Diaries and Intelligence Summaries are contained in F. S. Regs., Part II. and the Staff Manual respectively. Title pages will be prepared in manuscript.

(Erase heading not required.)

Place	Date	Hour	Summary of Events and Information	Remarks and references to Appendices
H.Q. 2H NB.C.93 104 MDP Sht 51 B	7/11/17		Company employed mending existing tracks on NEW DALE TK. Repairing & widening CANISTER AV. & PER. AV. Building & repairing approach corduroys for gun pits at various areas on PER CAVE. Coys. relieved employed mending & laying horse standings on Our transport lines.	
— do —	8/11/17		Company employed mending tracks & mending front line tracks & duckboards near NEW DALE TK. Building & repairing NEW DALE TK. Formations for 2nd Battn. got also completed on PER. AVE. Building & repairing PICK & MINSTER AV. Per. section mending tracks & horse standings on our transport lines.	
— do —	9/11/17		Company employed mending trackboards, existing tracks & cubby holes in NEW DALE TK. mending approaches to Wing Pill AV. & approach Nº 125 completed. New section mending FLORIAH tracks on transport lines, 1 bed completed.	
— do —	10/11/17		Company employed mending, existing tracks in front line mending existing tracks & mending stations in DALE TR. Building & repairing PILATE AV. & approach. Repairing & improving H.Q. Dug Out in SHRAPNEL TK. New section mending tracks & horse standings on transport lines. 1 MISSEN HUT completed.	
— do —	11/11/17		Company building existing tracks & frame stations in NEW DALE TR. Building & repairing Pilate AV & PILATE AVE granaries. Repairing & mending N.G supplies in SHRAPNEL TR. 1 CAMAS shelter completed for Green Road & coys. in PER. CAVE.	
— do —	12/11/17		Company employed existing tracks of first flights in DALE TK. & mending T.H. Empt'n in HILL SUPPORT. N.G. supplies completed in SHRAPNEL TK. Building & mending PICK AV. & Supt Sections granaries on dug-outs.	
— do —	13/11/17		Company employed mending & existing tracks & ext'by running stations on NEW DALE TR. mending & mending Sap. front line & PICK AV. Nos. 4 & 5 approach completed. 2 O.P. frames mint from BASE. CAIRNS.	

A.P.O 6 (Refence) Field Coy. R.E.

Major R.E.

/ Army Form C. 2118.

WAR DIARY
or
INTELLIGENCE SUMMARY.
(Erase heading not required.)

Place	Date	Hour	Summary of Events and Information	Remarks and references to Appendices
N490 A N24 B3 Ref Map Sheet 51 B Gine	14/7		Working parties employed revetting & framing T.M. Empts in HILL SUPPORT entrance bay, framing fronts in DRIE 7A revetting & revetting 2 frames in sap & front line trenches, enemy would front in Gun Boot store in BENTAVE NR 430193 Sergt Reid H 430301 L/Cpl Miles S } Wounded 412996 Sapr Cunningham A } (Gassed) Shell T.M. 3 O.R. gassed send from Base	
- do -	15/7		Company employed revetting & framing saps, revetting & clearing P.O. AH. Revetting storeholdings & erecting loopholes & cubby holes in DRIE 7A framing for G.B. store in PICK CAVE erected, Loophole erected, 6 holes cubby points in DRIE 7A completed in PICK CAVE	
- do -	16/7		Company employed revetting cubby holes loopholes & entering pumping points in DRIE 7A. Revetting & clearing PICK AH, revetting saps & front line trenches	
- do -	17/7		Company employed revetting front line & Saps nos 9&12 also completed trenches cubby holes & revetting DRIE 7A. Excavating & framing pumping points in sector 1 & 13 others completed in PICK CAVE.	
- do -	18/7		Working parties revetting & clearing BENFAVE & super Revetting & revetting. Excavating, framing pumping points & drainage of DRIE 7A.	
- do -	19/7		Working parties employed revetting & clearing PICK AH & Pick AH Excavating & framing pumping points in Front Line & DRIE 7A. Taking dets: L/Cpl Miles, Sapr. Cunn A/S	
- do -	20/7		Company employed making clearing & laying track from SWORD LANE through MENSHY to GREEN LANED. Clearing & Laying CAVE at LE FOSSE Fm for Coy H.Qrs. No work done in the line owing to operations.	

[signature] Major R.E.
O.C. 406th (Renfrew) Field Coy R.E.

WAR DIARY or INTELLIGENCE SUMMARY

Army Form C. 2118.

403rd (RENFREW) FIELD COMPANY, R.E.

Place	Date	Hour	Summary of Events and Information	Remarks and references to Appendices
Hyvart N2.c.8.3. Ref Map 51.B.	21/4/17		Working parties employed clearing & marking out Mule Track in MONCHY Trench System & clearing front line trenches & dugouts. Building & laying Track boards in PER HVE. Clearing & building FOSSE AVE. accommodation dugouts for a section. No. 3 Sect moved into FOSSE CAVE.	
-do-	22/4/17		Parties working on Mule Track through MONCHY. Clearing & forming and DOLE PR Building front line trenches & dugs. Building & Track boards PER HVE. Clearing & making accommodation in FOSSE CAVE. No. 1 Sect moved & billeted on FOSSE AVE.	
-do-	23/4/17		Parties employed marking & clearing front line Trenches & extension of pumping points making & laying Track boards in PER AVE. Gun test stores in PER AVE completed. Clearing & building accommodation in FOSSE CAVE.	
Hqrs at FOSSE CAVE No. 1 & 2 Sect Nos. 3 & 4 Sections SHEET St. B.	24/4/17	11-0pm	Hqrs 4th Sect moved to FOSSE CAVE. Parties employed extending pumping stations in DOLE 78 & front lines marking & clearing saps. Building & clearing PER AVE. Building accommodation in FOSSE CAVE.	
-do-	25/4/17		Parties employed marking front line Trenches & accommodation revetting & forming pumping points. Extending pumping points & revetting DOLE 78. Building & trench-boarding of saps completed.	
-do-	26/4/17		Parties employed revetting front line Trenches & extending pumping points in front line TRISTER & DOLE 78. Building & clearing PER AVE & Building DOLE 78.	
-do-	27/4/17		Parties employed revetting & sinking pumping points in DOLE & front line Trenches. Building, Trenchboarding & repairs of PER AVE. Elephant shelter at 1890.4930 started.	
-do-	28/4/17		Elephant shelter at 1890.4930 completed. Work on main CAMBRAI RD & MONCHY DEFENCES taken over from the 526th (Durham) Yth Fd. Cy. R.E. Work on C.T's & front line trenches from PER AVE to CASEMILEY handed over to 9th Field Coy R.E. Work of work on drainage & maintenance & repair of MONCHY Defences, repair of main CAMBRAI Rd., Rest to work on drainage & maintenance of DOLE 78 front line trench not CASEMILEY with BRIDDON & HIGHLAND SUPPORT.	

M. Mashall Major R.E.
O/C 403rd (Renfrew) Field Cy R.E.

WAR DIARY
or
INTELLIGENCE SUMMARY.

Army Form C. 2118.

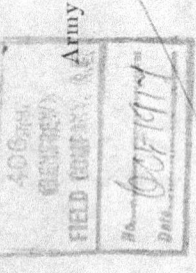

Place	Date	Hour	Summary of Events and Information	Remarks and references to Appendices
HQ at N11.A.n.3 Fosseaux By Hqs J.1.B.25.20	29/7		Company employed on repair & maintenance of CIRCLE TR, EAST RESERVE & ORCHARD TR including cook-houses in VINE AVE & EAST RESERVE. erection of salt for dead changing also repair & maintenance of DALE TR. erecting new observing posts in CANISTER AVE & Sap 12. Killing in & stamping eater track on AMBARI RD. 3 O.R. found unit from Base.	
-do-	30/7		Working parties revetting EAST RESERVE & ORCHARD TR. Cleaning & revetting CIRCLE TR. Erecting cook-house in VINE AVE & EAST RESERVE. Excavating jumping points in DALE TR. Company just completed filling in crater & shell holes on AMBARI RD & CRATER SUNK. Strength at next day 205 Other Ranks.	

F Marks Major RE
O.C. 406th (Renfrew) Field Coy R.E.

Army Form C. 2118.

WAR DIARY
or
INTELLIGENCE SUMMARY.

(Erase heading not required.)

Instructions regarding War Diaries and Intelligence Summaries are contained in F. S. Regs., Part II. and the Staff Manual respectively. Title pages will be prepared in manuscript.

406TH (GENFIELD) FIELD COMPANY, R.E.

406 4th Army CA sh 26

Place	Date	Hour	Summary of Events and Information	Remarks and references to Appendices
Hqrs at FOSSE CAVE Map. Ref. N.12.a.3.3 Sheet 51B 40000	1/12/17 to 4/12/17		STRENGTH OF UNIT 4 Officers, 203 O.R. Company employed on repair & maintenance of MONCHY DEFENCES, DOLE & CANISTER TR. repair & filling in shell holes on CAMBRAI RD between LA BERGERE & CRATER SUBWAY. Clearing & filling in shell holes on MULE TRACK from SWORDLANE through MONCHY to GREEN LANE. Repair of CAMBRAI RD completed on 22nd 4 Tank. 2/Lieut C.L. Stuart evacuated sick to U.K. 2/12/17.	
-do-	5/12/17 to 15/12/17		Wiring of reserve line. MONCHY DEFENCES started, parties employed on repair of MONCHY DEFENCES, DOLE & CANISTER TR. repair & upkeep of tank road from SWORDLANE to MONCHY & VINE PRE. erecting two curtains & Lurking dug-outs in sector. 4 O.R. joined unit from Base on the 4/12/17	
-do-	16/12/17 to 23/12/17		Company employed on wiring of RESERVE LINE. repair & maintenance of MONCHY DEFENCES. Erecting two curtains & bunks in dug-outs. repair & upkeep of W.R. tracks. Relaxation of RIFLEE TR from O.1.d.15.95. to O.1.b.26.15. started on the 16/12/17. Electric lighting of FOSSE CAVE Hqrs completed on the 31st Decr. Evacuation of Day-outs at H.36.C.1.1.5. started on the 21st Decr. Roads on TWIN COPSE recommended & gravel laid to DOLE TR. Dumps formed in DOLE with stores for proposed communication trench to TWIN COPSE. Wiring of reserve line completed on the 22 Decr. Work in O9 B TR. Sector handed over to 556th Durham Field Coy R.E. 2/Lieut E.J Ingleby joined unit 17/12/17 as reinforcement	

J. Crawhall Major R.E.
R.C.M.O. 406th Genfield Field Coy. R.E.

Army Form C. 2118.

WAR DIARY
or
INTELLIGENCE SUMMARY.
(Erase heading not required.)

Instructions regarding War Diaries and Intelligence Summaries are contained in F. S. Regs., Part II. and the Staff Manual respectively. Title pages will be prepared in manuscript.

Place	Date	Hour	Summary of Events and Information	Remarks and references to Appendices
FOSSE CAVE	1/4/17 to 23/4/17		Company employed on the repair & maintenance of MINING DEFENCES. Extension of Rgtl Aid Post in CIRCLET started, overhauling trench frames. Track from SWORD LANE to VINE. Excavation of dug-outs at H.34. Q.4.R. Work on improving accomodation on BROWNLINE started on 24 inst Work on trench aids & erecting fire steps on new intermediate line started on the 26 inst.	
N.12. a 3.3 Sheet N° 51.B.	24/4/17 to 31/4/17		Mining in front of network line at GORDON avenue started on 30 inst. Lieut R. Thomson admitted to hospital 24/4/17. Strength of Unit, 7 Officers, 194 O.R.	

J. Marshall
Major R.E.
O.R. 206th Bigadeer Field Coy R.E.

4th Division

406th Field Company R.E.

~~January to December 1918~~

~~Jan - Dec 1919~~
     June

1918 JAN — 1919 JUNE

Vol 26

War Diary
January 1918

406th
(RENFREW)
FIELD COMPANY, R.E.
No.
Date

Army Form C. 2118.

[Stamp: 496TH (RENFREW) FIELD COMPANY, R.E.]

WAR DIARY
of
INTELLIGENCE SUMMARY.
(Erase heading not required.)

Instructions regarding War Diaries and Intelligence Summaries are contained in F. S. Regs., Part II. and the Staff Manual respectively. Title pages will be prepared in manuscript.

Place	Date	Hour	Summary of Events and Information	Remarks and references to Appendices
Headquarters At No Boscourt camp N.23.3 Sheet 51BNW 11140.0.00	1/1/18 to 5/1/18		Strength of Company on 1st January 1918 - 4. Officers 197 Other Ranks. Company employed on the Repair and maintenance of the trenches forming the MONCHY DEFENCES, including the reclamation of CIRCLE TRENCH. Shelter excavated for Air Raid in CIRCLE TRENCH, - complete 5/1/18. Work continued on the excavation of artillery dugout at H.34.d.4.8. Recess sinking and gas proof doors in dugouts in EAST RESERVE. Commencing up de Brosse Work North Bank, Lance by an underground tunnel under CAMBRAI ROAD - length excavated to 5/1/18 - 28'6". Increasing and improving accommodation at BROWN LINE - North North side of CAMBRAI ROAD. Continued work on mining INTERMEDIATE LINE, in front of GORDON AVENUE. Mining in front of the Boeta Lapre (not in France) Mentum to Coy from J.B. MUNDELL admitted to hospital 4/1/18. Four Sappers reinforcements joined unit on 4/1/18. Lieut R. STEVENSON discharged from field ambulance 6/1/18 and proceeded on leave to U.K. 4/1/18 to 21/1/18 and since officially notified to be granted extension of leave on medical grounds until 4/2/18.	

J. Mitchell
M. U. Coll (Renfrew) Field Co RE
Major RE

Army Form C. 2118.

WAR DIARY
of
INTELLIGENCE SUMMARY.
(Erase heading not required.)

409TH
RENFREW
FIELD COMPANY, R.E.
No.
Date.

Instructions regarding War Diaries and Intelligence Summaries are contained in F. S. Regs., Part II. and the Staff Manual respectively. Title pages will be prepared in manuscript.

Place	Date	Hour	Summary of Events and Information	Remarks and references to Appendices
Headquarters at Rea to Boyelle bank N12.a.3.3. Sheet 51 B NW 1/10,000	6/1/18 to 14/1/18		Continuation of work on the drain and maintenance of the trenches forming the MONCHY DEFENCES and the drain with duck-board tracks. Work continued on the excavation for artillery dugout at H3 a d A.8. Excess bunking and gas screen doors at dugouts in CIRCLE TRENCH and ORCHARD RESERVE. Increasing and improving accommodation at BROWN LINE on the north and south sides of CAMBRAI ROAD. Wiring in front of Boyelle bank, from a point N12.c.15.85. to N.b. H.O. #5, completed 8/1/18. Tracing out Intermediate Line (lately called) Reserve Line - 2nd system. - Trench dug 1 foot deep by Infantry, under R.E. supervision. Excavate for machine gun emplacement (I4) at Boyelle north bank completed 14/1/18. Excavate for machine gun emplacement shelters (R1+R2) in GORDON AVENUE. Tracing out SUPPORT LINE. 2nd system. completed 13/1/18. Infantry under R.E. supervision. Underground tunnel connecting up the Boyelle north bank caves completed 13/1/18. Total length 1/2 feet. Excavating machine gun dugouts R6 at O.4.a. H.Q.29.-R.7. at O.a. 40.95. Off.J.B. Rundell officer from trench 12/1/18 12/1/18 J Marshall	2/Lieut R.E. 2/Lieut R.E. H Saper unsuccessful 2/Lieut R.E.

WAR DIARY
INTELLIGENCE SUMMARY.
(Erase heading not required.)

Army Form C. 2118.

406TH (RENFREW) FIELD COMPANY, R.E.

Instructions regarding War Diaries and Intelligence Summaries are contained in F. S. Regs., Part II. and the Staff Manual respectively. Title pages will be prepared in manuscript.

Place	Date	Hour	Summary of Events and Information	Remarks and references to Appendices
Headquarters at kn. Boris bar p N.D.a.3.3. Sheet 51B. N.W. 1/40,000	15th To 22nd		Continued repairs and maintenance of the tracks forming the MONCHY DEFENCES and the repair of the dick-board tracks. Work continued on the excavating for artillery dugout at HEAD H.8. Increasing and improving accommodation at BROWN LINE - North-West side of CAMBRAI ROAD. Tracing out SUPPORT LINE, 2nd system, in preparation for Infantry to dig. Tracing out RESERVE LINE, 2nd system, in preparation for Infantry to dig. Excavations continued for small elephant shelter at M.G. Emplacements R.1, R.2. - GORDON AVENUE, shelter at R.4 completed 18/1/18 and at R.1 - 19/1/18. Excavations at M.G. dugouts. R.6 - O.Y.a. 40.20, & R.7, O.a. 40, 95, completed 22/1/18. Repair and maintenance of water pipe track at BROWN LINE, taken over on 20/1/18. Lieut. C. McN. H. BROWN - M.C. admitted sick to Field Ambulance on 18/1/18 and evacuated to b.C.S. 19/1/18. Two Sappers and two driver reinforcements joined unit 22/1/18.	

J. Marshall
O.C. 406th (Renfrew) Field Coy R.E.
Major R.E.

Army Form C. 2118.

WAR DIARY
INTELLIGENCE SUMMARY.
(Erase heading not required.)

Instructions regarding War Diaries and Intelligence Summaries are contained in F. S. Regs., Part II. and the Staff Manual respectively. Title pages will be prepared in manuscript.

[Stamp: 406TH (GENFREW) FIELD COMPANY, R.E. 3 Aug 1918]

Places	Date	Hour	Summary of Events and Information	Remarks and references to Appendices
Headquarters at Reserve Line N.12.a.3.3 Sheet 51BNW 1/10,000	21/1/18 to 31/1/18		Continuation of work on the repair and maintenance of the tracks forming the MONCHY DEFENCES, and the repair of the duckboard tracks.	
			Continuation of work on the excavating for dugout at H.3u.d. M.R. artillery increasing and improving accomodation at BROWN LINE — north, which since the CAMBRAI ROAD. Erecting bunking and gas screw doors in dugouts in ORCHARD TRENCH.	
			Repairs to deanville railway at 248 Battery, completed 25/1/18. Repairing and maintaining water pipe track at BROWN LINE. Burying M.M.G. dugout in GORDON AVENUE, completed 24/1/18. Forty two notice boards. "GAP" fixed, to denote gaps in wire in front of Reserve Line - 2nd system. Erecting bunks in dugouts at Rly Breeze, also erected cookhouses. Completed excavation (already started) at M.G. dugout H.76.b, 2.0. wounded (shell) 24/1/18.	
			No. 143301 Sapper KIDNEY, J., wounded (shell) 26/1/18. One Sapper reinforcement joined unit 31/1/18. Notification received on 31/1/18, of the award of the CROIX DE GUERRE (Belgian decoration) to No. 420234 Sapper (acr.cpl.) TOWNS. W. Strength of Company at 31/1/18 — 4 Officers (including 2 officers in hospital) — 219. Other Ranks.	

J.C. Campbell Major R.E.
O.C. 406th (Renfrew) Field Coy R.E.

Vol 27

Mr Deans

406th
(RENFREW)
FIELD COMPANY, R.E.
2 May 1918

WAR DIARY or INTELLIGENCE SUMMARY

Army Form C. 2118.

(Erase heading not required.)

Place	Date	Hour	Summary of Events and Information	Remarks and references to Appendices
Hqrs at Les Fosses Farm N.11.a.3.3 Sheet 51BNW 1/40,000	1/2/18 to 6/2/18		Company employed on the repair and maintenance of the trenches forming the Northern Defences. Increasing accommodation at the BROWN LINE - Work kept back since MCAMBRAI ROAD. - Maintaining the spare H water pipe track to the BROWN LINE water supply. Continuation of work on Artillery dugout at H 3.d.4.8. Commenced O.P. at HUSSAR LANE, N.8.a.0.65. Commenced Barra "Gap" denuding gaps in wire of the Intermediate line, erected complete on 5th inst. Company relieved by the 132nd Field Coy RE 15th Division and moved to SCHRAMM BARRACKS PERP on 6th inst. Move completed 8/30pm - 6/2/18; and Headquarters established at SCHRAMM BARRACKS ARRAS. 1 Officer reinforcement - 2nd Lieut D.R. BALFOUR joined unit 6/2/18. Strength of unit on 1st inst - Officers 9. Other Ranks 218.	
Coy Hqrs SCHRAMM BARRACKS "ARRAS" LENS II Sheet	4/2/18 to 16/2/18		Company employed on the general cleaning up of temporary parade and marching Order Kit also on Physical training. Lectures instructional parade also on Trainings Machine Gun and Lewis Gun. Inspection of Company march forward by C.R.E. 4th Division on 11th inst. Inspection of Company with transport by G.O.C. 4th Division on 15th inst. Capt J.B. MUNDELL - to R.E. School Rouen on 8/2/18. Lieut W. MOON - recalled from School on 9/2/18. Company moved from SCHRAMM BARRACKS ARRAS, to No.11. RUE DE L'ABBE HALLUIN, ARRAS on 16th inst. Company Headquarters established at No.1. RUE DE BEAUFORT ARRAS. Move completed 10 pm	

WAR DIARY
or
INTELLIGENCE SUMMARY

Army Form C. 2118.

406TH (RENFREW) FIELD COMPANY R.E.

Month: February 1918

Place	Date	Hour	Summary of Events and Information	Remarks and references to Appendices
Bjiv of No 1. at RUE DE BEAUFORT ARRAS	11/2/18 to 28/2/18		Company employed on manly bathing at GORDON AVENUE. and wiring at LESFOSSES. — completed 24/2/18. Commenced work on dugouts L2 and L3 at ORANGE HILL on 19th inst. and dugouts R1 + R4 at BROWN LINE on 25/2/18. Company billet bunker to sapper in course of construction for living quarters. Lewis gun received from Ordnance on 24/2/18 for use in firing line against hostile aircraft. LIEUT. R. STEVENSON unable to return from U.K. on account of prolonged influenza and struck off strength units with effect from 9/2/18. (authority W.O. letter G/Engrs/222 aug 7 dated 9/2/18). LIEUT. R. BALFOUR and no 420041 of Reel Campbell R. wounded (shells) 23/2/18. no 420041 a/Cpl Campbell P died from wounds at no. 19 C.C.S. 25/2/18. Sent MOON W. nominal from leave 26/2/18. — Baps J.B. MUNDELL rejoined from R.E. school of instruction 28/2/18. Strength of Company at 28/2/18. Officers 7. other ranks 216 (including 2 Officers w. attached)	

J Burgess Capt RE
pp O.C.
406TH (RENFREW) FIELD COMPANY R.E.

4th Div.

WAR DIARY

406th (RENFREW) FIELD COMPANY, R.E.

MARCH

1918

WO 95
WA 28

War Diary -
406th (Renfrew) Field Coy RE

406TH
(RENFREW)
FIELD COMPANY, R.E.
No.
Date March 1916

SECRET

Army Form C. 2118.

403RD (RENFREW) FIELD COMPANY, R.E.
Month: March 1918

WAR DIARY

INTELLIGENCE SUMMARY.
(Erase heading not required.)

Instructions regarding War Diaries and Intelligence Summaries are contained in F. S. Regs., Part II. and the Staff Manual respectively. Title pages will be prepared in manuscript.

Place	Date	Hour	Summary of Events and Information	Remarks and references to Appendices
Coy HQrs situated at No 1 Rue de Beaufort ARRAS. Reference maps LENS. 11. 1/100,000 and sheet FRANCE. 51BNW and 51BSW 1/20000	1/3/18 to 22/3/18		Strength of Company on 1st March 1918 = Officers 7, Other Ranks 212. Wiring on own line at GORDON AVENUE complete on 1/3/18. Company working on the excavation for four dugouts situate at ORANGE HILL H.34.B.8.5. & H.34.b.8.7. and at BROWN LINE N4.04.7. + N.4.c.N.2.) Wiring on RESERVE LINE - THIRD SYSTEM, at SWORD LANE, sect. of 51st ARRAS: CAMBRAI ROAD. Captain J.B.MUNDELL rejoined unit on 11/3/18 on completion of course of instruction at R.E. School of Instruction. ²/Lieut. R. BRAND and ²/Lieut. J. CHADWICK joined unit as reinforcements on 1/3/18. MAJOR J.S. CRANDALL, M.C. proceeded on leave to U.K. on 3/3/18 - Capt J.B. MUNDELL assumed temporary command of unit during the absence on leave of Major J.S. Crandall M.C. ²/Lieut. G.D.MACADAM, joined unit as reinforcement on 6/3/18. LIEUT. W. MOON, transferred to No.8. Railway Coy R.E., 9/3/18 19 Saprs transferred to Railway Base Depot 11/3/18. LIEUT. H.K.ABRAM proceeded on leave to U.K. 19/3/18. Notification received that LIEUT C.M.N.H.BROWN. M.C. was evacuated sick to U.K. on 25/2/18 MAJOR J.S. CRANDALL, M.C., rejoined unit from leave on 19/3/18 and re-assumed command of unit. Company moved to STIRLING CAMP. - BLUE LINE, on 27/2/18 and relieved 45th. Field Coy R.E., 15th Division, in work on the line. Work completed by H R.M. 27/3/18, and Company Headquarters established at H.13.b.40.10.) Reference Map. - FRANCE. 51B N.N.- Nos 3 and 4 section moved from STIRLING CAMP at 6 R.M. 27/3/18 to forward billets in PUDDING TRENCH.	

J.S. Crandall Major R.E.
OC 403rd (Renfrew) Field Coy R.E.

SECRET

WAR DIARY
or
INTELLIGENCE SUMMARY
(Erase heading not required.)

Army Form C. 2118.

408TH (RENFREW) FIELD COMPANY, R.E.

Month: March 1918

Instructions regarding War Diaries and Intelligence Summaries are contained in F.S. Regs., Part II. and the Staff Manual respectively. Title pages will be prepared in manuscript.

Place	Date	Hour	Summary of Events and Information	Remarks and references to Appendices
Coy HQrs at RAILWAY EMBANKMENT (H13.b.90.10) Sheet 51c SQ 8 NW 1/20,000	23/3/18		Orders received for transport to move forward to AREAS - ST POL ROAD. Transport move at 4.20.a.m. and were completed 4.40.a.m.	
	24/3/18		Dismounted personnel and Headquarters moved from RAILWAY EMBANKMENT at 12.45.a.m. to ETRUN. Transport moved from ARRAS - ST POL ROAD at 1.30.p.m. Company moved to ETRUN completed 6.15.p.m. and headquarters established at billets no.5. ETRUN	
Coy HQrs at 24/3/18 ETRUN Reference Sheet 51c 1/40,000	25/3/18		The whole of the dismounted personnel some drivers working on defence line 2 miles WEST OF ARRAS.	
	26/3/18		410135 Cpl Cpl LINDSAY J. wounded (shell splinters) 26/3/18 - (Remains at duty)	
	27/3/18		Sappers working on same defence line between ACHICOURT and DAINVILLE.	
	28/3/18		Sappers moved from ETRUN at 8.a.m. to the trenches held MISSOURIE TRENCH Casualties - 410243 Sapper CRANFORD R Killed (shell) and the following sappers wounded by shell, 410354 Sapper CALLENDER W., 420230 Sapper STEWART T.G., 420030 Sapper BRODLEY J, and 340618 Sapper CROPP W (Remained at duty). Company reliefs in trenches at 4.p.m. by Provincial Battalions and on relief marched back to STIRLING CAMP.	
	29/3/18		STAND TO - All day. Erected barbed wire fence from RIVER SCARPE at H13.C.45.45 boundary - 410017 Sergeant (A/S. Sergeant) BOYD wounded H20.b.5.5.p DUNBAT + B (shell)	
	30/3/18		STAND TO - In morning. Excavating & wiring on RESERVE LINE.	
	31/3/18		In morning party preparing for demolition of bridge on GAVRELL ROAD at H.8.c.10.10. and loading of Railway Arch H.14.a.0.30.	Appx. Y. Other Ranks 190.

Strength "H" Company on 31/3/18 - Officers 7.

J. Crutchall
M. Woot (Renfrew) Field Coy R.E.

4th Divisional Engineers

406th (Renfrew) FIELD COMPANY R. E.

APRIL 1918.

WAR DIARY

409th (Renfrew) Field Coy R.E.

April 1918

Army Form C. 2118.

WAR DIARY
or
INTELLIGENCE SUMMARY.

(Erase heading not required.)

Instructions regarding War Diaries and Intelligence Summaries are contained in F. S. Regs., Part II. and the Staff Manual respectively. Title pages will be prepared in manuscript.

408TH (RENFREW) FIELD COMPANY, R.E.
Month April 1918

Place	Date	Hour	Summary of Events and Information	Remarks and references to Appendices
Army Hdqrs. Situated at STIRLING CAMP. (NEAR FAMPOUX) H.13.d.90. to Sheet 51B N.W. FRANCE.	1/4/18		Strength of Company on 1/4/18 — Officers 7. Other Ranks 184. Company employed on wiring and excavating Army Reserve Line and prepared demolition charges at Railway Crossing H.18.C.1.0 and Railway Bridge. H.14.a.2.3. Headquarters and dismounted personnel moved from STIRLING CAMP to ST LAURENT BLANGY - G.18.C.6.4 on 3/4/18. Company arrived fow wagons with Line, on 8/4/18, by Canadian truck on R.E. and marched to SIMENCOURT - move completed 12 P.M. 8/4/18.	
Coy Hdqrs. SIMENCOURT. LENS II 1/100,000	9/4/18 to 12/4/18		Company employed on general cleaning up and recreational training. Company moved with 17th Infantry Brigade group on 12/4/18. to BUSNES. — move completed dismounted personnel and transport by motor, and transport by road. - move completed 2 a.m. 13/4/18.	
Coy Hdqrs. BUSNES. Sheet FRANCE 36A 1/40,000	13/4/18 to		Transport moved on 13/4/18 to CORNET BRASSART O.23.d.5. Hdrs and dismounted personnel marched with 17th Infantry Brigade group to CANTRAINES, at 6.30 p.m. Outposts established outside village on arrival. On the night 14/4/18 one 4.5 Howitzer gun was recovered by the unit from the village of RIEZ DE VINAGE, belonging to 515th Divisional Artillery sent to Musicourt Hdqrs. Remaining 2—4.5 Howitzer guns belonging to Reinforcement Battery R.F.A. were also recovered from RIEZ DE VINAGE, on night of 16/4/18, and brought to GONNEHEM, where they were handed over to 51st Divisional Artillery. For service rendered in the recovery of these guns, the following N.C.O. and man were commended by the G.O.C. 4th Divisional — twice awarded the Military Medal. — 420239 Lance Corporal THOMSON J. - 420243 Sapper McLELLAN M5 and 420051 Driver COOPER J.	
CANTRAINES. Sheet FRANCE 36A 1/40,000	16.4.18		On 16/4/18 Hdqrs. & transport personnel moved to GONNEHEM - V.23.b.1.8. and marched to LE HAMEL - V.22.a.2.4. on 14/4/18. and thence to CENSE-LA- VALLEE, V.11.c.0.8. on 17/4/18. Company employed in erecting pontoon bridge across LA BASSEE CANAL, using bridge heads on Canal & wiring on Reserve Line.	
GONNEHEM, V23-b.1.8. Sheet FRANCE 36A 1/40,000				

J. A. Mitchell
O.C. 408th (Renfrew) Field Co. R.E.

WAR DIARY or INTELLIGENCE SUMMARY

Army Form C. 2118.

406th (RENFREW) FIELD COMPANY, R.E.

Place	Date	Hour	Summary of Events and Information	Remarks and references to Appendices
GONNEHEM V 23 c 4 8 Sheet FRANCE 36A 1/40,000	18/4/18		In the early morning of 18/4/18 about 1-45 am a party of about 38 Sappers of No 1 and 4 sections under 2 LIEUT R. BRAND were employed wiring the BRIDGES on NORTH SIDE of LA BASSEE CANAL at Q 33 c 9.0, whilst the enemy opened a heavy barrage in front of and on the canal bank. Our men were obliged to leave their work and took up their position in the trenches on either side of the bridge on the south bank, along with 8 sappers of 9th SUSSEX R.E. and some of the 2nd Seaforths. At 4 am the barrage lifted on to the rear line behind the canal. There was then an interval of 5 or 10 minutes before a party of about 70 Germans with 3 machine guns made a rush for the bridgehead. They appeared to hesitate and collected in a mass and very effective rifle fire was opened upon them. Some tried to dash across the bridge but were shot down half way across, while the others were being mown down on the Spricis bank. Three of the enemy who were able disappeared over the far bank, neither was a lull in the fighting for about 5 minutes. Then about 20 enemy on the bank carrying a specially made pontoon bridge with them which they launched intact but only reached 3/4 of the way across the canal. Some of the enemy dashed along this light bridge but were shot down or when jettying, emergio and expired at the 9th Field Co. R.E. dashed on to the bridge with grenades and ran their into the pontoon but in order to prevent a crossing on and subjected they into the pontoon but in order to prevent a crossing on the bullets. 2 LIEUT R. BRAND got two of our men to help him and they broke up the pontoon right out on our side. There until any break the fighting the bridge. Greatly to the east of the enemy who continued across the canal, about 6 am a party of Seaforths were lying constantly exposed himself on the wire. A whole platoon was lying on the northern bank, about Q 33 c 4 0. 2 LIEUT R. BRAND jumped into the water, swam out to a drift in the canal, and made it fast to a cable which was stretched the pontoon and made its stage he saved about 25 Seaforths and 8 Kings along this state he saved one of the enemy on the north bank stood above the water. About 7 am one of the enemy on the North bank finally about 200 on own men. Then others put up their hands and came out about 30 attempted to surrender hands up. The transportation homes in the but were going machine gunned brought by twenty half hundred men retired were 100 to 150 mowers were at scene. brutes from machine fire. The Renfrew Sappers were withdrawn about 10.30 am	

Army Form C. 2118.

WAR DIARY
or
INTELLIGENCE SUMMARY.
(Erase heading not required.)

Instructions regarding War Diaries and Intelligence Summaries are contained in F.S. Regs., Part II. and the Staff Manual respectively. Title pages will be prepared in manuscript.

[Stamp: 408TH (RENFREW) FIELD COMPANY, R.E.]

Place	Date	Hour	Summary of Events and Information	Remarks and references to Appendices
Vicinity of GONNEHEM V.23.6.8. Sheet FRANCE 36A 1/40,000 and CENSE LA VALLEE V.11.C.0.8. Sheet FRANCE 36A. 1/40,000	18/4/18 to 30/4/18		For gallantry in the operations of 18/4/18 the following N.C.Os. were commended:- WPS/15651 L/Sgt. Ferguson A. – 420081 L/Sgt. McLaren D. – and 420215 2/Cpl. Stevenson D. While the following Sappers were also commended by the G.O.C. 14th Divn. and awarded Military Medals:- 170444 Roberts R.T. 420031 Boyle J. – 224164 - Pearce C and 230415 Price F. From the 18/4/18 onwards company was employed constructing barrel bridges across LA BASSEE CANAL, erecting and setting RAVEN & NAVE RIVER, excavating in Reserve Line, CLARENCE RIVER; Clearing timber from BOIS DE PACAUT; Installed two pairs of tracks, digging cover in machine gun emplacement at W.I.A.S. – locks visited O.P. at W.14.b.6.4 (completed 23/4/18) ; erecting aid post at W.I.d.4.2; strengthened cellar in GONNEHEM; and maintenance daily on the bridges across the BASSEE CANAL. Reconnaissances and dismounted pursuit moved to CENSE LA VALLEE V.11.C.0.8. on 19/4/18. Casualties during the month – 1 Other Ranks wounded (Inshaw) December at duty and 2 died of wounds – 1 O.R. killed. Reinforcements - 1 O.R. on 3/4/18 - 34. O.R. on 10/4/18 - 2 O.R. on 18/4/18 and a 3 O.R. on 26/4/18 Other Ranks 192. Strength of Company at 30th April 1918 - Officers - 7 Other Ranks 192.	

J. Musk(?)
Major R.E.
O.C. 408th (Renfrew) Field Coy R.E.

18th April 1918.
2.30 p.m.

C.R.E. 4th Division.

Brief Report on Operations of No 4 Section and ½ of
No 1 Section.

****

   The party of about 38 Sappers under 2/Lieut BRAND relieved
the first wiring party at the bridgehead Q.33.c.9.0. about 1 a.m.
About $\frac{3}{4}$ of an hour after commencing work the enemy opened a heavy
barrage in front of and on the LA BASSEE CANAL Bank. The party was
obliged to cease work and took up their positions in the trenches
on either side of the bridge on the South bank, along with about
8 sappers of the 9th Field Company R.E. under 2/Lieut McKAY and
some of the 2/Seaforths.

   At 4 a.m. the barrage lifted on to the new line behind the
Canal. There was then an interval of 5 or 10 minutes before a
party of about 70 Germans with three machine guns made a rush for
the bridgehead. They appeared to hesitate and collected in a mass,
and very effective rifle fire was opened upon them. Some tried to
dash across the bridge, but they were shot down half way across
the bridge whilst the others were being mown down on the opposite
bank. Those of the remainder who were able disappeared over the
far bank, and there was a lull in the fighting for about 5 minuted.
Then about 20 dashed over the bank carrying a specially made
pontoon bridge with them, which they launched intact but it only
reached $\frac{1}{4}$ of the way across the canal. Some of the enemy dashed
along this light bridge but were shot down to a man.

   Following this a Corporal of the 9th Field Company R.E. dashed
on to the bridge with grenades and threw them into the pontoons,
but in order to prevent a crossing on the submerged bridge, 2/Lieut
BRAND got one or two men to help him, and they pulled the bridge
right in to our bank. From this time until daybreak the fighting
continued across the Canal greatly to the cost of the enemy who
constantly exposed himself.

   About 6 a.m. a party of Seaforths were seen on the Northern
bank about Q.33.c.7.0. A whole pontoon was lying adrift in the
Canal, so 2/Lieut BRAND jumped into the water, swam out to the
pontoon and made it fast to a cable which was stretched across
the water. Along this cable he ferried about 25 Seaforths and 8
Kings Own men.

   About 7 a.m. one of the enemy on the North bank showed a white
handkerchief then others put up their hands and finally about 200
or 300 attempted to surrender. During the transportation of
prisoners in the pontoon some machine gunners opened fire on our
men and several were hit, this renewed the fighting but eventually
about 100 to 150 prisoners were got across. Some of the enemy
attempted to get back into the wood again and offered fine targets
for our rifles in doing so. The Renfrew sappers were withdrawn
about 10.30 a.m.

            (sd) J.S.CRAWHALL.
               Major R.E.
       O.C. 406th (Renfrew) Field Company R.E.

Army Form C. 2118.

WAR DIARY
or
INTELLIGENCE SUMMARY
(Erase heading not required.)

408TH (RENFREW) FIELD COMPANY. R.E.

Instructions regarding War Diaries and Intelligence Summaries are contained in F. S. Regs., Part II. and the Staff Manual respectively. Title pages will be prepared in manuscript.

Place	Date	Hour	Summary of Events and Information	Remarks and references to Appendices
Offices at MENSE LA VALLEE Sh M.A.P. Sheet M36A Appx VII 2147	1/5/18		Strength of Unit: 7 Officers 192 Other Ranks. Company employed on Maintenance of Bridges on Canal LA BASSEE & CLARENCE RIVER. Sudeley Retained on water supplement R.G. at M.M.V.F. Everything going for GIBBS at M.9.B.57 at M.9.12 Field shed in PERNICHEM Field Bridge erected at V.10.L.S.2. Finisher erected on BASSEE Canal at Q.32.C.7.4.	
	6/5/18		Experimental mats fitted for LONNEHEM BRIDGE. 1st Two Bays made & erected over canal at Q.33.C.44. Gabions of Brush wires. Wattlers & A.P. erected at HINGES. Decunille track re-laid from PLAN CROCHE to FORT DE VINETTE. So. m. th. entre length HWELP laid at LONNEHEM. Wrung HELENIE MINE. CASUALTIES 1 in 5 - by C.A. persons send from area 2/5 3/5 O.C.A. persons send from area 3/5 " " " 1 " " " Lieut R. BEARD Killed in Action	
			430165 Ft Coll YOUNG H. Gunshot Shell.	
			N2653 Sgt RICHARDS H. " " "	
			N30071 " DOWNIE G. " " (Returned to duty)	

J.C.Russell
Major R.E.
O.C. 408th Renfrew Feld Coy R.E.

WAR DIARY
or
INTELLIGENCE SUMMARY.
(Erase heading not required.)

Army Form C. 2118.

406TH (RENFREW) FIELD COMPANY, R.E.

Place	Date	Hour	Summary of Events and Information	Remarks and references to Appendices
Hqrs at SENSE LA VALLEE Ref Map Sheet 11.S.W.	9/18 to 18/18		Company employed on incendment of bridges on CANAL BAS BASSEE. Preparation of CLARENCE RIVER bridges for demolition & repairs of bridges & river bank. Pill boxes erected on PANAL at Q.31.a.8.3. Seeking M.G. Emfs at M.A.N.F. Strengthening & revetting cellars in LES HARISOIR'S for aid post. Dugout Deanville track from DOUE CREME FM to PIEZ DE VINAGE. Seeking shelter for Lest horses on Signal lines. Patrol & repair of roads in forward area. Erection of O.P. on HINGES started. Dusting Re-Saquery plant at BAS MISERE. Water point sunk in BUSNETTES. Baths cleaned from BOURECHEM & re-erected at BUSNETTES.	
V.11.C.19	18/18		Casualties for period. No 517297 Sgr Cottingham J (wounded in action shell) (Sheld) 420159 " Park S " " " " (Sheld) 450101 Crmar Ball N.J. " " " " (Sheld)	

J.S. Crushell
Major R.E.
R.L. HO 6th (Renfrew) field Cy 132

Army Form C. 2118.

WAR DIARY
or
INTELLIGENCE SUMMARY.
(Erase heading not required.)

Instructions regarding War Diaries and Intelligence Summaries are contained in F. S. Regs., Part II. and the Staff Manual respectively. Title pages will be prepared in manuscript.

406th (COMPANY?) FIELD COMPANY R.E.
Date 26.5.17

Place	Date	Hour	Summary of Events and Information	Remarks and references to Appendices
HQrs at EPPSETTE VALLEE Ref Map Sheet No 36A Zone VIII. C.17.	19/5		Company employed on reconnaissance of bridges on LA BASSÉE CANAL & CLARENCE RIVER. Pte Tripp ended on PANOL at G.32.d.1.5. A dummy bridge of known widths. M.G. Empt at M.10.1.8 completed 19/5. Haversay track from DOUVE CREME F14.f. PIEZ DE VINAGE completed 19/5.	
	26/5/15		Sinking signal post. Loopes strengthening saltan for MG Posts on LEHARCOIS. Sinking reinforced concrete O.P. with dugouts of RES BRITES in trenches at SINGES, Map Ref M.19.B.55,35; Making double aeroplane pier for 2nd Squadron & Reserve Lines. Location of enemy potholes at BUF REUX & Officers Baths at PIRIS LA VILLAGE. Site alia for Aid Post at CENSELA VOLICE K.10.d.2.9. Sinking saps protection anothers on M.G. Biupla & MID Posts. Repairing roads & trackways & making more permanent roads. Dismantling & Manure huts at camps A PATACHE DE WEPPES M.19.P.	Lieut H.V. BIGNELL Joined Unit 19/5 from 12 DR posted Unit from Park 26/5

Assembled:
Lieut A.K. ABRAM
420071 — Lieut McFARLANE D.
ND0171 — Sgt McFARLANE D.
220399 — Sqt BURNSIDE A.E.
420339 — " SPIERS A.
420363 — " WALLACE L.   Wounded
213096 — " MURRAY D.
329715 — " DENHAM J.   Spr DELL
130029 — " ROGERS M.   30/5
132044 — " WRATHALL B.
80007 — " ANGILL W.
536039 — " ROBERTS H.
18150 — Cpl RILEY C.

K.K. Walshall
Major R.E.
6.6.17 Major R. English 2nd Lt. R.E.

Army Form C. 2118.

WAR DIARY
or
INTELLIGENCE SUMMARY
(Erase heading not required.)

Instructions regarding War Diaries and Intelligence Summaries are contained in F.S. Regs., Part II. and the Staff Manual respectively. Title pages will be prepared in manuscript.

Place	Date	Hour	Summary of Events and Information	Remarks and references to Appendices
HQ. OF (ENGELS) YPREE VILL. M.Y. BH My-FULL 30H XYPM	24/5 h 31/5		Company employed on the defence & maintenance of bridges on LA BASSEE CANAL & YPRES-YSER RIVER. Section of Bgn. Pks. & reinforced console O.P. at HINGES M.Y. E.53.35. Working dept & drawing stores for Bg. posts in N° BERGUEMON. Erecting de Jonghy plant at BAC RIEUR. Infantry had cover on M.G. Posts. Mason hut erected at BAC RIEUR. Many supply de Repense thus. Repair of road in area. Excavation & repairing switchline at G.25. Casualties, nil. Strength of Unit 31/5 9 Officers 204 Other Ranks. Lieut R. MacNAUGHTON joined Unit as reinforcement 29/5.	

J. C. Crandall
Major RE
O.C. 406 (Telegraph) Field Co. RE 125

Army Form C. 2118.

WAR DIARY
of
INTELLIGENCE SUMMARY.
(Erase heading not required.)

Instructions regarding War Diaries and Intelligence Summaries are contained in F. S. Regs., Part II. and the Staff Manual respectively. Title pages will be prepared in manuscript.

Place	Date	Hour	Summary of Events and Information	Remarks and references to Appendices
HQRS OT CENSEETH VILLERS Y11C6.7 Map 36.B 1/25,000	1/6/18 to 14/6/18		Strength of Unit. Officers 4, Other Ranks 209. Company employed on the maintenance of bridges on LA BASSÉE CANAL & CLARENCE RIVER. 2 Pale Bridges erected at P.36.a.19 & P.30.15.1 at Q.33.c.63 & 73. Bailey bridge worked on CLARENCE RIVER at Y.11.a.35. Repair & maintenance of roads in forward area. Member over of Nozzle Visors Facings. Existing reinforced concrete M.G. Empts at Mesnil. Existing concrete O.P. at Mt BERNENCHON M.C. able with Eyes. Shift covering. New Shelter with concrete Screen constructed for M.D.S. at LENNE LA MALLE. Steel Shelter erected at HINGES L.R. Circuit Blocks Eight dug-out erected at S.t LES HARISOIRS. M3.B.80. Repair & extension of Light Railway to Pt.1046 L.R3 Bridge from LES HARISOIRS. Excavation of gallery for dug-out at Mt BERNENCHON. Excavation & revetting of Gun-pits on ROBECQ SWITCH. Excavation & revetting of Gun-pits in ROBECQ SWITCH. Existing & laying shelving racks in AID POST at LES HARISOIRS. Existing road from intersection on RIVER BANK & RESERVE LINE together from LE TAUROY to Mt BERNENCHON DOUVE TRENCH to the Exit Boundary. CASUALTIES. No 73698 Sapt. GRAYSON (WOUNDED GAS) 14/6 HONOURS M2.20018 Capt. 4/Sgt BEITH R.L received the and REWARDS. Distinguished Conduct Medal No 70.437 R.S.M. WINCH J.R. Received the Meritorious Service Medal. King's Birthday Honours, 1918.	

J Marshall Major R.E.
OC 400th (Renfrew) Field Coy R.E.

WAR DIARY or INTELLIGENCE SUMMARY

Army Form C. 2118.

406th (RENFREW) FIELD COMPANY, R.E.

Place	Date	Hour	Summary of Events and Information	Remarks and references to Appendices
HDQRS AT RENSE LAVALLEE Y.11.B.1.7 Sheet No 36 A 1/40000	15/6 to 30/6		Company employed on maintenance of bridges on EMBRASSEZ CANAL & CLARENCE RIV. Laying footbridges on Infantry Tracks. Work of Pont out of Rd. bridge erected over CANAL at P.9.9.65.35. Decoration of old & erecting new concrete shell shelter for R.T. Bde posted M.7.B.94. Sinking reinforced concrete M.G. Empl. Mt BERNENCHON M. central Enghefield 31.75. Entry concrete O.P. with Byp. look canopy at M' BERNENCHON M.1.a.6.6. Enghefield 27.5. Sinking concrete shelter at HINGES O.P. Repair of Railway truck & permanent way from RESERVOIRS to M.03 Bridge. Spurs Decauville track from Walking RESERVOIRS to CANAL. Erecting reinforced concrete shelter with cured steel shelter canopy for Bde H.qrs / FOUCHE V.H.B.0.3. Marers Reserve Line 1st & 2nd Systems. Maintenance of Tracks and forward roads in area. Casualties No H.1H 657 Sapr TAYLOR. W. Mountainous Action (Shell) 29/6 Died of Wounds 29/6 Strength of Unit Officers 7 Other Ranks 200	

J.P. Crawshall
Major R.E.
O.C. 406th (Renfrew) Field Coy R.E.

WAR DIARY or INTELLIGENCE SUMMARY

Army Form C. 2118.

Instructions regarding War Diaries and Intelligence Summaries are contained in F. S. Regs., Part II. and the Staff Manual respectively. Title pages will be prepared in manuscript.

(Erase heading not required.)

WO 32

Place	Date	Hour	Summary of Events and Information	Remarks and references to Appendices
HDQRS AT YPRES IN YPRES V.14.9.17 B/SHEET N°36	1/7/15 to 16/7/15		Strength of Unit Officers 9 Other Ranks 202. Company employed on the following work:— Maintenance of Bridges on BUCKINGHAM'S & BRIE RIVER. Maintenance of Bridges on CANAL LA BASSEE & CARBENTIER. Bridges on BUCKINGHAM'S BRIE detonated by shell fire on the morning of the 10th inst. Bridge constructed over gap & opened for horse transport at 5 pm night of 11th. Shell fire damaged shelter on the 17th for Motor traffic. 5 Cart piers bridge for temporary works on CANAL. Election of concrete shed the POST WESTWARDINGS (Completed 9th inst) at W.A.74. Sentry concrete cubby hole for AID POST Completed 13th. Sentry reinforced concrete shelter shelters at L.1.80. HDQRS V.14.a.3. Laying tramway track from 16.6 HDQRS to sides of shelters on CANAL BANK. Excavation of sites & erecting concrete block shelters on CANAL BANK — 3 Shelters completed 18th inst at Q.33,4,10,9,5. Wiring entrance on RESERVE LINES, CANAL BANK & LE PADROY & AT BERNENHMON. Patrol & repair of Infantry tracks, roads & tramways in area. Excavation of sites for M.G. Emp. between REIZ DE VINAGE. CASUALTIES No 430315 A/Corpl STEVENSON. D (Wounded in Action) of 7/5 Shell & O.R. reinforcements joined unit from Base 7/15	

Signed: J. Mitchell
MAJOR R.E.
A/Lt.Col (RENFREW) Field Coy R.E.

WAR DIARY
or
INTELLIGENCE SUMMARY.
(Erase heading not required.)

Army Form C. 2118.

Instructions regarding War Diaries and Intelligence Summaries are contained in F.S. Regs., Part II. and the Staff Manual respectively. Title pages will be prepared in manuscript.

Place	Date	Hour	Summary of Events and Information	Remarks and references to Appendices
HQ 49 at CENSE LA VRILEY	19/7		Company employed on the following work:— Maintenance of bridges on MARENE Rd. & BRISSÉE CANAL. R.E. park built on same at Pol 5/7a to replace hand pen bridge.	
Y/116,14, Sheet M36A 2000	to 31/7		Heavy girder drawn for bridging forces at M3.2.53 and 9.33.544. Section of concrete blockhouses on ROMMEL BRANCH & shelters completed on the go to section of reinforced concrete shelters at BISHOPS WOOD completed & 1 steel corrugated shelter erected at ROUPER HARBOUR & 1 framed only lais complete. 1 steel corrugated shelter erected at ROUPER HARBOUR & 1 framed & laid complete. Engrs. tramway back from LES HENSOIRS to CHELSEA BRIDGE (POTIZE DE VINAGE), & site of shelters on ROMMEL BRANCH. M.G. Emps. RETZ DE VINAGE. Reconnoitring works for M.G. Emps. HUSHES ROAD & MANAYUNK RR. area. Patrol & repair of Infantry tracks in area. Military Tramline LE POUROY N'BERNENCHON, DOUVE PIÈME & CONGE BANK.	

(CASUALTIES NIL DURING Sapper DOWN N.I. (Wounded in Action) 19/7) Strength of Unit: 7 Officers 202 O.R.

[Signature]

MAJOR R.E.
O/F 106th Regiment Field Coy R.E.

YR 33

War Diary - August 1918
406th (Kentish) Field Coy RE

Army Form C. 2118.

WAR DIARY or INTELLIGENCE SUMMARY

(Erase heading not required.)

Instructions regarding War Diaries and Intelligence Summaries are contained in F. S. Regs., Part II and the Staff Manual respectively. Title Pages will be prepared in manuscript.

Place	Date	Hour	Summary of Events and Information	Remarks and references to Appendices
CENSE-LA-VALLÉE VII.C.1.7. Sheet FRANCE 36A. 1/40,000	1-8-18 to 23-8-18		Strength of Company on 1st August 1918 - Officers 4 - Other Ranks 201. Company employed on the following works:- Maintaining 11 bridges on LA BASSÉE CANAL and CLARENCE RIVER. - Pile bridge for pack transport lifted at W.3.b.5.3. and Q.33.c.3.5. and opened for traffic 8th August. - Crib Pier bridge erected at Q.31.a.8.3. and opened for traffic at PONT LEVIS, Q.32.a.6.5 on 9th August. Steel girder bridge built on canal on abutments at PONT LEVIS, Q.32.c.6.5 on 13th August. - CHELSEA BRIDGE lifted, strengthened and relaid 16th August. - Excavating abutment at WATERLOO BRIDGE Q.31.a.55.30. commenced 21st August. - Reinforced raft and pile piers for bridge at W.3.a.9.9. - Laid tramway to site of proposed machine gun emplacement at W.3.a.9.9. - Dismantled trestle in CLARENCE RIVER 20th August. - Erection of concrete block shelters in LA BASSÉE CANAL bank, located as follows:-	
			No 1. Q.32.d.10.45 No 2. Q.32.d.60.65 No 3. Q.33.c.0.55 No 4. Q.33.c.3.3 No 5. Q.33.c.0.7.0 No 6. W.3.a.9.8 No 7. W.3.b.5.5. No 8. W.3.b.7.2.	No 6, 7, 8 shelters not completed. 3 - Excavation only.
			Clearing growth from bo stem of RIVER NOC. LE CHUROY - Mt BERNENCHON - DOUGE CREME - CANAL BANK. Wiring Reserve Line - Nt BERNENCHON. Patrol and repair of infantry tracks, roads and tramways in the area. Repair and drainage of BELLE ROAD. Clearing and draining wells in GONNEHEM. Company relieved in this sector 23rd August by 2nd Field Coy R.E., 19th Division - LA BASSÉE CANAL - CLARENCE RIVER bridges handed over to 82nd Field Coy R.E. Concrete shelters handed over to XIII Corps R.E.	
RELY Sheet HAZEBROUCK 1/100,000	24.8.18		Company left CENSE LA VALLÉE at H.20 am 24.8.18 by march route to RELY - transport joined company at BUSNETTES - Moved to RELY, Company arrived 9.30 am 24.8.18 - Transport arrived at 8.15 PM 24.8.18, from RELY to CROIX, out. area.	
			MAJOR J S CRAWHALL, M C on leave to PARIS - 4/8/18 to 19/8/18.- CAPTAIN J B MUNDELL, assumed temporary command in the absence of MAJOR CRAWHALL.	

J B Crawhall Major R.E.
O.C. 400th (Bedford) Field Coy R.E.

WAR DIARY or INTELLIGENCE SUMMARY

Army Form C. 2118.

(Erase heading not required.)

Instructions regarding War Diaries and Intelligence Summaries are contained in F.S. Regs., Part II. and the Staff Manual respectively. Title Pages will be prepared in manuscript.

Place	Date	Hour	Summary of Events and Information	Remarks and references to Appendices
HERICOURT	25.8.18		Company left RELY at 4.15 P.M. 25.8.18 for internment at BERGUETTE - Entrained at 8 a.m. Returned at WAVRANS at 2.30 P.M. and marched to HERICOURT arriving there at 4 P.M. - Transport arrived at 3 P.M.	
WAR LENS II. 1100-000	26.8.18		Company and transport moved from HERICOURT by march route at 4.30 A.M. 26/8/18 to ACQ via ST POL, SAVY and upper ARRAS ROAD - Company and transport arrived at ACQ at 7 P.M. 26/8/18	1/8/18 to 23.8.18 XIII Corps 5th Army
ACQ. ENS II	27.8.18		Company at ACQ.	
1100-000	28.8.18		Company left ACQ at 3.15 P.M. and entrained on main ACRQ-STPOL ROAD and detrained at ROND POINT ARRAS and marched to SPADE TRENCH. Headquarters established in SPADE TRENCH at O.4, d.4.1. - Wt 51B J.4.0-0-0-. Transport moved at G.28.d.8.6. ARRAS.	23.8.18 to 25.8.18 XXII Corps
SPADE TRENCH 04.b.4.1	29.8.18		Reconnaissance in CAMBRAI ROAD from FOSSE FARM to VIS-EN-ARTOIS. Company employed on repair of this part of road. - Reconnaissance of bridge at O.23, c.60.85.	26.8.18 to 31.8.18 Canadian Corps 1st Army
Sheet 51B/40000	30.8.18		Company employed on maintenance and road repair of BOIRY LANE and CAMBRAI ROAD.	
	31.8.18		Company employed on clearing CAMBRAI ROAD from FOSSE FARM to O.4.a.2.1. Repair and maintenance of bridge at O.18.a.8.5. O.18.c.6.a. and O.18.b.4.0. Bridge opened at P1, a.3.1. and P.4.a.5.4 over SENSEE RIVER.	

2 LIEUT A MACNAUGHTON to Field Ambulance sick on 27/8/18. Reported 31.8.18
MAJOR J S CRANHALL MC to Field Ambulance sick on 31/8/18. Reported 3.9.18
CAPTAIN J B MUNDELL resuming command of unit whilst MAJOR CRANHALL 31/8/18 to 3/9/18 LIEUT H V BIGNELL, to Field Ambulance sick on 24/8/18 - rejoined 31.8.18.
O.R. reinforcements during month - 3 O.R. 9/8/18 - 3 O.R. 14/8/18 - 3 O.R. 21/8/18 and H.O.K. 31/8/18
Casualties during month 3/60283 Spr CHAS WOLFE W. wounded (shell) 30/8/18 at duty.
WILLIAMS H.E. wounded [illegible] 31-8-18.

J B Crushall [signature]
Officers - 19 Other Ranks

2449 Wt. W14957/M90 750,000 1/16 J.B.C. & A. Forms/C.2118/12

Army Form C. 2118.

403RD (RENFREW) FIELD COMPANY, R.E.

WAR DIARY
or
INTELLIGENCE SUMMARY.
(Erase heading not required.)

Instructions regarding War Diaries and Intelligence Summaries are contained in F. S. Regs., Part II. and the Staff Manual respectively. Title pages will be prepared in manuscript.

Place	Date	Hour	Summary of Events and Information	Remarks and references to Appendices
By HQrs at O7.d.4.1. R/My Sheet 51.B.	1/9/18		Strength of Unit. 4 Officers - 203 Other Ranks 1 ℞. Company employed on repair & maintenance of Park Bourt. Reinforcement 1 Sect on repair of tracks in ETERPIGNY.	
⎯⎯⎯ HQRS SPACE 7B.		6-0pm	N°3 Sect. moved to Ronvelly area E of ETERPIGNY. 6-0pm 1 ℞.	
		6-30pm	N°4 Sect. moved to O.9.c.54 on BOIRY R°. 1 ℞.	
By HQrs at O.9.c.54	2/9/18	4-30am	2 Sections in assault on DROCOURT-QUEANT Line, for examination of any-carts & wants for traffic. 1 Section on reconnaissance of wells & roads. 1 Section in reserve.	
—do—	3/9/18		Coy employed on repair of roads & estby overland track from P.13.d.17 - P.13.d.77 to P.9.a.7.0. & reconnaissance of wells. Company relieved by 409 th Field Coy R.E. All roads & reports handed over. Company personnel in concentrated at H4.d.34 on ARRAS - PARGNY R° to PALLUEL in old trench system.	
		5-0pm 7-0pm		
		1/9/18	Casualties:- Lieut. N. CHADWICK Wounded G.S.W. " Lieut. J.B. MUNDELL " Remained at duty Sapper CADDY. J " Remained at duty " ARMSTRONG. G " Burying Wounds ℞.	2/9/18 2/9/18
			A20395 M865653 Sgt ROBINSON R.N. MISSING 154566 Coldwell R. Returned Wounded 349599	2/9/18
			M420365 Cpl YOUNG H. Wounded G.S.W. A20300 Sgt HOLMES W. " " 2/9/18 315533 " SIMPSON G " Remained at duty H34251 " GREGSON Y.S. " 2/9/18 A20009 " ANDERSON W " Bullet 359534 " NASH H.E. " Remained at duty	

D/D HQ G 4th/Infantry Field Coy R.E.

Army Form C. 2118.

WAR DIARY
or
INTELLIGENCE SUMMARY.
(Erase heading not required.)

[Stamp: 405th (RENFREW) FIELD COMPANY R.E.]

Place	Date	Hour	Summary of Events and Information	Remarks and references to Appendices
HdQrs &	11/9/18		Company at old transit system off main ARRAS-CAMBRAI Rd.	
H.4 M 3 4 Ref Map Sheet 51B 1/40000	5/9/18	6-30am	Transport left ARRAS for HOUVELIN by direct route via SAVY - FREVILLERS arrived HOUVELIN at 5-0pm.	
		1-15pm	Dismounted personnel marched from H.4.a.9.30. to ARRAS Stn entrained with 13th Bn Group at 3-30pm for TINQUES detrained 7-30pm & marched to HOUVELIN via CHELERS - MAGNICOURT arrived & billetted 10-30pm.	
HdQrs at HOUVELIN.	6/9/18 to 19/9/18		Company in training at HOUVELIN. Equipment, vehicles overhauled & overcome. Orders received to be prepared to move to XXII Corps area on the 19th inst.	
	20/9/18	3-30 AM	Transport left HOUVELIN by march route for area East of ARRAS at Q.30,Q.29. arrived 11-30pm.	
		4-30 AM	Dismounted personnel marched from HOUVELIN to embussing point on the BOILEUL Rd. enbussed at 7-0am, debussed at FEUCHY 10-15am and marched to MONCHY LE PREUX. arrived at 12 noon.	
			Casualties Nil. Lieut W.A. ROBERTSON joined unit from P.E.B.O. 12/9/18 " " " " 13/9/18 10 O.R.	

John Lee (Capt R.E.)
O/C 405th (Renfrew) Field Coy R.E.

Army Form C. 2118.

WAR DIARY
of
INTELLIGENCE SUMMARY
(Erase heading not required.)

Instructions regarding War Diaries and Intelligence Summaries are contained in F. S. Regs., Part II. and the Staff Manual respectively. Title pages will be prepared in manuscript.

Place	Date	Hour	Summary of Events and Information	Remarks and references to Appendices
H'qrs at MOHENY LE PREUX	21/9/18		Company employed on repair of roads in Moheny area.	
		11 am	2nd Section moved to billets in 15"B area at R.13.c.4.2.	
			Major J.S. Crandall M.C. proceeded to H.Q. II Div on O/duty.	
			Capt. W.G. Bunnell 2nd in command assumed command (Temp.)	
H'qrs at P.13.c.4.2 Ref Sheet 51.B 1/20,000	22/9/18 to 30/9/18		Company employed on reconnaissance of bridges, wells, roads & sufficiency of forthnight accommodation & transport over the 8 divisions in PERUISE & ETAING for H.Q.s & other personnel. Enemy dugouts improved & casual areas noted for housing depots for wheeled transport & Battn. loads taken forward & handsown to Details.	
			WELLS. Samples of water taken from wells in area & tested and types reported in ETERPIGNY, ETAING & DURY.	
			Sluice Gates at J.36.8.60.65 destroyed by demolition at 2-30 am 26 inst to allow water to run from flooded area above into Ecole L'habie daily.	
			Infantry billets for Infantry at P.18.C.31. Shelter erected for Brigade office at P.15.7.74. Bunks erected in dugouts in Baraca dugouts cut in Canadé type at P.10.B.10.90. for O.P. Loopholes and for M.G. Emplts J.36.d.15.60. & J.36.d.40.65.	
			Enemy dugouts in Inf & Artillery dug-outs. Salvaging timber for works from deserted huts in ETERPIGNY & DURY.	
			Patrol & repair of roads in same. Tank traps filled in at P.20.a.9.5. ETAING.	
			CASUALTIES NIL.	
			HONOURS 420306 Sapr MURDOCH D.C.M.	
			420053 Sapr 1/Cpl FULTON D.C.M.	
			420039 2nd. Cpl. CAMPBELL R. Military Medal.	
			309534 Sapr NASH M.E. " "	
			1 O.R. proceeded on course from R.E.B.D. 28/9	
			" " " " 30/9	
			6 O.R.s proceeded on leave from R.E.B.D.	
			STRENGTH of Unit. 4 Officers 206. O.R.	

Army Form C. 2118.

WAR DIARY
or
INTELLIGENCE SUMMARY.
(Erase heading not required.)

Instructions regarding War Diaries and Intelligence Summaries are contained in F. S. Regs., Part II. and the Staff Manual respectively. Title pages will be prepared in manuscript.

Place	Date	Hour	Summary of Events and Information	Remarks and references to Appendices
H.Q. at EVERPIGNY Pts C.42	1/11		Strength of Unit. Officers 7 Other Ranks 204.	
Ry Head 51.B. at PURO	5/11		Company employed on patrol & repair of roads in ETERPIGNY - DURY-LEICLUSE ETAING.	
	6/11		Reconnaissance of bridges, gaps & railway works. Crater in PLOUICH area. Trestle bridge proposed & started on site at G at P.13.c.75.55.	
			Preparing accommodation for Coy by employing 4 artillery on area, excluding See section.	
	6/11	3.30pm	Company arrived in new H.Q. at Hoot Caraclan Inf. All ranks in Nissen huts. Dismounted personnel marched to MONCHY to relieve 9 Battn. Boats taken up to MONCHY area, arriving on my of G/11. Re-assembled & Coffee. Boats used next morning for purpose of crossing moats & offices.	
H.Q at MONCHY-PREUX	7/11	7-0am	Company left MONCY to R.D.B by march route for HOPELETTE via TILLOY. HARRIS & MILNAM. Unit assembled at 2-30pm.	
H.Q at HOPELETTE Coy Hqs LENSII.	8/11 9/11 10/11		Company in training at HOPELETTE. Cadre personnel of Bridge Reconnaissance of roads between LENS and DOUAI. Unloading Eng Equipment.	
	11/11		Dismounted personnel left HOPELETTE & reached St HORBERT & entrained at 13 hours. Debussed at BOUZON & encamped at E.9.E.91. Rest of Coy & Tools & transport left HOPELETTE at 12 noon & reached WANCOURT & stayed for the night 11/12th.	
H.Q at E.9.E.91 2ndSection at G.YE.4050	12/11 13/11		Company arm handed twenty minutes worship parade ordered from WANCOURT at 4P.M. Major R Burnett appointed under from Essex Engs. M.P.C.	

J W Lee Capt R.E.
O.J.C 207 Workshop 1st 14 Coy R.E

Army Form C. 2118.

WAR DIARY
or
INTELLIGENCE SUMMARY.
(Erase heading not required.)

Instructions regarding War Diaries and Intelligence Summaries are contained in F.S. Regs., Part II. and the Staff Manual respectively. Title pages will be prepared in manuscript.

Place	Date	Hour	Summary of Events and Information	Remarks and references to Appendices
N° of BOURLON	13/11		Company employed clearing road to Havres Via BOURLON - HAYNECX - CUPPEL ROAD FORMING MAIN CANE - CAMBRAI AVENUE. Shelled in NAYES at 3.30 am.	
E. 9, c, 9, 1, Map Sheet 57C N.W.	14/11		Company employed clearing debris of destroyed railway bridge at T.6.c.3.2. Work on bridge completed on 14/11.	
Area at NAVES 7.23.c.4.9 Mapsheet 57A	15/11		Erection of water & washing shelters for Gen. H.Q. at USA Station completed on 15/11.	
	16/11		Company employed on repairs & placing up "Nissen Sons" at Souezin shown for Mudur Field bridges & pontoon at R.5.a.4.6.	
N° at IVERSEN (NORD 20.16) V.B.9.C.9.9 Map Sheet 57A, N.W.	17/11	2 am	Company moved into Viersen at 2 a.m. 4 Light truck bridge erected over River Seine at P.2.6.a.9.1, of 3 bays. Bridge completed for traffic at own times. Motor traffic bridge with wit at P.9.b.0.3 completed at own times. Transport returned from Naves + Onnaies at 1600 hours.	
N° at VIXLERS EN COUCHE	21/11		The A.O.H. girder bridge taken up at SAETZON for erection at P.2.6.a.9.1. Bol. started on bridge at 01.30 & opened for traffic at 19.30 hours. Work continued on society chapel, placing huts, water supply extension of bridge at P.9.b.0.3.	

CASUALTIES	N° 312231	Sapper CUNNINGHAM. J.	Killed in Action 14/11 (Shell)
	212,677	" MCPARTNEY. G.	WOUNDED 15/11 (Shell)
	N8626	SCARSBROOK. F.	WOUNDED (Died of Wounds) 22/11 (Shell)
		Sapper MARSH.	Wounded this Military 23/11 (Shell)

HONOURS " Lieut G.D. MARSH Wounded this Military 23/11 (Shell)

STRENGTH 2 Lieut 2 O.R. Joined unit from R.E.B.D. 21/11
         1 Lieut AMMIRLAND Joined unit from R.E.B.D. 19/11

405TH (RENFREW) FIELD COMPANY, R.E.

Army Form C. 2118.

WAR DIARY
or
INTELLIGENCE SUMMARY.
(Erase heading not required.)

Instructions regarding War Diaries and Intelligence Summaries are contained in F. S. Regs., Part II. and the Staff Manual respectively. Title pages will be prepared in manuscript.

Place	Date	Hour	Summary of Events and Information	Remarks and references to Appendices
HQRS at SAULZOIR R.20.a.7.3 Bd/Maj 51A Div'n	24/10/18		2 Infantry footbridges made + thrown across FURTESCAULOT at P14a.9.5, P14d.7.1, P20.9.5.70 ? / 3 Medium Trestle bridges built over PIEBE SAULZET at P.14.9.14 + P.13.9.77 / Bridges constructed for traffic at 1.4.0.a known as Maltese Bridge P.2.0.a.9.5 and P.20.a.d.8.9.3 commenced at about same time to load out heavy traffic on time a tramway	
	25/10/18		In P.12.a.7.3. Then at VERCHAIN + work started at 9.0a.m. Menin 26 fr railway girder bridge built + apptment 25ft stone culvert rebuilt + abutments to [?] courses built completed opposite for traffic at 14.00 hours 24/10. Bridges assisn nickel Trestle bridge at P.20.a.7.3 Commenced + possibly ready to carry forward 26/10	
Hd.qrs. at VERCHAIN P.12d 6.6 Hy/Maj 51A Div'n	26/10/18		+ VERCHAIN. / continuing works on their esscribed support of Army heights at P.16.c.93. Looks after existing and new bridges and further 2 bridges erected in Martin Trestle bridge semi permanent on RIVER ESCAILLON at P.12.a.24 on the 29th (completed at 17.00 hrs) with heavy traffic. New stones + dust bottom had an apprx radius of bridge. Completed. A heavy girder bridge in process of P.20.a.31	
same	31/10/18			

CASUALTIES:
	WOUND	DIED		
	416584	Sapper Simmonds W.R. Woundinham J. Nov 25th (Bullet)		
	3 P.M.49	Marr L. Woundill in ? Plaine 17th (C. of Fpsmm 258)	21/4 ? received at Duty	
	341988	Cox B.H.	26/10	
		Kemp R.F.N.		

Capt J.B. Nicoll took over command of sunt during absence of Major O Campbell on leave 27/10

Shariffs of Sund Officers of GR 903.

JB.Nicoll Capt RE
OC
405th (RENFREW)
FIELD COMPANY R.E.

WAR DIARY
or
INTELLIGENCE SUMMARY

Army Form C. 2118.

(Erase heading not required.)

Instructions regarding War Diaries and Intelligence Summaries are contained in F. S. Regs., Part II. and the Staff Manual respectively. Title pages will be prepared in manuscript.

403rd (RENFREW) FIELD COMPANY R.E.

Place	Date	Hour	Summary of Events and Information	Remarks and references to Appendices
Hqrs at VERNEUIL BILLOR Map Ref. 57d Sh.2 S/5	1/4/18 to 2/4/18		Strength of unit Officers 4 Other Ranks 203. Company employed preparing abutments for heavy girder bridge at HAIRES R.29.a.2.8. Bridge for Buffer taken up to site from PBD on lorries of 7th & 2nd Stores Coys. Wind started on bridge at 08.00 hours & opened for traffic at 10.15 hours. Bridge completed at 12.30 hours.	
	2/4/18	15.00	15th Pontoon returned by the 6th Divn. by Rly & returned to Hqrs.	
		15.30	Dismounted of company marched from VERNEUIL to SAUZOIR remainder of company marched from VERNEUIL to SAUZOIR arriving at Hqrs at R26.d.4.3 Ref map sh.51 zone.	
Hqrs at SAUZOIR Map Ref. 51b Sh.1A Zone 6 2/5	3/4/18 to 8/4/18	17.00 hrs	Company at SAUZOIR Road & Tramway Overhauling of equipment.	
Hqrs at SAUZOIR	9/4/18		Company moved by Road East from SAUZOIR to PRESEAU arriving at 17.00 hrs.	
Hqrs at PRESEAU	10/4/18		Embky mend by Rush of March Made Km Vacated 5th to PRESEAU. Move completed at 16.15 hrs.	

J Marshall Major
O.C. 403rd (Renfrew) Fd Coy R.E.

WAR DIARY or INTELLIGENCE SUMMARY

Army Form C. 2118.
400th (RENFREW) FIELD COMPANY, R.E.

Place	Date	Hour	Summary of Events and Information	Remarks and references to Appendices
N[?] at ROISIN ISBERGUES			Company employed on hauling of infantry stores. Work started on North side of ANTIGNY Bridge. Constructed 18 ft Single Single Way approach to abutments. Approach to bridge at BROGEE completed 18 Nov 1918.	
N[?] at ROISIN	18/11		Relics of work in ROISIN at BROGEE. Roof Repair and rebuilt & broken over etc. of small Wing wall – Bridge at FLOBECQ. Guardrails 18/11.	
	19/11	0900	Company moved by March Route to ST SAULVE VALENCIENNES to join 13 H&H Group. Move completed by 1300 hrs.	
N[?] at ST SAULVE VALENCIENNES	20/11 to 29/11		Dismounted personnel inspected with Division on parade ground at SAULTAIN by G.O.C. 11 Div on 20/11. Company employed overhauling equipment. Drill & Education. Workshops at ST SAULVE preparing mounted personnel, animals & wagons inspected on Grand Route by G.O.C. 11 Div on 29/11.	
	30/11		Dismounted personnel marched to SAULTAIN for inspection by Army Commander with Division on 30/11.	

CASUALTIES. 1 O.R. joined Unit from R.E.BD. 9/11

HONOURS. No 671st Sapper BROWNE A.O. – Military Medal
No 1931 A/L/Cpl LEWIS R.
No 71575 Pte BARCLAY W.
No 30304 "D" McDONALD A.

[signatures]
Major R.E.
O/C 400th (Renfrew) Field Coy R.E.

WAR DIARY
INTELLIGENCE SUMMARY

Army Form C. 2118.

(Erase heading not required.)

Place	Date	Hour	Summary of Events and Information	Remarks and references to Appendices
Coy HQ situated at ST SAULVE VALENCIENNES Ref Map VALENCIENNES 1/100 000	1/12/18 to 31/12/18		Company strength at 1st December 1918. = Officers 7 O. Ranks 203. Company housed at ST SAULVE - VALENCIENNES. The employment of the Company during month - was Education, musketry, drill, ceremonial drills, and general regimental duties within the unit. On 7th December the company fired on rifle range at MARLY. On 11th December the company paraded with 12th Inf any Bayal Bregaed Groupy for presentation of medal ribbons by the Corps commander XXII Corps. *LIEUT H.M. KIRKLAND - proceeded on 7th December for attachment to Labour with Labour commandant XVII Corps. LIEUT. W. ROBERTSON - proceeded on 16th December from a/y of HQ Divisional RE - workshops. MAJOR J.S. CRANWELL - M.C. attached HQ Divisional Engineers as acting C.R.E. 6th A.C. to 9th A.C.C. CAPTAIN J.B. MUNDELL - took over command of unit during the period in which MAJOR J.S. CRANWELL M.C. was attached to 4th Divl Engineers M.G. - 6th to 24th A.C.C. CAPT. J.B. MUNDELL on lve. 031/2 LIEUT. R.N. ADEN - reported from leave 27th Dec. 1918. HONOURS announced during month = STRENGTH 420207 JARM STIRLING H. = MILITARY MEDAL. ELIEUT J. CHADWICK - MENTION 420111 SERGT HOGG J.B. } IN DESPATCHES.	6 Officers unforcasts on 9th Dec 4 O.R. ogalannews suggested to UK O.R. going despatch during 8th, 9th, 10th Dec. for ROMALIS Sth. N. Their ranks 199. STRENGTH OF UNIT AT STALIS

WAR DIARY
or
INTELLIGENCE SUMMARY.
(Erase heading not required.)

Army Form C. 2118

Instructions regarding War Diaries and Intelligence Summaries are contained in F. S. Regs., Part II. and the Staff Manual respectively. Title pages will be prepared in manuscript.

Place	Date	Hour	Summary of Events and Information	Remarks and references to Appendices
Hqrs at ST SOUPLET	1st		Strength of Unit. Officers 9. Other Ranks 199.	
			Company employed on studies & physical training.	
VAUCHENNES	1/9		Transport left ST SOUPLET 0700 hours on 1/9 for move to MARCHIENNES arrived & parked at JEMAPPES for the night 3rd 4th.	
	4/9		Dismounted personnel entrained at ST SOUPLET at 1030 hours, detrained at MARCHIENNES 15.00 hours.	
			Transport left by march route at 0500 hours, arrived MARCHIENNES at 16.00 hours.	
Hqrs at MARCHIENNES BELGIUM.	5/9 to		Company employed on education & physical training.	
SHEET H.G.			Changes intertakines from enemy mine at LA HESTRE H14.C.9.5 & T.5.C.2.7 by M.G.I & 4 G. Coys. BELGIUM.	
			Erection of NISSEN HUTS at CARNIERES started on the 28/9.	
			Company inspected by D.R.E. 4th Div. on the 16/9.	
			Strength of Unit. Officers 9. Other Ranks 126 on the 31st.	
			70 Other Ranks proceeded to U.K. for demobilization during the month.	
			Honours Nil.	
			Casualties Nil.	

J M Crawhall
Major R.E.
406th (Renfrew)
Field Company R.E.

WAR DIARY
INTELLIGENCE SUMMARY

Army Form C. 2118.

408TH (RENFREW) FIELD COMPANY, R.E.
No. .... Feb/1919.

Instructions regarding War Diaries and Intelligence Summaries are contained in F.S. Regs., Part II. and the Staff Manual respectively. Title pages will be prepared in manuscript.

(Erase heading not required.)

Place	Date	Hour	Summary of Events and Information	Remarks and references to Appendices
Coy H.Q. NORLANWELZ BELGIUM MAP 46 1/40000	1/2/19 to 28/2/19		Strength of Unit on 1/2/19 :— OFF. 7 O.Rs. 128.	
			Company employed on the location of wooden huts for officers' mess at CARNIÈRES. — Completed	
			Company equipment overhauled.	
			Demobilization.	
			MAJOR J.S. CRAWHALL M.C. proceeded to U.K. on 10/2/19 — for demobilization.	
			CAPTAIN J.B. MUNDELL M.C. took over command of unit vice MAJOR J.S. CRAWHALL M.C. proceeding on demobilization 10/2/19	
			37 O.Rs. demobilized during month =	
			4H. Animals evacuated for demobilization purposes during month.	
			CASUALS	
			2 LIEUT G.D. MACADAM M.C. rejoined from leave 12.2.19	
			LIEUT W.A. ROBERTSON — proceeded on leave 2.2.19, and rejoined 20.2.19	
			Strength of Company at 28/2/19 :— OFF. 6 O.Rs. 92	

J.B. Mundell Capt. R.E.
O.C. 408th (Renfrew) Field Co. R.E.

406 2nd Corps Sigs. Army Form C. 2118.

WAR DIARY
or
INTELLIGENCE SUMMARY
(Erase heading not required.)

Place	Date	Hour	Summary of Events and Information	Remarks and references to Appendices
HQ at BINCHE BELGIUM Map Ref. 1/5000	1/6/19		Strength of Unit Officers 2 — Other Ranks 38. (CADRE STRENGTH)	
	to 10/6/19		Cadre employed on general duties, guards. (etc)	
	12/6/19		Equipment packed & transport prepared for entrainment.	
	13/6/19		Vehicles & equipment entrained at BINCHE STATION. Cadre personnel entrained at 2100 hours for ANTWERP & detrained wagons, equipment & personnel at 1000 hours 14/6/19 at ANTWERP	
	14/6/19 15/6/19 16/6/19		Cadre bathed & medically inspected clothing disinfected 15/6/19. Cadre entrained. Vehicles & equipment loaded on Barge P.D.14. for BOULOGNE at 1815 hours 16/6/19.	
	17/6/19		Cadre arrived at BOULOGNE & detrained & marched to ST MARTINS (Camp) & camped at 2015 hours.	
	18/6/19 to 21/6/19		Cadre bathed medically inspected. Cadre moved from ST MARTINS Camp to MARLBOROUGH CAMP at 1300 hours to await orders for dispersal.	
			Embarked SS Princess Victoria for Dover. Finally 406 2/Corps Sigs Cadre dispersed from No 1 Dispersal Unit Wimbledon at 1300 13/7/19	

2 Offrs. 37 ORs

R. H. Bull Major
for officer i/c Leslie G/S
406.)

www.ingramcontent.com/pod-product-compliance
Lightning Source LLC
Chambersburg PA
CBHW080847230426
43662CB00013B/2039